WILHELM TELL POSTER	THE CBS EYE LOGO
SELECTED BY	SELECTED BY
IVAN & STEFF CHERMAYEFF GEISSBUHLER	**SAGI & WOODY** HAVIV PIRTLE

STEVEN HELLER

I HEART DESIGN

ROCKPORT

REMARKABLE GRAPHIC DESIGN SELECTED BY DESIGNERS, ILLUSTRATORS, AND CRITICS

THE ROLLING STONES STICKY FINGERS ALBUM	TYPOGRAPHY AS DISCOURSE	PININFARINA MAGAZINE
SELECTED BY	SELECTED BY	SELECTED BY
STEFAN SAGMEISTER	**RUDY VANDERLANS**	**STEPHEN DOYLE**

POSTERS • OBJECTS • FILM TITLES • TYPOGRAPHY • MAGAZINES • LOGOS & SYMBOLS

BANCO TYPE	THE @ SYMBOL	HAPPY FACE	VIBE COVERS	TYPE SCULPTURE	PEACE POSTER
CYRUS HIGHSMITH	PAOLA ANTONELLI	ART CHANTRY	AREM DUPLESSIS	GAIL ANDERSON	KEN CARBONE

Text © 2011 by Steven Heller

All rights reserved. No part of this book may be reproduced in any form without written permission of the copyright owners. All images in this book have been reproduced with the knowledge and prior consent of the artists concerned, and no responsibility is accepted by producer, publisher, or printer for any infringement of copyright or otherwise, arising from the contents of this publication. Every effort has been made to ensure that credits accurately comply with information supplied. We apologize for any inaccuracies that may have occurred and will resolve inaccurate or missing information in a subsequent reprinting of the book.

First published in the United States of America by
Rockport Publishers, a member of
Quayside Publishing Group
100 Cummings Center
Suite 406-L
Beverly, Massachusetts 01915-6101
Telephone: (978) 282-9590
Fax: (978) 283-2742
www.rockpub.com

Library of Congress Cataloging-in-Publication Data

I heart design : significant graphic design selected by designers, illustrators,
and critics / edited by Steven Heller.
　　p. cm.
　Includes bibliographical references and index.
　ISBN-13: 978-1-59253-682-5 (alk. paper)
　ISBN-10: 1-59253-682-4 (alk. paper)
　1. Design. 2. Graphic arts--Themes, motives. I. Heller, Steven. II.
Title: Significant graphic design selected by designers, illustrators, and critics.
　NC703.I2 2010
　741.6--dc22

　　　　　　　　　　　　　　　　　　　　　　　　　　　　　2010041709
　　　　　　　　　　　　　　　　　　　　　　　　　　　　　CIP

ISBN-13: 978-1-59253-682-5

ISBN-10: 1-59253-682-4

Digital edition published 2011
eISBN-13: 978-1-61058-032-8

10 9 8 7 6 5 4 3 2 1

Design: Rick Landers
Printed in China

{ACKNOWLEDGMENTS}

First, thanks to Emily Potts, my editor at Rockport, for continued support (good-natured nudging) and her dedication to design. Gratitude also to Regina Grenier for her invaluable contributions to this and other projects.

The book would be shapeless if not for the keen eye and skilled craft of designer Rick Landers, with whom I've worked on many books.

Of course the vessel would be empty if not for the wonderful contributors to this volume, whose words and selections are smart and vivid.

Various people have helped me to do this and other work over the years. Thanks to my wife, Louise Fili, for her support and contribution to this book; and my friends Seymour Chwast, Mirko Ilić, Veronique Vienne, Marshall Arisman, Gail Anderson, and Lita Talarico. Also I cannot do this at all if not for the generosity and support of David Rhodes, president, and Anthony Rhodes, executive vice president, of the School of Visual Arts in New York City.

For help in acquiring some of the images, thanks to Scott Hamilton, Chisolm Larsson Gallery in New York, and Nick Heller.

Finally, thanks to Milton Glaser for inspiring the title with his beloved "I Heart New York" logo.

—Steven Heller

{CONTENTS}

006/ **INTRODUCTION: WE HEART DESIGN**
Steven Heller

008/ 1. BANCO TYPE
Selected by Cyrus Highsmith

010/ 2. PININFARINA MAGAZINE
Selected by Stephen Doyle

014/ 3. LONDON UNDERGROUND GRAPHICS
Selected by J. J. Sedelmaier

016/ 4. TYPOGRAPHICA MAGAZINE
Selected by Ed Fella

018/ 5. LA FONDA DEL SOL RESTAURANT
Selected by Sean Adams

020/ 6. HIROSHIMA APPEALS
Selected by Katherine McCoy

022/ 7. SUPERMAN TITLE SEQUENCE
Selected by Brian Collins

024/ 8. THE HAPPY FACE
Selected by Art Chantry

027/ 9. CRAVEN "A" CIGARETTES POSTER
Selected by Seymour Chwast

030/ 10. ISOTYPES
Selected by Michael Maharam

032/ 11. THE @ SYMBOL
Selected by Paola Antonelli

034/ 12. I OBJECT DEFY MYSELF
Selected by Edwin Schlossberg

036/ 13. PLAYPOWER
Selected by Rick Poynor

040/ 14. THE SAVOY COCKTAIL BOOK
Selected by Arnold Schwartzman

044/ 15. I, LEONARDO
Selected by Anita Kunz

046/ 16. WILHELM TELL POSTER
Selected by Ivan Chermayeff

048/ 17. WILHELM TELL POSTER
Selected by Steff Geissbuhler

050/ 18. THE BUFFALO NICKEL
Selected by R. O. Blechman

052/ 19. GENERAL DYNAMICS POSTERS
Selected by Steven Heller

057/ 20. VALENTINE / OLIVETTI POSTER
Selected by Gerrit Terstiege

060/ 21. THE ROLLING STONES
STICKY FINGERS ALBUM COVER
Selected by Stefan Sagmeister

064/ 22. APARTHEID MUSEUM
Selected by Warren Lehrer

070/ 23. HISTORY OF RUSSIA
Selected by Christoph Niemann

072/ 24. EVERLAST LOGO
Selected by Ralph Caplan

074/ 25. TYPOGRAPHY AS DISCOURSE
Selected by Rudy VanderLans

076/ 26. STEDELIJK CATALOGS
Selected by Adrian Shaughnessy

082/ 27. EBERHARD FABER MONGOL 482 PENCIL
Selected by Liz Danzico

084/ 28. ALBERTUS (1935)/ THE PRISONER
(1967–1968)
Selected by Kerry William Purcell

088/ 29. THE NATIONAL PARKS SERVICE
Selected by R. Roger Remington

090/ 30. LIGHTNIN'!
Selected by Jason Godfrey

092/ 31. VIBE COVERS
Selected by Arem Duplessis

096/ 32. PEACE POSTER
Selected by Ken Carbone

098/ 33. COCA-COLA BOTTLE
Selected by Tim Hossler

100/ 34. THE EQUIVALENT SERIES
Selected by Allen Hori

102/ 35. AD CUTS FROM A–Z
Selected by Charles Spencer Anderson

106/ **36.** POSTER FOR THE 50TH ANNIVERSARY OF THE UNION INTERNATIONALE DE LA MARIONETTE, 1978 Selected by James Victore	143/ **52.** TOMATO: SOMETHING UNUSUAL IS GOING ON HERE, 1978 FROM POPPY WITH LOVE, 1968 Selected by Beth Kleber	180/ **66.** COLLAGE Selected by Deborah Sussman
108/ **37.** THE CBS EYE LOGO Selected by Sagi Haviv	146/ **53.** KODACHROME II Selected by Jeff Scher	182/ **67.** LILLIPUT Selected by Ken Garland
111/ **38.** THE CBS EYE LOGO Selected by Woody Pirtle	148/ **54.** NEWSWEEK Selected by Bonnie Siegler	186/ **68.** PONTRESINA Selected by Reto Caduff
112/ **39.** STP & MOONEYES LOGOS Selected by Geoff McFetridge	150/ **55.** COLORS MAGAZINE, NO. 1, 1991: "IT'S A BABY" Selected by Omar Vulpinari	188/ **69.** SIGNS OF ITALY Selected by Louise Fili
115/ **40.** MY BOOK HOUSE Selected by Ross MacDonald	152/ **56.** "ADOLPH THE SUPERMAN SWALLOWS GOLD AND SPOUTS JUNK" AIZ MAGAZINE, JULY 17, 1932 Selected by Robbie Conal	192/ **70.** REQUIEM FOR 500 THOUSAND Selected by Krzysztof Lenk
118/ **41.** VH PLAKATE Selected by Jan Wilker	156/ **57.** CERTIFICATE OF APPROVAL Selected by Jessica Helfand	194/ **71.** MOTORWAY SIGNS Selected by Monika Parrinder
120/ **42.** L'INTRANSIGÉANT POSTER Selected by Kim Elam	158/ **58.** JIMI HENDRIX Selected by Jim Heimann	196/ **72.** MORTON SALT UMBRELLA GIRL Selected by Debbie Millman
122/ **43.** BLUE, JONI MITCHELL Selected by Allan Chochinov	161/ **59.** HET BOEK VAN PTT Selected by Martha Scotford	198/ **73.** PROCES, KAFKA, 1964 Selected by Mirko Ilić
124/ **44.** DYLAN POSTER Selected by Andrea Rauch	164/ **60.** POLAR BEAR (1928) Selected by George Tscherny	200/ **74.** SEEING IS NOT BELIEVING Selected by Marshall Arisman
128/ **45.** JOHN M. WARD BASEBALL CARD, 1887 Selected by Mark Lamster	166/ **61.** BIFUR Selected by Steven Heller	204/ **75.** COMMERCIAL ART OF PALESTINE, 1938 Selected by David Tartakover
130/ **46.** THE MAN WITH THE GOLDEN ARM Selected by Christian Annyas	168/ **62.** XIII SECESSION EXHIBITION, VIENNA 1902 [COLOR LITHOGRAPH] Selected by David Raizman	206/ **76.** LETTERS IN POMPEII Selected Mauro Zennaro
132/ **47.** DR. SEUSS Selected by Laura Guido-Clark	172/ **63.** McCARTHY: PEACE POSTER Selected by Ward Sutton	208/ **77.** THE CENTURY DICTIONARY FIRST ISSUED 1889–1891, FINAL EDITION 1914 Selected by Scott-Martin Kosofsky
134/ **48.** TYPE SCULPTURE Selected by Gail Anderson	174/ **64.** YENI MOSQUE, ISTANBUL (1597–1640) Selected by Marian Bantjes	210/ **78.** MUSICA VIVA Selected by Chris Pullman
136/ **49.** THE CHROMOLITHOGRAPHIC POSTCARD Selected by Monte Beauchamp	176/ **65.** KORANIC EXEMPLA Selected by Majid Abbasi	212/ **79.** IRON MAIDEN: PIECE OF MIND Selected by Charles Wilkin
138/ **50.** THE HIP Selected by Jonny Hannah		214/ **80.** HIGHLY PRIZED, 1967 Selected by Alissa Walker
140/ **51.** PINNACLE HENDRIX POSTER Selected by Shepard Fairey		

WE HEART DESIGN

The most common question asked of designers from design school students (usually to fulfill a class assignment) is, "What is your favorite piece of design?" Oh, what a dreaded question it is. Although it is fairly easy to select five or ten designed things that have long-term importance or resonance, can one choose just one? It is like asking what is one's favorite book, movie, or record—or worse, what is one's favorite color? Can there be just one? I don't think so.

The answer must be rooted in context. What is a favorite now may not be in a year or two. As we mature and are introduced to new (old) things, our opinions invariably change. Of course, there are always those things that have an incredible influence on our work and perceptions. That is, I suspect, what the student asking the question is going for (whether they know it or not).

One thing I do know for certain, we would not be designers or engaged in the design practice as teachers, critics, journalists, scholars, etcetera, if we did not love design. We can love the entire practice or a specific aspect or a unique method, but *love* is the operative word. Of course, the reasons for such a charged emotion varies from individual to individual, but there are certain commonalities regarding form, function, outcome, and more. Design triggers something in all of us that may be solely aesthetic or decidedly content driven, but in the final analysis, we are drawn to it through the heart and mind.

I don't see this as a monogamous relationship. We may have preferences, like modern over postmodern, serif over sans serif, decorative over minimal. We may prefer one aesthetic school over another, or a particular approach captures our fancy. But can we put all our passion on just one single object or thing? Maybe not, but the contributors to this volume were asked to take the plunge.

The aim of this book, *I Heart Design*, an obvious twist of Milton Glaser's beloved, ubiquitous, and frequently copied trademark, is to explore what many of us believe to be a significant designed object, artifact, or thing—something with resonance and implications beyond the context in which it was made. The initial request of the participants was to select work other than their own, but a few contributors offered their own work anyway, and that is fine.

The book is not an objective history but, rather, a subjective reflection that will supplement the historical record. Some of the selections are indeed historically beyond reproach, but others are new to the cannon, (or maybe will never be part of the cannon). The selections were based on the following criteria:

1. Why is this graphic design important in the continuum of design history?
2. What makes this object unique among all other objects?
3. Are there any key components or anecdotal information associated with this object?
4. Why is this so important to your work or thinking?
5. What has this object influenced or what influenced this object?

The responses do not always cover all these bases. Some are brief and extremely subjective. Others are more expansive and analytical. The common thread is the heart. What is it that touches the heart, as well as brain and eye, equally?

Like every art form, functionality is not the only criteria for success or appeal. As the following responses reveal, there are many predictable commonalities that underlie the reasons for a given selection, but there are also quite a few from left field. Personally, I Heart the Answers.

no. 1

SELECTED BY CYRUS HIGHSMITH | BANCO TYPE | DESIGNED BY ROGER EXCOFFON

When someone asks me what my favorite typeface is, I reply, "Banco." The follow-up question is almost always, "No really, what's your favorite typeface?" "Banco," I say again. I admit that Banco is unusual and not found in the most prestigious places. However, it's a daring, imaginative design that has had a big impact on some of the most important type designers working today.

Banco was drawn in 1951 by Roger Excoffon for Fonderie Olive. Excoffon's other typefaces include Mistral, Choc, Calypso, and Antique Olive. These are all primarily advertising typefaces, designed to catch the reader's eye. Their outspoken flair makes them effective.

Excoffon had a fine arts background and a passion for drawing and painting. When he applied himself to type design, this passion showed itself in the dynamic shapes he devised to represent the familiar forms of the Latin alphabet. He often broke the rules in his typefaces, but he always did it in a skillful and meaningful way.

Excoffon's typefaces were once widely used, especially in his native France, but they're becoming harder to find in the wild. Hair salon logos and advertisements for escort services are some of the only places left where you can see Banco and friends. They are often subjected to extreme scaling and letterspacing. Consequently, these typefaces have lowbrow associations for many designers.

But I'm not the only one with an appreciation for Excoffon's unique contributions. His influence is in the subtle flair of Matthew Carter's masterly historical series Galliard and Miller. It's in the fast curves of Gerard Unger's practical designs like Swift. Banco exemplifies Excoffon's flamboyant style.

So I'll say it again: Banco is my favorite typeface.

In 1997, **Cyrus Highsmith** graduated with honors from Rhode Island School of Design and joined the Font Bureau. As senior designer, he concentrates on development of new type series. A faculty member at RISD, he teaches typography in the Department of Graphic Design. He lectures and gives workshops across the United States, Mexico, and Europe. In 2001, Highsmith was featured in *Print* magazine's New Visual Artist Review. His typefaces have won awards in national and international design competitions including Bukva:Raz!, the AIGA, and the Type Directors Club.

ABCDE
FGHIJK
LMNOP
QRSTU
WXYZ

no. 2

SELECTED BY STEPHEN DOYLE | PININFARINA MAGAZINE | DESIGNED BY ORGANIZZAZIONE SANGUINETI

Indecipherable but delightful, somehow ... That's how I felt in 1978 about finding a perfect-bound, card-covered copy of a magazine called *pininfarina* from 1965, completely in Italian, unintelligible—to me—but seductive in that its articles segued from one illustrated with Kandinsky and mathematical formulas, to another with tetrahedrons and maps drawn in the fourteenth and fifteenth centuries, and wait—there's an engraving of Gutenberg and his press, then a foldout of the *Mariner* Mars spacecraft. In this curious magazine, the article "Front Transverse Engines" (even in English, this is a foreign language to me) bumped up against Morandi and the Bayeaux Tapestry, and the finale is an exquisite portfolio of cars. Ah, the photo of the Fiat Abarth 1000 Speciale (silver convertible with red interior) perched by a misty canal somewhere in Italy made my heart beat, and I don't even like cars!

pininfarina

Anyone who knows me is double-checking the author slug on this piece (a typo perhaps?), because Stephen Doyle is definitely not a car guy. It's true, but get this: The book is interspersed with vellum sheets, printed in red and black with things like heavily bordered title pages to fourteenth-century title pages of treatises on geometry, in blackletter Latin, which hits both my graphic design G-spot as well as the Jesuit-education one. Another vellum sheet overlays a drawing of a horseshoe crab on an Arabian diagram of eyes, and the *systema visivo dell'uomo* from the year 965. I am still baffled and intrigued with this printed artifact, which only now—thirty-two years later—I will admit to stealing from my workplace at the time.

Did I tell you about page 13? A black-and-white page of text, headlined with an awful (okay, retro and fun) font, but wait—someone has pressed a pansy blossom in this old magazine. And you reach for it, to lift it. Bingo! It's printed!

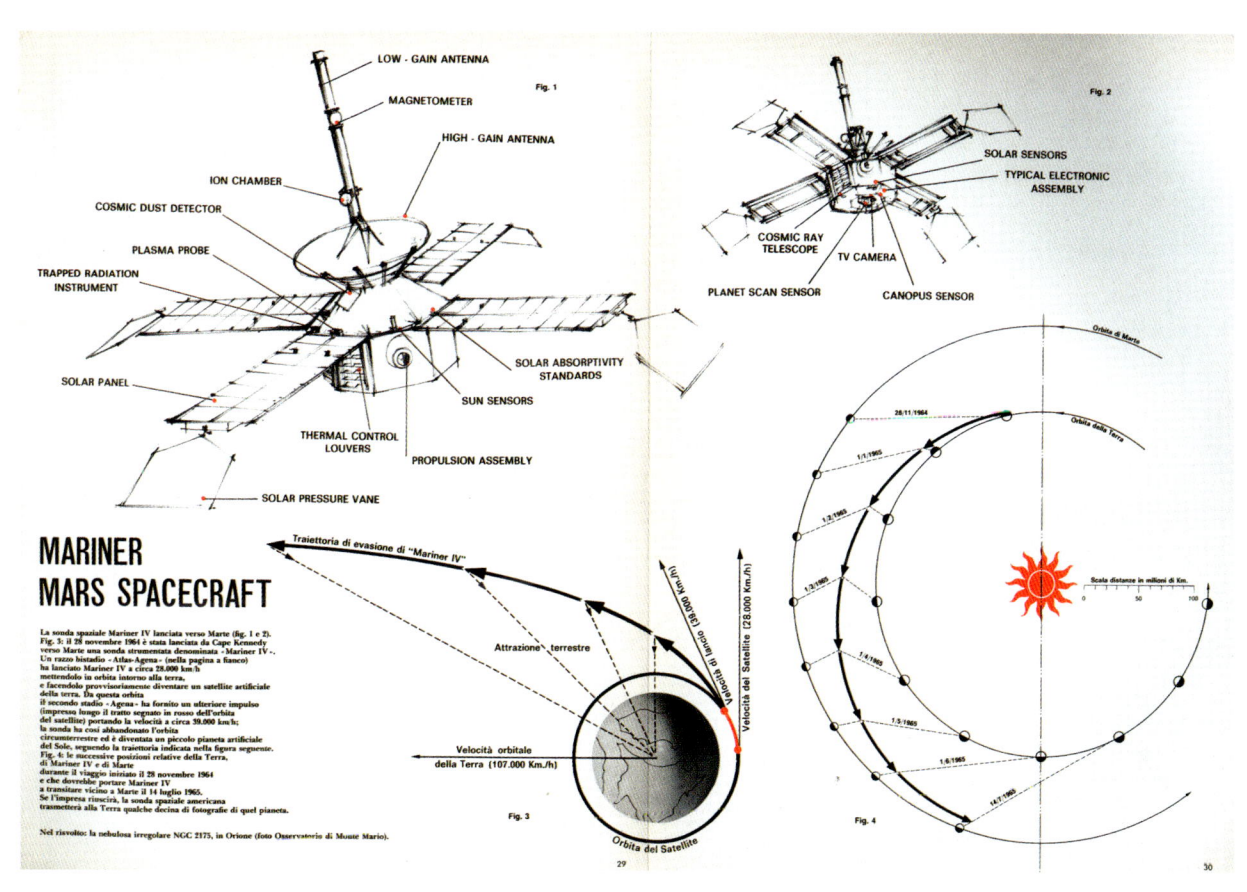

Stephen Doyle is the creative director at Doyle Partners, a design studio specializing in identity, packaging, signage, environment, and editorial design. Doyle's unique ability to give words a deeper meaning in graphic form results in an intelligent, provocative body of work for clients including the *New York Times*, AIGA, *Vanity Fair*, and publisher Alfred A. Knopf. Doyle previously served as art director at M&Co. and as associate art director at *Rolling Stone* and *Esquire*.

no. 3

SELECTED BY J. J. SEDELMAIER | **LONDON UNDERGROUND GRAPHICS** | **DESIGNED BY** VARIOUS DESIGNERS

I can't think of a more substantial and influential collection of posters designed under one company's umbrella than the posters of the London Underground. Beginning in 1908, and continuing now for over a century, this graphic approach of using a variety of design styles to advertise and brand a company's image had to have served as inspiration to corporations like MTV when devising the most effective means of reinforcing their image in the public's eye.

Another block of work that was clearly inspired on several levels by the LU approach was the 1920s Chicago Utilities posters. From 1922, and continuing throughout the decade, the Chicago region's elevated railway platforms, stations, and coach interiors were emblazoned with graphic art, advertising everything from railway transit to electric utility service. Frank Pick was the one who ran the show for the London Underground and commissioned not only the artists to do the poster but Edward Johnston to design the Johnston Underground typeface in 1916—our studio's font as well!

In Chicago, it was utilities tycoon Samuel Insull and his assistant, Britton Budd, who organized and employed the same poster approach as in the U.K. It's good to know that Insull was a Brit who retained close ties to London throughout his life and was undoubtedly well acquainted with the success of Pick's approach to transit advertising. Insull and Budd arranged for well-known artists like Ervine Metzl and Leslie Ragan to design the lithographed graphics but also employed young regional artists—such as Oscar Rabe Hanson and Walter Graham, to name a couple. The Chicago posters went almost forgotten until David Gartler curated an exhibition of the Insull posters at his vintage poster shop, Poster Plus, on Chicago's north side in 1975.

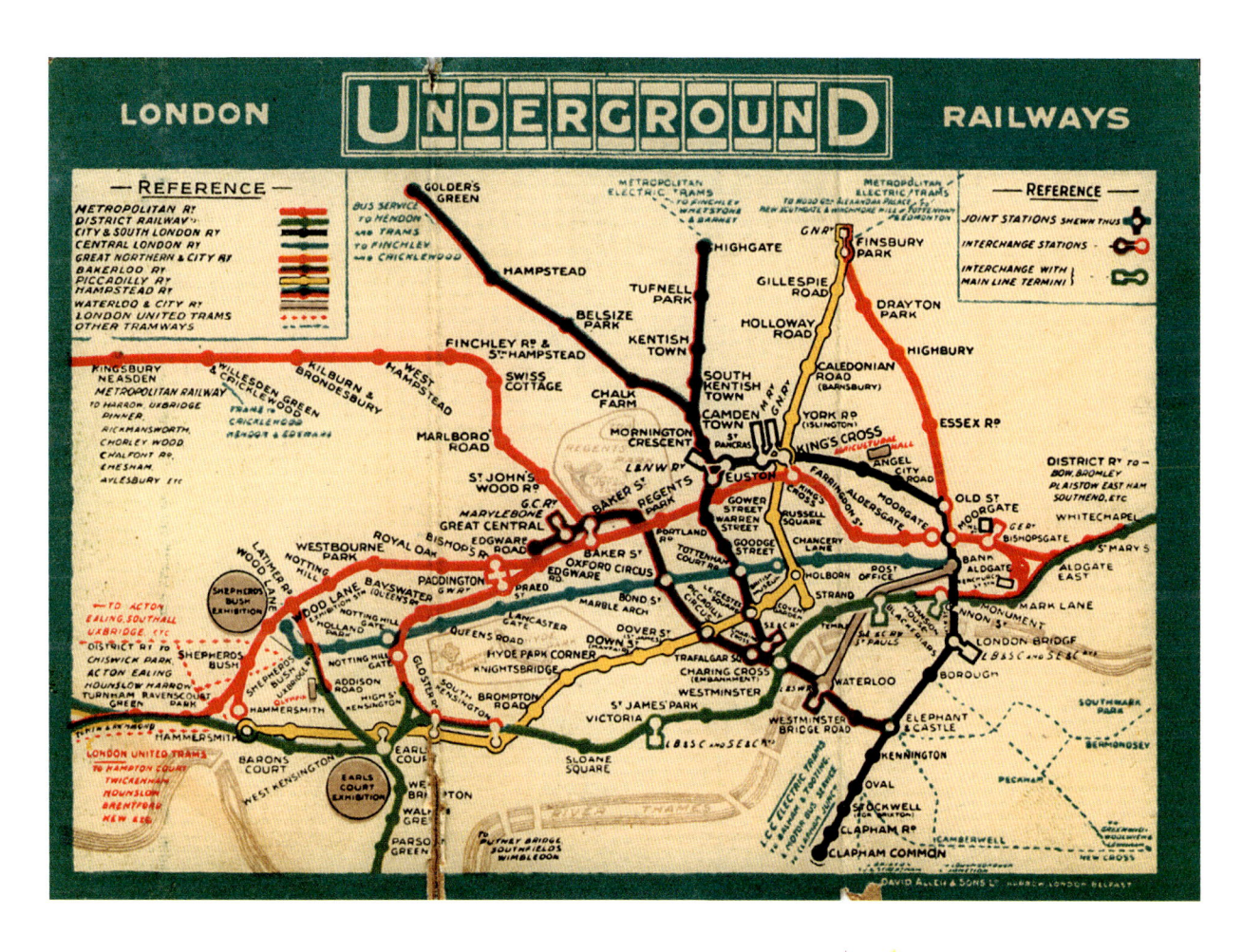

J. J. Sedelmaier is an American animation director, designer, and producer. He and his wife, Patrice, run J. J. Sedelmaier Productions, Inc., an animation/graphic design studio they established in 1990 in White Plains, New York, to create and produce television commercials utilizing print illustrators as designers. His studio's more recent works, which are more parody-oriented, include animation for Saturday TV Funhouse on *Saturday Night Live*, the pilot episode of *Harvey Birdman, Attorney at Law*, the Tek Jansen series for the *Colbert Report*, and a series of interstitial cartoons for the USA/NBC live-action series *Psych*. Sedelmaier collaborated with Robert Smigel on creating the *Ambiguously Gay Duo*, the *X-Presidents*, and the *Fun with Real Audio* cartoons for SNL. JJSP also launched the first season of MTV's acclaimed *Beavis and Butthead* series in 1993.

no. 4

SELECTED BY ED FELLA | TYPOGRAPHICA MAGAZINE | DESIGNED BY HERBERT SPENCER

Typographica No. 5—a special issue containing over eighty illustrations of postwar printing—is devoted to an exhibition, *Purpose and Pleasure: A review of book, magazine, and commercial printing from fourteen countries.* Contributors include Max Bill, Paul Rand, Herbert Simon, James Shand, and W. J. H. B. Sandberg.

I can't quite remember when I acquired this issue, other than sometime during the 1960s. I put it into a frame and it hung in my studio cubicle for many years, probably up until the early '80s. Actually, I wasn't that interested in what was in the issue or what it espoused back in 1952, as these ideas and the work shown were already part of my student education by the late '50s At the time I started my professional career in 1957, the American modernists like Rand and Beal were also not as much of an influence for me as an interest in revival styles, eclecticism, Pop art, and the vernacular. (We were part of the so-called "push pin" generation.) This cover, with its strongly connotative typography (I think it's the first time I really understood what that meant, even if I wouldn't have used the term), within a very modern and structured layout, is what appealed to me. And of course, the statement, which perfectly described what the practice of graphic design meant to me, and still does, even if the pleasure part is all I have or use nowadays, as an exit-level designer!

Ed Fella, age 72, has called himself an exit-level designer for the last twenty years as he no longer competes with the present generation. "I had my time (thirty years as a graphic designer and illustrator from 1957 to 1987), so it's their turn to earn the money and the glory—and whatever the current downside of all that might be!" For the past twenty-two years, Fella has taught graphic design for the graduate program at CalArts.

Typographica: An Occasional Review of Typography and the Graphic Arts was edited by Herbert Spencer and published by Lund Humphries in London in 1952.

Typographica No. 5 – a special issue containing over eighty illustrations (many in colour) of post-war printing design – is devoted to

PURPOSE AND

an exhibition

PLEASURE

A review of book, magazine and commercial printing from fourteen countries. Contributors include Max Bill, Paul Rand, Herbert Simon, James Shand, W. J. H. B. Sandberg

Lund Humphries   5/-

no. 5

SELECTED BY SEAN ADAMS | LA FONDA DEL SOL RESTAURANT | DESIGNED BY ALEXANDER GIRARD

Alexander Girard's design for La Fonda del Sol Restaurant in 1961 is a wonderful synthesis of modernist concepts paired with a sense of joy and play. Traditional Mexican handcrafts and materials were reconsidered within a contemporary urban context. This combination takes the rigor and discipline of European Bauhaus thinking and reinterprets it for the new world. The result is not as much Mexican as it is a representation of the American process of incorporating multiple cultures into its identity. The color palette rejects a European aesthetic and embraces a Mexican and South American palette.

Girard's work on La Fonda del Sol gave me the permission to move beyond the small confines of pure Bauhaus modernism and create work that is optimistic, joyful, and celebratory without descending into chaos and disorder.

Sean Adams is a partner at AdamsMorioka in Beverly Hills, California. He has been recognized by every major competition and publication, including *Step Inside Design*, *Graphis*, AIGA, the British D&AD, and the NYADC. Adams has been cited as one of the forty most important people shaping design internationally in the I.D. 40. Adams is president ex officio of AIGA and a Fellow of the Aspen Design Conference and AIGA Fellow. He teaches at Art Center College of Design, and he is the author of *Logo Design Workbook*, *Color Design Workbook*, and the *Masters of Design* series, all published by Rockport Publishers.

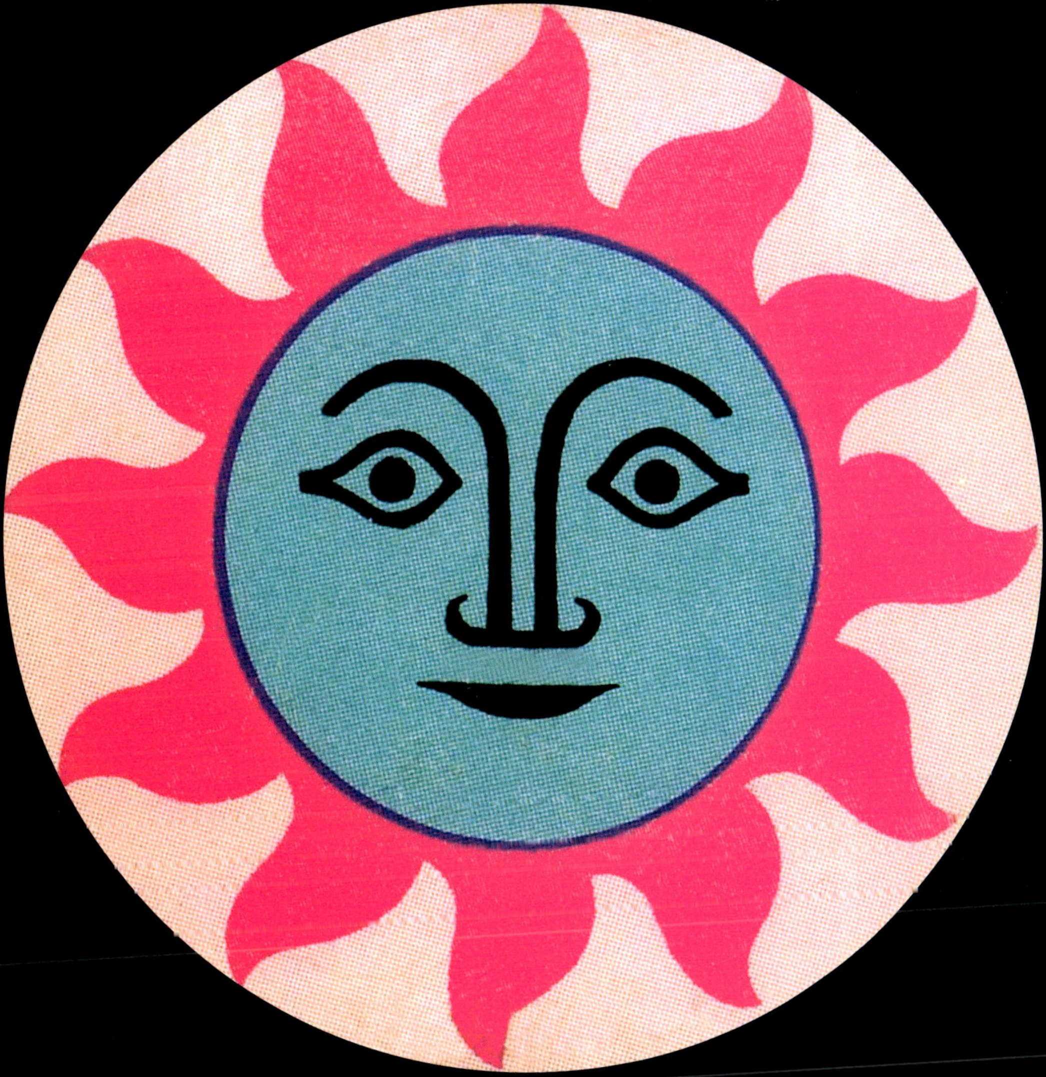

no. 6

SELECTED BY KATHERINE McCOY | **HIROSHIMA APPEALS** | **DESIGNED BY** KUNIOMI UEMATSU

This poster by the Japanese graphic designer Kuniomi Uematsu was part of the influential *Hiroshima Appeals* series of Japanese peace posters against nuclear war directed to an international audience.

The nonverbal communication of this poster's powerful imagery is masterful. Because of its global audience, the message cannot depend on words from any one language and must communicate using symbols. Visual symbols are more widely understood than verbal texts from specific languages, so symbolic images are important tools for communications designers.

This poster is not beautiful in the conventional sense, but to me (a perpetual student of visual communication) it is beautiful in its power and universality. Each element of this rather simple image carries two or more meanings. Taken literally, the image is an iconic photographic representation of a piece of burned toast with holes punched in it and jelly oozing through a hole. But this photo is packed with powerful symbolic associations. The toast is the shape of a nuclear mushroom cloud. It has been burned and damaged, suggesting the violence of nuclear holocaust. The toast is also a skull shape, and the holes make a face with eyes, nose, and a grimacing mouth—a frightening image of death. The jelly becomes blood and gore, or tears weeping from an eye. The poster demonstrates rhetorical irony, too—toast and jelly are very familiar and comforting breakfast foods, provided by our mothers when we were children. This suggests that nuclear war could surprise any of us, even in our sheltered homes and most domestic moments. There is even an embedded visual/verbal pun, although the poster's Japanese-speaking designer may have been unaware of it: In a nuclear war, "You're toast." In so many ways, this image makes us think deeply about the horror of nuclear war.

Katherine McCoy is best known for her work as the cochair of the graduate design program for Cranbrook Academy of Art. During her extensive career spanning education and professional practice, McCoy worked with groundbreaking design firm Unimark, Chrysler Corporation, and with Muriel Cooper in the early days of MIT Press while at the Boston design firm Omnigraphics. McCoy's career in education was similarly broad, teaching at Cranbrook Academy of Art, Illinois Institute of Technology's Institute of Design, and the Royal College of Art, London.

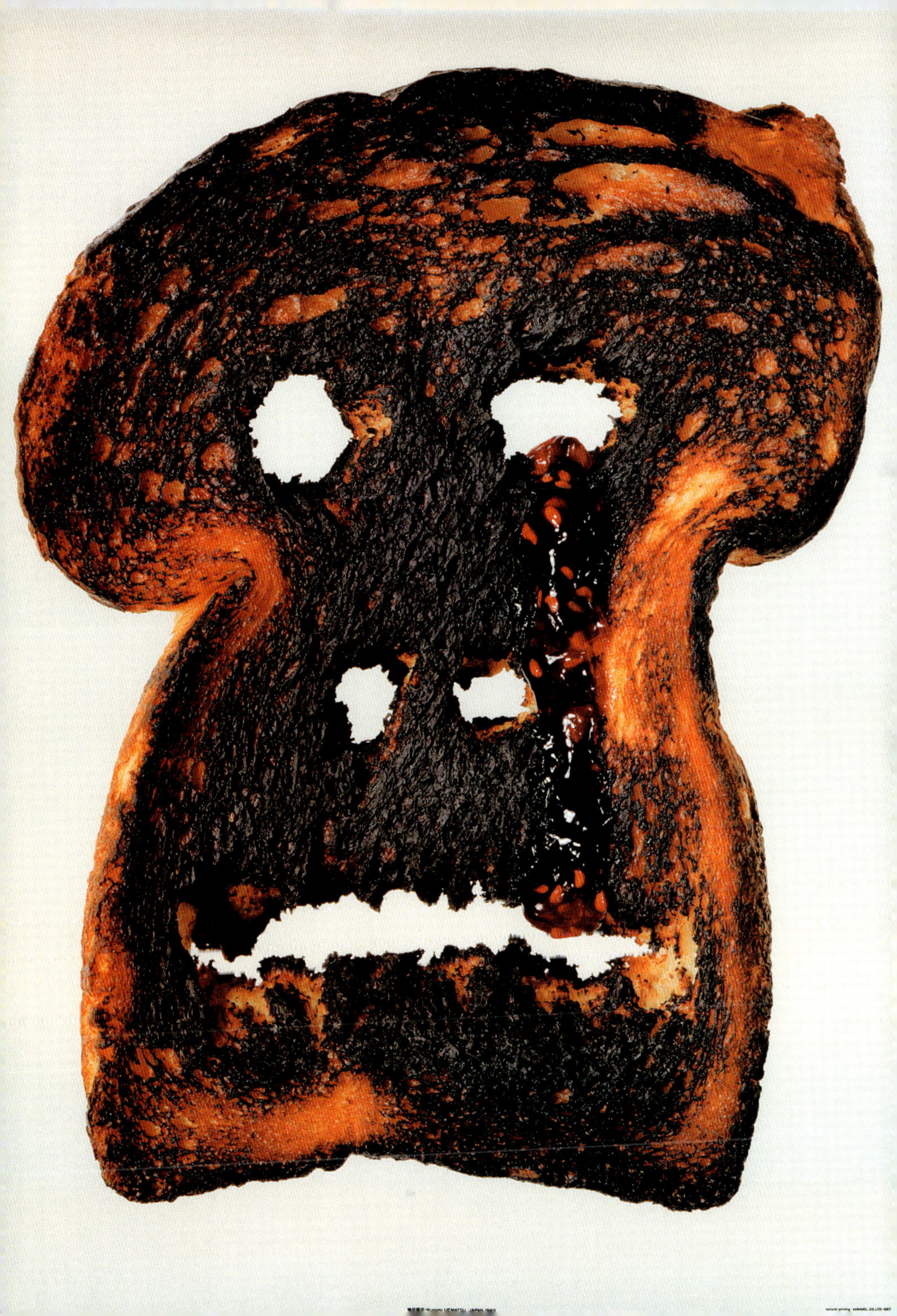

no. 7

SELECTED BY BRIAN COLLINS | **SUPERMAN TITLE SEQUENCE** | **DESIGNED BY** RICHARD GREENBERG

"This is no fantasy—no careless product of wild imagination … No, my friends, these are matters of undeniable fact." So speaks Marlon Brando in the first minutes of Richard Donner's 1978 film, *Superman.*

The design of the opening credits delivered on this promise, instantly transforming a dusty children's comic into a stirring American myth. In a blaze of flying blue typography amplified by John Williams's thundering, triumphant score, *Superman* arrives as a hero of epic proportions.

In mere seconds, this design accomplishes a major feat. Beyond setting the tone for what is to come by establishing a new emotional expectation for the audience, the opening sequence sends a very clear message that this Superman has gravitas.

It does so by honoring its subject's origins—opening with a black-and-white shot of a tattered comic book from the Great Depression. It grounds the story in what the audience knows. Next, it connects it to the present day and achieves verisimilitude via a flyover shot of the *Daily Planet* headquarters. Finally, as the audience soars through the stars toward the doomed planet Krypton, it reveals what is most beloved about our hero's story as the only son from another realm—its mythic power.

Great myths momentarily lift us into another plane of existence so we can see the world—and our own lives—with fresh eyes. And the design of these credits does just that—revealing timeless meaning to this story while also keeping it fresh. As designers often charged with reinventing companies and their products, this is a road map my team and I often use in our own work. This is a fine example of how revisiting a story's origins can revitalize its future. The movie's ad campaign exclaimed, "You'll Believe a Man Can Fly!" Well, sure. But by the end of this sequence, we believe we can fly, too. And that is no careless product, indeed.

Brian Collins is an American designer, creative director, and founder of the communications and branding firm COLLINS: in New York City. He was the chief creative officer of the Brand Innovation Group, Ogilvy & Mather, in New York for nine years (1998–2007) He teaches in the MFA design program at the School of Visual Arts.

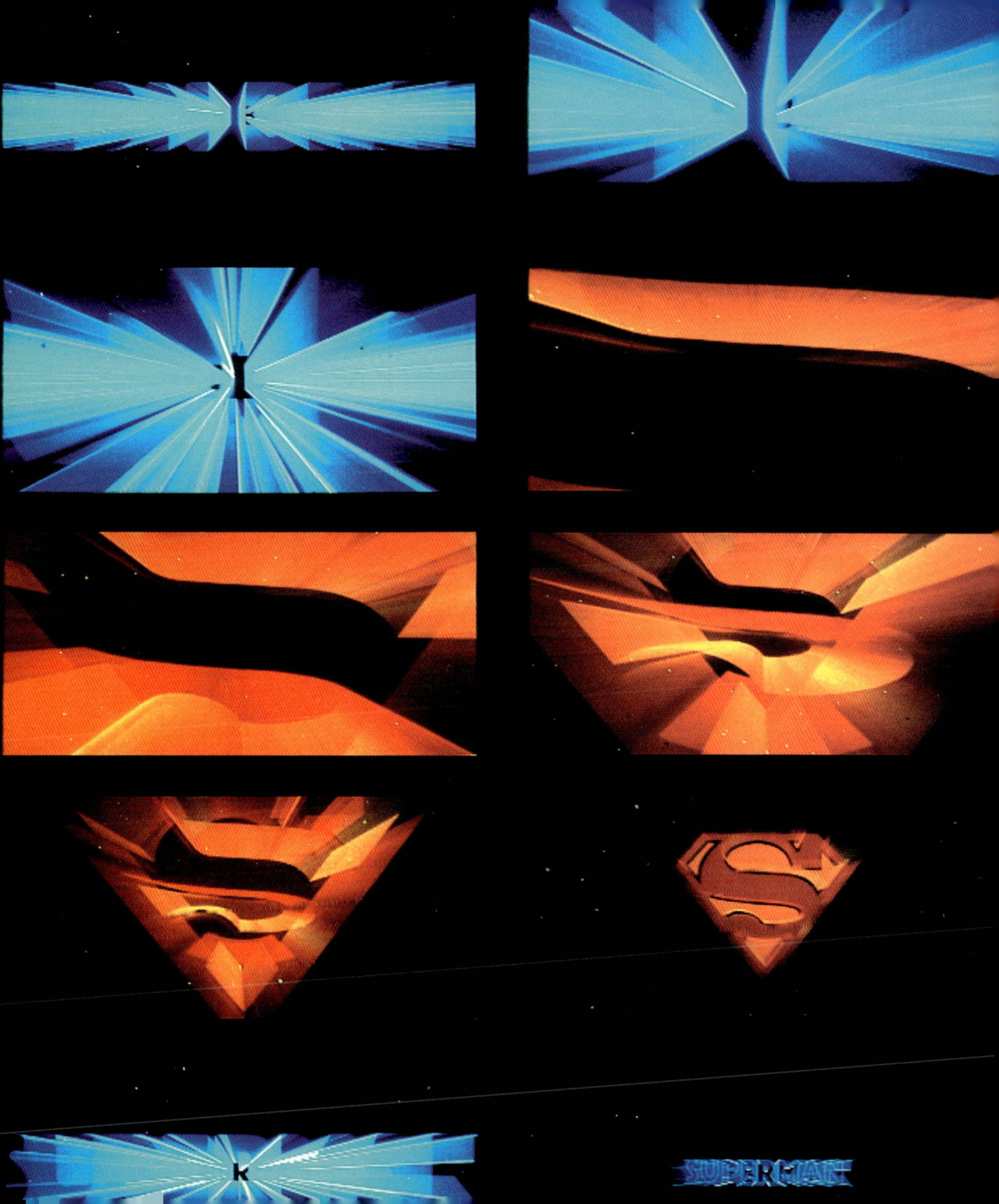
SUPERMAN

no. 8

SELECTED BY ART CHANTRY | THE HAPPY FACE | DESIGNER UNKNOWN

In graphic design circles, there is an ongoing and vociferous debate about the authorship of the happy face (a.k.a. "Mr. Smiley"). This image has been around so long and has been through so many permutations and redefinitions, that it has become one of the most basic and essential images in the dictionary of graphic design. It's possibly the most ubiquitous (and therefore most prominent) bit of graphic design of the last century.

The earliest current documentation of the happy face origins is its use as an advertising icon (not quite a logo) for the New York radio station WCMA (the "good guys") in 1964. There is even a photograph of a young John Lennon wearing one of the radio station's promo T-shirts featuring a happy face. Soon thereafter, a Mr. Harvey Ball penned the classic (East Coast) version of the happy face for a novelty company. It then exploded into the mid '60s Pop Art market and was picked up by every company selling Pop trash (greeting cards, buttons, clothing—basically all that graphic design stuff we try to ignore). It seemed to be the happy-go-lucky, kid-next-door version of the slightly frightening peace symbol; a sort of industrial psychedelia marketed to American teenagers by corporate America. We always have to cash in on what the kids are up to. It's what made America great.

There were regional variations as well. On the West Coast, in about 1967, Seattle marketing guru David Stern executed an ad campaign for University Savings and Loan using the happy face, most notably as a little button that became hugely popular. The actual design (slightly different from the East Coast version) of the happy face in that campaign was executed by George Tanagi, a venerated longtime Seattle graphic design grand master. To this day, most West Coast academics credit George Tanagi and David Stern for the creation of the happy face. Stern even ran for the mayorship of Seattle largely on the basis of his having created the happy face (no joke). Thank heaven he lost.

Turn the happy face upside down and make it green and he became Mr. Yuk, saving America's children from the evils of household poisons. Sneak him

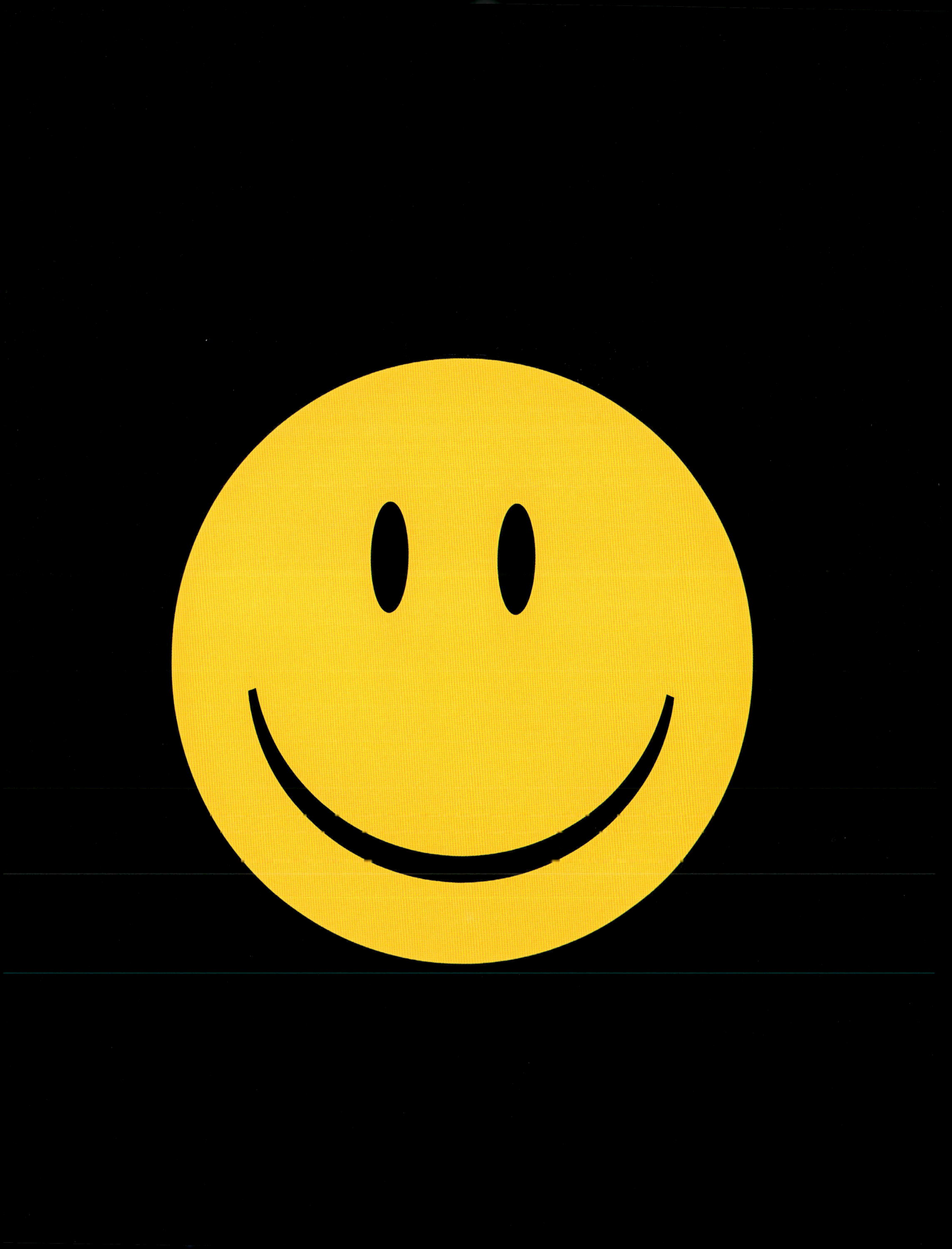

on tablets of the drug "xstacy" and the happy face became the underground logo for that notorious feel-good drug culture. Slap him into a megastore ad campaign for Walmart, and he became the virtual logo for that huge corporation. I imagine they even tried to file an exclusive copyright on its use. Pop a bullet hole in its forehead and you've got the dark ironic brand of the Watchmen. Bring on the Internet, and we have millions of happy face emoticons peppering the ether. The happy face is as available as belly buttons—I mean, everybody has one! My mom collects them and has hundreds of mugs, stuffed toys, dolls, place mats, and crap.

So who actually did the first one? Some high school cheerleader? The Dadaists? The Roman Empire? The earliest advertising use of the happy face that I've found is the logo for a small (but popular) store in Beulah, Michigan (cherry capital of the world), called The Cherry Hut. Founded in 1922, it uses not the classic yellow Mr. Smiley of 1960. However, I doubt the happy face was invented by The Cherry Hut.

Tibor Kalman's famous argument was that most important graphic design language grew from the vernacular. I always had a problem with that idea, not because I disagreed with it, but because it somehow felt like slumming, like anything deemed common or vulgar or authorless was to be dumped into the landfill of the vernacular to be exploited freely as source material for postmodernist genius. I think a definition of vernacular may have been helpful. If you loosely define the word as "of the people," then I would agree wholeheartedly with Tibor. In fact, I think of graphic design as *the* language of the people. We all understand what the happy face means. It doesn't even require a common spoken or written language to understand it.

I think that graphic design itself is a language—a language everybody speaks fluently but doesn't know they speak it at all. We all know what red means, what a circle means, what a ratty line or a smooth curve means, and we know what a happy face means. Through all of its scattered lives and constant "rebranding," its basic underlying meaning remains intact. So, who was the author? We'll never know, like we'll never really know who did the Coke bottle or the Oreo cookie. It's lost to a time when we didn't value authorship in graphic design; indeed, did not value graphic design.

Every little girl named Debbie who dotted her *i* with a smiley face is the author. Every person who slaps a smiley emoticon onto their comment on a blog or email is the author. Every ad agency hack who thinks they invented the concept of a smiling little face is the author. We are all the author. The happy face basically grew on a tree. Maybe a cherry tree.

Arthur S. W. Chantry II (born April 9, 1954, in Seattle) is a graphic designer known for expanding on the bristling low-tech aesthetic of punk music, in posters and album covers for bands like Nirvana, Hole, and the Sonics, as well as lesser-known groups like the Cramps, the Lord High Fixers, Mono Men, and Bert. His work has been exhibited at the Rock and Roll Hall of Fame, the Museum of Modern Art, Seattle Art Museum, the Smithsonian, and the Louvre.

SELECTED BY SEYMOUR CHWAST | **CRAVEN "A" CIGARETTES POSTER** | **DESIGNED BY** ACHILLE MAUZAN

Achille Mauzan (1883–1952) worked in Milan, Paris, and Buenos Aires. His fame as a poster designer never achieved the level of Cassandre or Hollwein, which may be due to the humor in his vast body of work. I relate to that humor but also to his ideas, use of color, and sense of scale. This image employed repetition and the abstract elements of a contemporary painting. Added to his design sense is his impeccable drawing skill: confident, forceful, and animated. There is nothing arty in his posters with the in-your-face, sans-serif typography. His work fits the art deco criteria, but it also includes the spirit of surrealism, futurism, and Dada. Unlike painting, drawing, and sculpture, which go on forever, poster design depends on a medium that is evolving. Conventional poster design is winding down, but it is a vital art form that must be studied and preserved.

Seymour Chwast is cofounder of Push Pin Studios and presently director of the Push Pin Group. Chwast reintroduced graphic styles and transformed them into a contemporary vocabulary. His designs and illustrations have been used in advertising, animated films, and editorial and corporate graphics. He has created over 100 posters, has written or illustrated more than thirty children's books, and has exhibited and lectured worldwide. He was inducted into the Art Directors Hall of Fame and is an AIGA medalist.

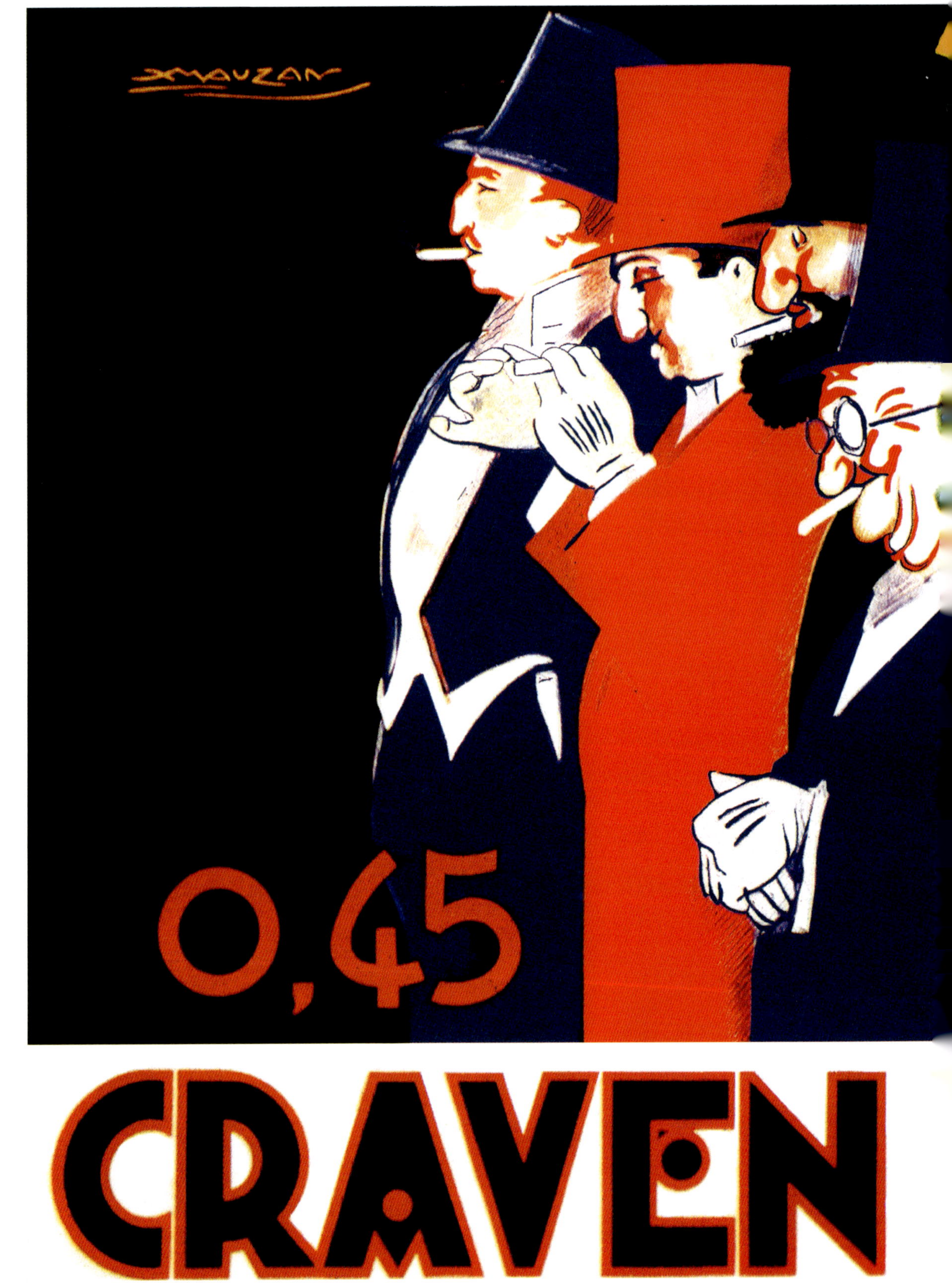
MAUZAN
0,45
CRAVEN

"A" Cigarettes
IMPORTADOS DE LONDRES

no. 10

SELECTED BY MICHAEL MAHARAM | ISOTYPES | DESIGNED BY OTTO NEURATH

El Lissitzky was commissioned by the government of the U.S.S.R. to create an album illustrating the organization, national economy, and demographic profile of the state for distribution at the 1939 New York World's Fair. This book exhibits the use of color and layout first encountered in the legendary Pickering edition of *Euclid* published in 1847, a forebear of the system of ISOTYPES (International System of Typographic Picture Education) developed under the auspices of Otto Neurath at the Gesellschafts und Wirtschafts museum in Vienna between 1925 and 1934.

The vivid contrast between dry Soviet statistics on such subjects as sanatoriums and rest homes and Lissitzky's lively and imaginative graphics is striking and illustrates the relevance and visual clarity of this simple form of graphic expression. ISOTYPES are the original analog GUI (graphical user interface) and reflect principles of information management and legibility, which virtually every business could benefit from in our increasingly content-rich world.

Michael Maharam is the principal of Maharam, a fourth-generation family business and the leading supplier of textiles to commercial architects and interior designers. He is a member of the MoMA A+D Committee, a trustee of the Chinati Foundation, and the 2007 recipient of the Cooper-Hewitt National Design Award for Design Patron.

SANATORIUMS AND REST HOMES

THE NUMBER OF WORKERS AND EMPLOYEES WHO RECEIVED FREE PASSES
(in thousands)

IN 1929–1937 OVER 12 MILLION PERSONS RESTED AND RECEIVED TREATMENT IN SANATORIUMS AT HEALTH RESORTS AND IN REST HOMES, ENTIRELY AT THE COST OF SOCIAL INSURANCE AND TRADE UNION FUNDS.

IN ADDITION, HUNDREDS OF THOUSANDS OF WORKING PEOPLE ANNUALLY RECEIVE FREE SANATORIUM TREATMENT AND REST AT THE EXPENSE OF MILLS, FACTORIES, ENTERPRISES AND INSTITUTIONS.

SANATORIUMS
1927/28 — 74.2
1938 — 555.0

REST HOMES (exclusive of one-day rest homes)
1927/28 — 437.2
1938 — 1,900.0

Each sign denotes 75,000 persons (in round figures).

96

PHYSICAL CULTURE AND SPORT

THE NUMBER OF PHYSICAL CULTURISTS WHO HAVE RECEIVED BADGES FOR PASSING THE STANDARD SPORT TESTS (in thousands)

1933 (on January 1)
Total 465
Men 429 Women 36

1938 (on May 1)
Total 4,978
Men 4,468 Women 510

Each group denotes 500,000 holders of badges (in round figures).

102

no. 11

SELECTED BY PAOLA ANTONELLI | **THE @ SYMBOL** | **REDISCOVERED BY RAY TOMLINSON**

The @ symbol has a long and disputed past. Some linguists believe that it dates back to the sixth or seventh century, an adaptation of the Latin preposition *ad*, meaning "at," "to," or "toward."

The @ ligature would have been formed by scribes in an attempt to lessen the number of pen strokes, exaggerating the upstroke of the letter *d* and curving it over the *a*. Others believe that the symbol has a later genesis in sixteenth-century Venetian trade, citing commercial documents where @ was used to mean amphora, a standard-size terra-cotta vessel employed by merchants that had become a unit of measure.

From the eighteenth century onward, @ meant "at the price of," similar to the Norman French use of à, which, incidentally, might be another source for @'s shape, with the grave accent eventually becoming @'s curl.

Due to a culmination of all these influences the @ symbol was known as the "'commercial a" when it appeared on the keyboard of the American Underwood typewriter in 1885, and it was defined as such, for the first time, in the *American Dictionary of Printing and Bookmaking* in 1894. From this point on, the symbol itself was standardized both stylistically and in its application.

In January 1971, @ was an underused jargon symbol lingering on the keyboard. By October, Ray Tomlinson had rediscovered and appropriated it, imbuing it with new meaning and elevating it to the defining symbol of the computer age. He chose the @ for his first email because of its strong locative sense—an individual, identified by a username, is @ this institution/computer/server, and also because…it was already there, on the keyboard, and nobody ever used it. The appropriation and reuse of a preexisting, even ancient, symbol already available on the keyboard is an act of extraordinarily elegant and economical design.

Paola Antonelli is one of the world's foremost design experts and was recently rated as one of the top 100 most powerful people in the world of art by *Art Review*. She is a senior curator in the Department of Architecture and Design at the Museum of Modern Art. The recipient of a laureate degree in architecture from the Politecnico di Milano University in 1990, Antonelli has curated several architecture and design exhibitions in Italy, France, and Japan. She has been a contributing editor for *Domus* magazine (1987–1991) and the design editor of Abitare (1992–1994).

From the top: Gotham Thin (175 pt), Adobe Clarendon Light (170 pt), The Sans Light (165 pt), Blackoak (134 pt), Helvetica Neue 65 (150 pt), Suburban Light (200 pt), Estilo Text Bold (145 pt), Hoefler Text Regular (135 pt), Linotype Didot (130 pt), Avenir Light (135 pt),

no. 12

SELECTED BY EDWIN SCHLOSSBERG | **I OBJECT DEFY MYSELF** | **DESIGNED BY** EDWIN SCHLOSSBERG

I made this in 1964. I was thinking about how words both separate and join people and how reflection is both a description of thinking and an action of rejection. I had started writing poems on aluminum foil because I loved the world that the reading and thinking and the sounds of turning the pages created. Then, I looked across the street and saw a new roof being installed made of heavy copper and I thought, "I object defy myself."

As an object, I defy my being, and as description, I separate myself from my experience. It was too good. I went and made this poem/drawing and it has hung at my desk ever since. It has influenced everything I have designed since then because it was/is so clearly interesting and reassuring. It has appeared in several shows and is always the object that is quoted. I love it.

Edwin Arthur Schlossberg, founder and principal of ESI Design, is an internationally recognized designer, author, and artist. Schlossberg specializes in designing interactive, participatory experiences, beginning in 1977 with the first hands-on learning environment in the United States for the Brooklyn Children's Museum. Schlossberg continues to work in the field and publishes frequently on the subject. Schlossberg is the author of *Interactive Excellence: Defining and Developing New Standards for the Twenty-First Century*, published by Ballantine Books.

I OBJECT
DEFY
MYSELF

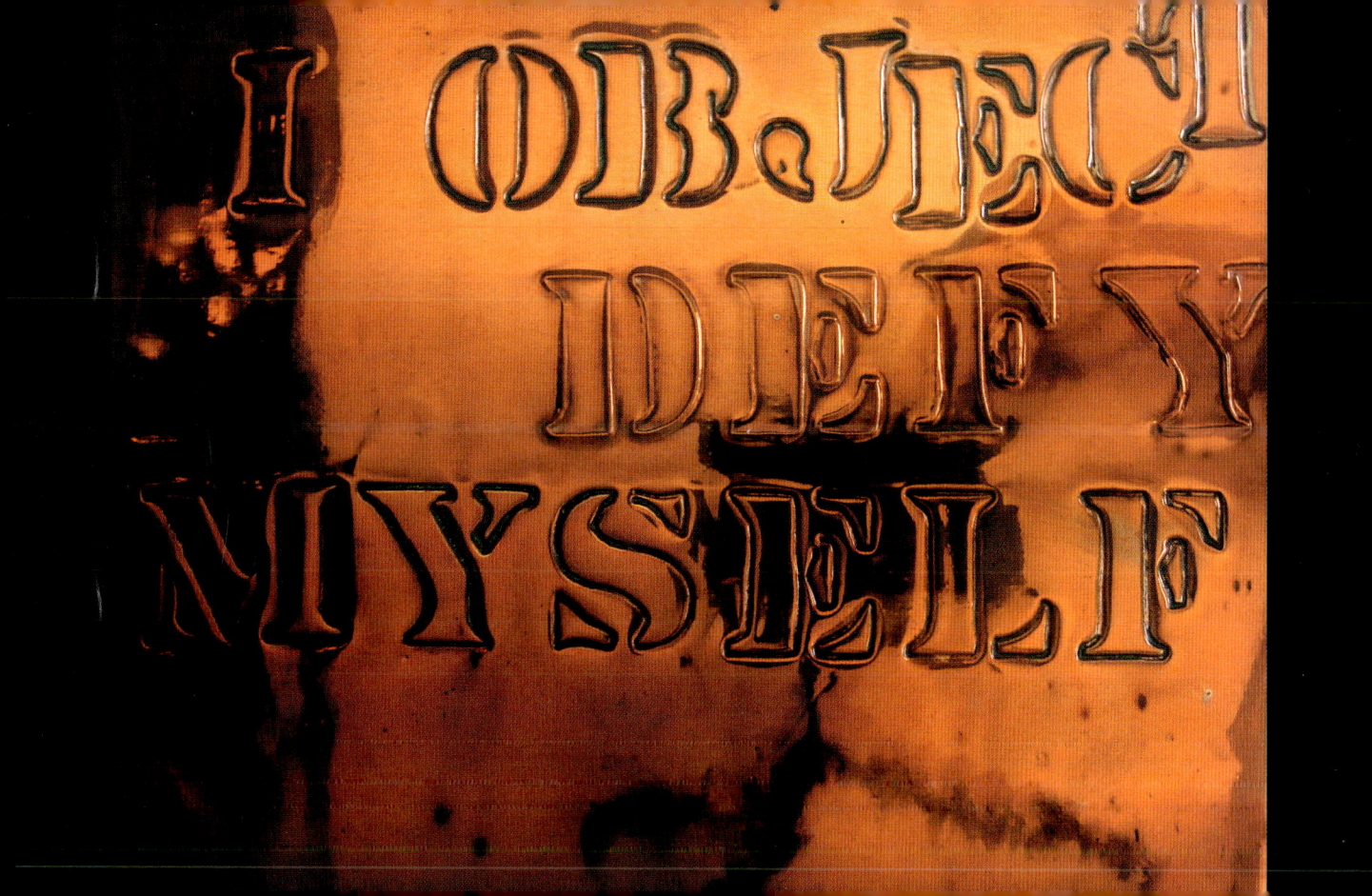

no. 13

SELECTED BY RICK POYNOR

PLAYPOWER

HARDBACK PUBLISHED BY **JONATHAN CAPE** | JACKET DESIGNED BY **MARTIN SHARP** | PAPERBACK PUBLISHED BY **PALADIN, LONDON** | COVER DESIGNED BY **RICHARD ADAMS**

I read Richard Neville's *Playpower* in 1972. I was fifteen and seriously disaffected. I took an unofficial day off from school and caught the bus to a distant park where I spent several hours at the top of a hill devouring Neville's racy, insider's guide to the counterculture and dreaming about sticking it to the man.

The author was the notorious Australian founding editor of *Oz*, a scandalous London underground magazine—I never missed an issue. My edition of *Playpower* was the Paladin paperback, though, and I didn't see the original 1970 hardback until many years later in an antiquarian bookshop. I had to have it. The jacket was designed by Neville's friend, Martin Sharp, who created wildly inventive layouts for *Oz* as well as classic album covers and posters.

PLAYPOWER
RICHARD NEVILLE

Playpower doesn't quite equal his best work, but it was a boldly iconoclastic image for Jonathan Cape, an establishment publisher with offices in Bloomsbury, then the heart of literary London. As with all of Sharp's underground art, an ambivalent satirical malaise taints the liberated psychedelic fantasy. This is a garden of queasily decadent delights where the joke is probably on the reader. The dope-smoking guitar alien twangs his pole obliviously, a long-nosed letter *A* (on the back) is about to screw a convenient red loop on the end of its tongue, and the smirking author reaches for a tab of acid from behind an erupting phallic column. "Sharp drew an exuberant cover—a flying circus of joints, flutes, exploding hearts and toothy smiles—though the book was not to his liking," Neville confides in his autobiography, *Hippie Hippie Shake*. Widely reviewed at the time, both celebrated and reviled, *Playpower* hasn't worn well. But Sharp's preemptive jaundiced vision (yellow!) still oozes menace. Its gleefully chaotic sarcasm is as far from modernist self-restraint as you can get: an antiprofessional rallying cry for the coming waves of punks, postmodernists, DIYers, and other graphic dissenters.

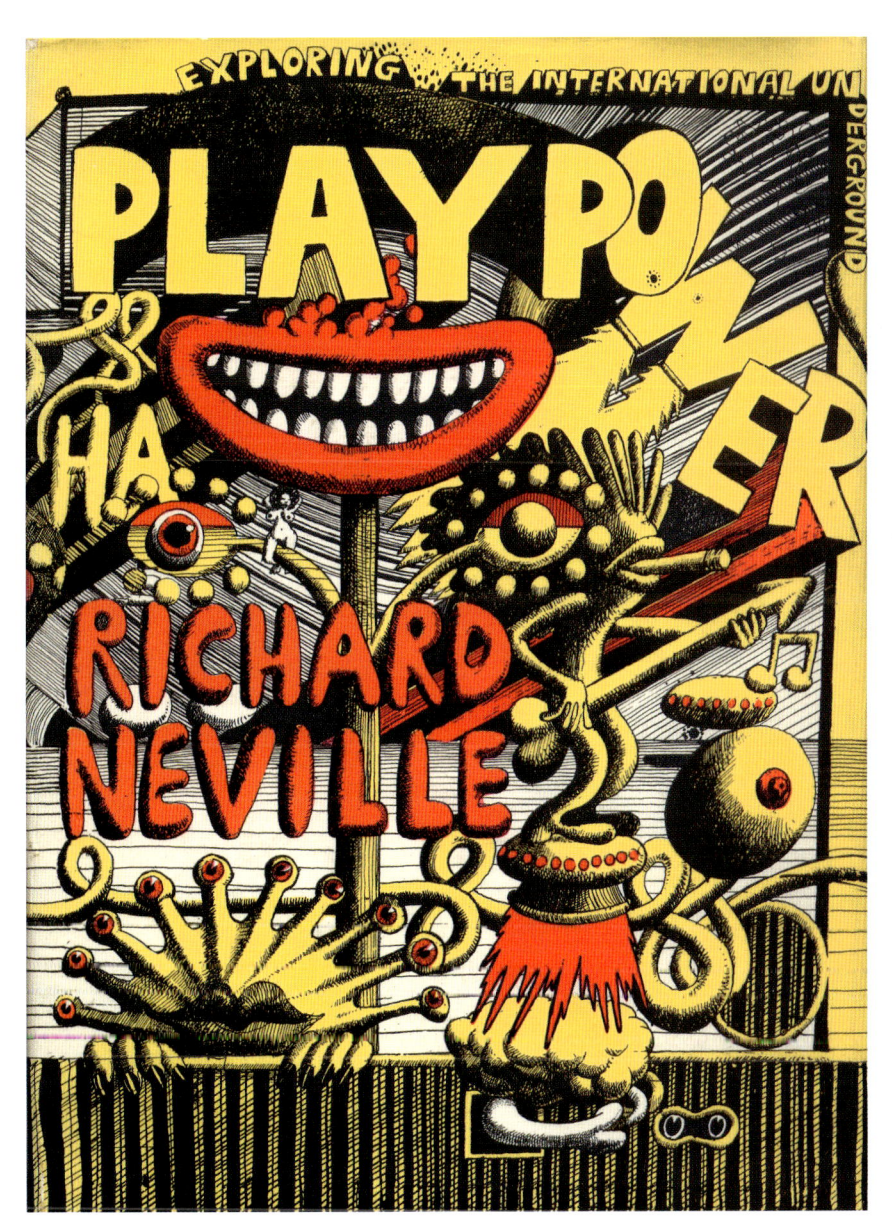

Rick Poynor writes about design, media, and visual culture. He was the founding editor of *Eye* magazine, a cofounder of the *Design Observer* weblog, and contributes columns to *Eye* and *Print*. He has written for *Blueprint, Icon, Frieze, Creative Review, Metropolis,* and *Adbusters*. His books include *Obey the Giant: Life in the Image World* (2001), *No More Rules: Graphic Design and Postmodernism* (2003), and *Jan van Toorn: Critical Practice* (2008). In 2004, he curated the exhibition, *Communicate: Independent British Graphic Design since the Sixties* at the Barbican Art Gallery, London.

no. 14

SELECTED BY ARNOLD SCHWARTZMAN | **THE SAVOY COCKTAIL BOOK** | **ILLUSTRATED BY** GILBERT ROMBOLD

As a born and bred Londoner, I cherish two beloved indigenous graphic objects. The first is *The Savoy Cocktail Book* by Harry Craddock. Craddock had been a cocktail barman in New York, but had left for London during Prohibition and set up shop at the American Bar in London's swank Savoy Hotel. His book, first printed in 1930 and illustrated by Gilbert Rumbold, is recognized today as an icon of Art Deco publishing. My copy was given to me by my father—he had acquired it during his days as a waiter at the Savoy Hotel—and I believe this elegant tome was my first exposure to the world of graphics. In fact, Rumbold's illustrations still bear outlined impressions caused by my childish attempt to trace his artwork.

My early life was inseparably entwined in the web of London's Underground train system. My parents and I slept on the crowded platforms of the tube stations after we survived a direct hit to our home by the Luftwaffe during an air raid in the London Blitz. Prior to World War II, the London Underground system had undergone a renaissance of design under the leadership of its chief executive, Frank Pick, who was responsible for the total "look" of London's Passenger Transport Board, including its architecture, furnishings, signage, and, most interesting to me, its magnificent posters from such artists as American-born Edward McKnight Kauffer.

The Savoy
COCKTAIL
BOOK

A year after the publication of *The Savoy Cocktail Book*, a twenty-nine-year-old London Passenger Transport Board engineer by the name of Harry Beck first envisioned his breakthrough color-coded Underground map, which compressed distances between stations and consisted of horizontal, vertical, and diagonal lines. He spent the next twenty-five years perfecting his design. His diagrammatic solution has become a landmark in the world of information graphics and the inspiration for a plethora of rapid transport maps around the globe, from D.C. to Delft, from Madrid to Montreal, and, of course Massimo Vignelli's now-iconic map for the New York Transit Authority. Still retained today are Edward Johnston's LPTB "bull's-eye" trademark and the Underground Railway Sans typeface of 1916, which predates Paul Renner's Futura of 1927 and was also emulated by his pupil Eric Gill in his design of Gill Sans in 1928.

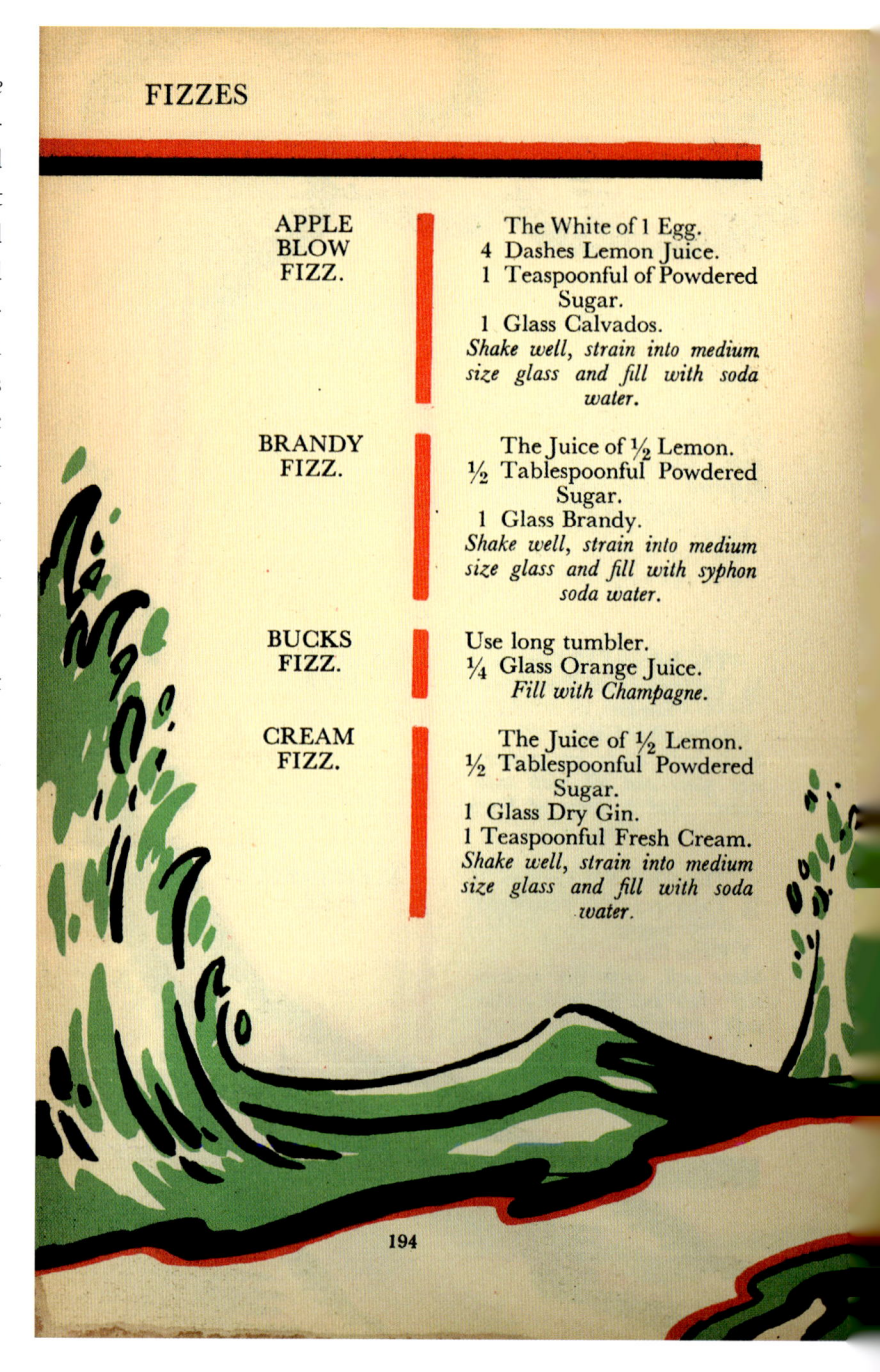

FIZZES

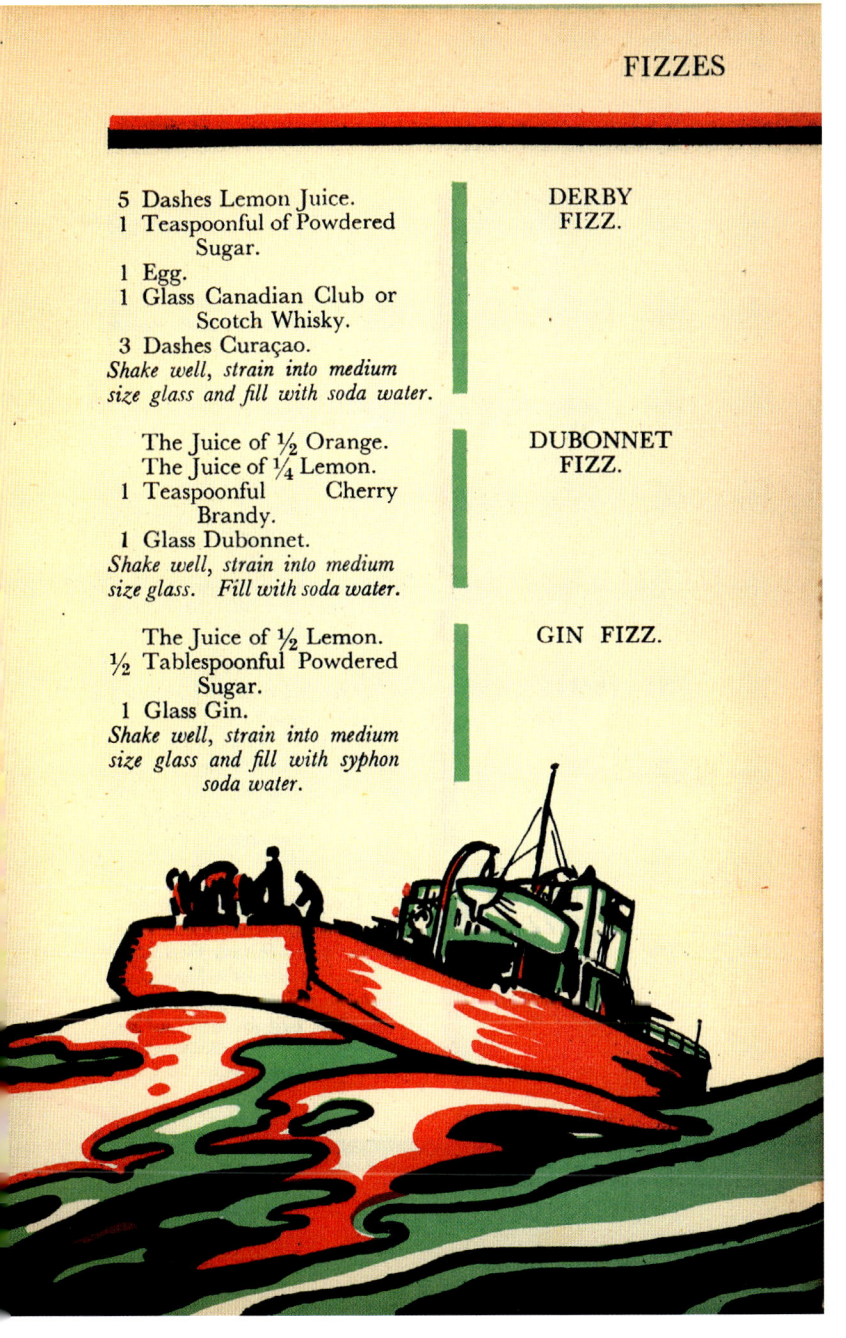

DERBY FIZZ.
5 Dashes Lemon Juice.
1 Teaspoonful of Powdered Sugar.
1 Egg.
1 Glass Canadian Club or Scotch Whisky.
3 Dashes Curaçao.
Shake well, strain into medium size glass and fill with soda water.

DUBONNET FIZZ.
The Juice of ½ Orange.
The Juice of ¼ Lemon.
1 Teaspoonful Cherry Brandy.
1 Glass Dubonnet.
Shake well, strain into medium size glass. Fill with soda water.

GIN FIZZ.
The Juice of ½ Lemon.
½ Tablespoonful Powdered Sugar.
1 Glass Gin.
Shake well, strain into medium size glass and fill with syphon soda water.

London-born **Arnold Schwartzman** is an Academy Award–winning filmmaker and noted graphic designer. He moved to Hollywood in 1978 to become the design director for Saul Bass and Associates. In 1982, Schwartzman was appointed the director of design for the 1984 Los Angeles Olympic Games. Since 1996, he has designed many of the key elements for the annual Academy Awards, including commemorative posters, billboards, cinema trailers, and printed programs for the awards ceremony and Governor's Ball.

no. 15

SELECTED BY ANITA KUNZ | **I, LEONARDO** | **AUTHORED & ILLUSTRATED BY RALPH STEADMAN**

When I was a young artist, I struggled to create a unique visual voice. I found great inspiration in the work of Ralph Steadman. His work is authentic, audacious, hilarious, and, of course, exquisitely drawn. The ideas were brilliant as well. Ralph was and remains a great artist, writer, and insightful thinker. Although he is best known for his *Fear and Loathing* work with Hunter S. Thompson, I admire him most for his compassion and work having to do with human rights.

I chose his book, *I, Leonardo,* as one of my most beloved objects. Who else but the great Ralph Steadman would choose another genius to interpret? The book contains a world of wit and wisdom, and I revisit it again and again. It is a triumph of personal expression, acerbic insight, and artistic brilliance.

Anita Kunz has worked as an artist, illustrator, and educator for almost thirty years. Her clients include *Time* magazine, *Rolling Stone*, *Vanity Fair*, the *New Yorker*, *GQ*, the *New York Times*, Sony Music, Random House Publishing, and many others. She has won numerous awards for her work and has exhibited internationally. She was the first woman and the first Canadian to have a solo show at the Library of Congress in Washington, D.C. Kunz has been made an Officer of the Order of Canada, Canada's highest civilian honor, "for her contributions as an illustrator whose insightful works have graced publications around the world."

I · LEONARDO

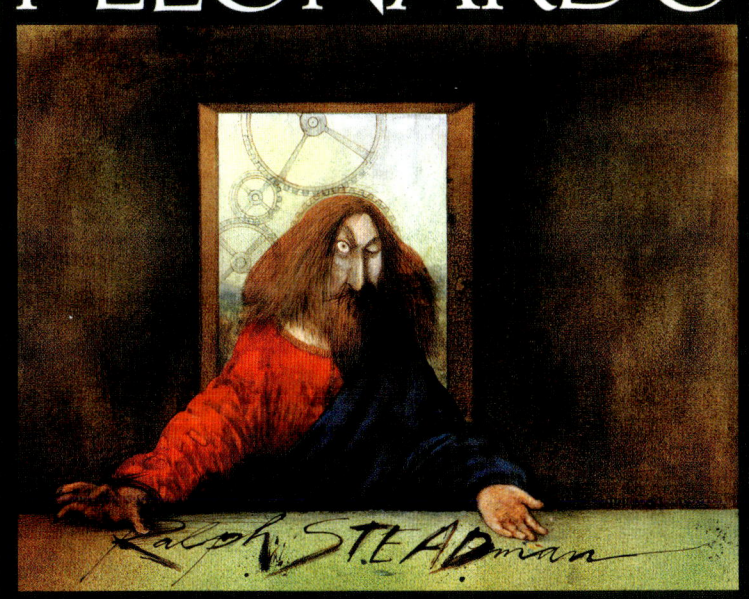

Ralph STEADman

no. 16

SELECTED BY IVAN CHERMAYEFF | **WILHELM TELL POSTER** | **PHOTOGRAPHED BY** ARMIN HOFMANN | **DESIGNED BY** ARMIN HOFMANN

Armin Hofmann was a visitor at Yale, invited by Paul Rand when I was there, and a teacher when I visited Brissago as a student in Switzerland. Armin was kind, calm and insightful, subtle, and generous with his thoughts in my memory.

The poster for the Basler Freilichtspiele has most of the important qualities of great graphic communications. It is ambiguous, playful, and is built upon the knowledge and memory of its audience about the legend of Wilhelm Tell putting an arrow through an apple placed on top of someone's head.

Hofmann skipped the actual arrow and put the letters of *TELL* into deep perspective, pointing to the center of a giant apple, larger than the poster, sitting on the top of a hint of a head with the disconnected but important stem in place appearing in a glow of light.

The entire image is very three dimensional.

A further wonder is the motion and placement of the small type, with the shortening of the month of August to VIII. Wilhelm Tell is no larger than the theater name, as there was no need for it to be larger with *TELL* so prominently in focus. It's a brilliant and memorable work of graphic design.

Ivan Chermayeff studied at Harvard University, the Institute of Design in Chicago, and graduated from Yale University, School of Art and Architecture. His lyrical, expressive style has resulted in iconic images for literally hundreds of clients. As a founding partner of Chermayeff & Geismar, his trademarks, posters, publications, illustrations, and art installations for contemporary buildings are widely recognized and have received nearly every award bestowed by the profession in the United States.

Basler Freilichtspiele
beim Letziturm im St. Albantal
15.-31. VIII 1963

Wilhelm Tell

no. 17

SELECTED BY STEFF GEISSBUHLER | **WILHELM TELL POSTER** | **PHOTOGRAPHED BY** ARMIN HOFMANN | **DESIGNED BY** ARMIN HOFMANN

The Wilhelm Tell poster is important on many levels. Armin Hofmann blends image and typography with the simplest means. The symbol of an apple, sitting wobbly atop a headlike form, is penetrated by the telescopic letterforms spelling out *TELL*, indicating the shot from the crossbow.

Using a very familiar set of symbols, especially in Switzerland, the essence of the legend is reduced to the absolute minimum. Its abbreviation of form and content is at its absolute best. It is "constructive, expressive, abstract poetic, objective and unemotional, apparent, and inescapable," according to Hofmann.

What makes it unique is the fact that the story of Wilhelm Tell has been depicted in books, film, opera, and theater in a superrealistic, often kitschy way, and the very theater play this poster advertises is often performed in natural surroundings with a cast of real farmers, cows, and horses and is everything but abstract. In contrast, this poster succeeds with the simple means of black-and-white symbolism intriguing and seducing the viewer.

Hofmann says, of the advertising industry, "Historically it was common in commercial advertising to design posters reflecting the requirements of the market. But for me, it was important to develop a new formal language. Furthermore, my posters should have a didactic effect. The industry had only limited interest in such an approach."

This poster is very important to me because Hofmann was my teacher and designed this poster in 1963, one year before I graduated from the Basel School. It encompassed everything Hofmann is about and everything we had learned. It also epitomizes to me what pure Swiss Design was and what it contributed to our profession.

This, and other Hofmann, posters helped change the perception of Swiss Design as a rigid, gridded, and austere form of typography and graphics, to a playful, experimental, and sophisticated form of expression. It also changed Switzerland as a cute place of alps, cows, banks, chocolate, and watches to a technologically advanced, education-, science-, and art-focused, modern and relevant country.

Basler Freilichtspiele
beim Letziturm im St. Albantal
15.-31. VIII 1963

Wilhelm Tell

Steff Geissbuhler received his diploma in graphic design from the School of Art and Design, Basel, Switzerland. Prior to forming C&G Partners, he was a partner at Chermayeff & Geismar for thirty years. He has designed print materials, posters, architectural graphics, sign systems, and exhibits for a variety of clients. In 2005, Geissbuhler's work was honored with the AIGA Medal for his sustained contribution to design excellence and the development of the profession.

no. 18

SELECTED BY R. O. BLECHMAN | THE BUFFALO NICKEL | DESIGNED BY JAMES EARLE FRASER

Back in the '30s and into the early '50s, this coin, minted in 1913, was something you touched every day, barely looking at it. But if you did, what you would see was a perfectly balanced, well-proportioned design bearing a finely crafted image (something a St. Gaudens might have done). It was handled daily, so its qualities must have insinuated themselves—by osmosis, if nothing else—to generations of Americans: the qualities of harmony, proportion, and craftsmanship.

Now compare this nickel to its 2010 counterpart. What we see is a bisected face of Thomas Jefferson, rendered in low relief, the missing half floating somewhere in the ether. Arching off to the side of Jefferson (his visible half) is an asymmetric "In God We Trust." It's an off-center coin for an off-center world, so I suppose it's appropriate. But no thank you.

Brooklyn-born **R. O. Blechman** says he has handled thousands (make that millions) of nickels since his birth in 1930. He stumbled into his art career, first by entering the High School of Music and Art (his mother's suggestion), then by having to make a living. In his long career as an artist–illustrator with several gallery shows here and abroad, and an animated filmmaker, he recently tried his hand at writing, *Dear James: Letters to a Young Illustrator* (Simon & Schuster).

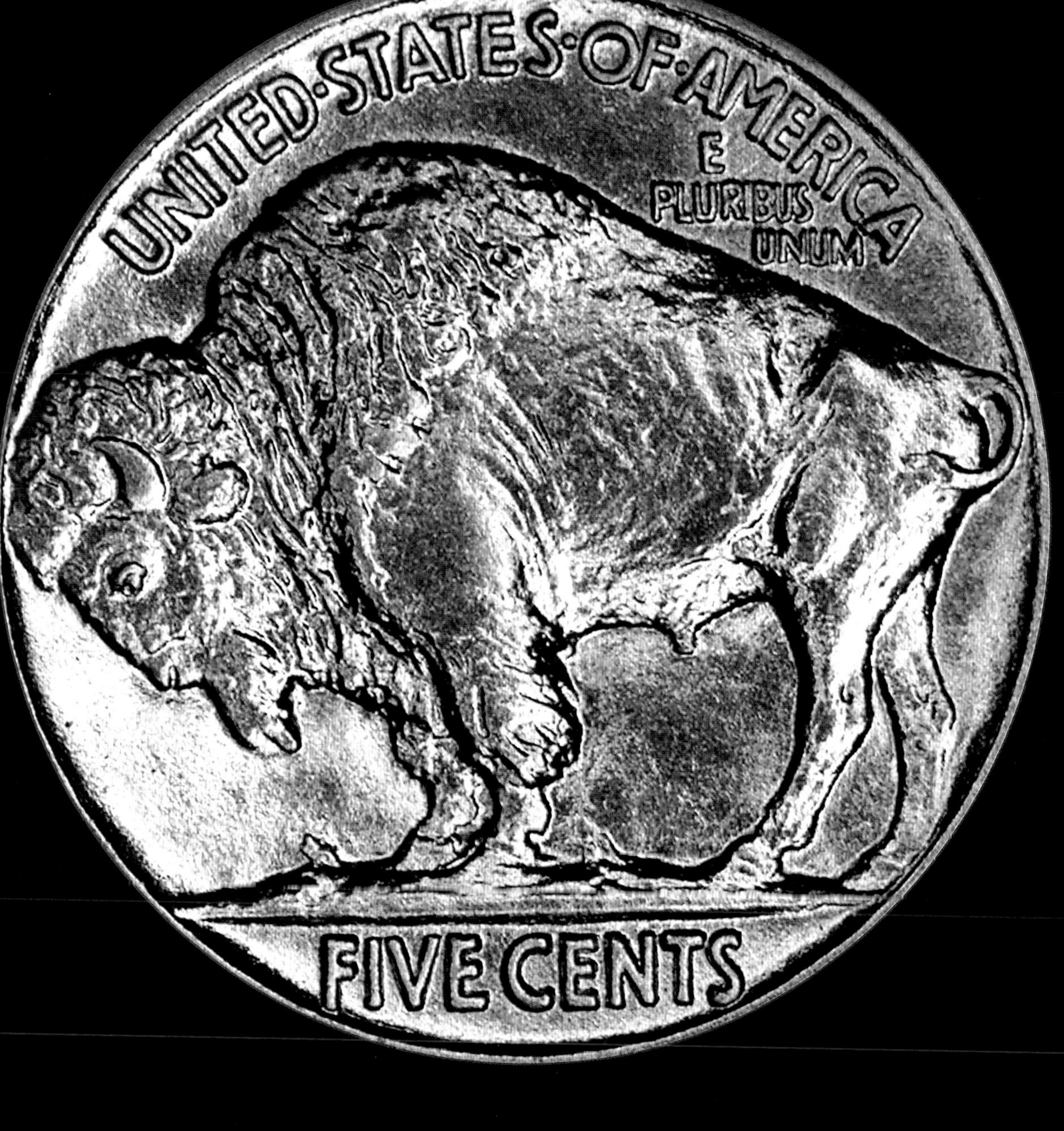
UNITED·STATES·OF·AMERICA
E
PLURIBUS
UNUM
FIVE CENTS

no. 19

SELECTED BY STEVEN HELLER | GENERAL DYNAMICS POSTERS | DESIGNED BY ERIK NITSCHE

Erik Nitsche did for General Dynamics Corporation what Paul Rand did for IBM and Westinghouse, in creating the total identity for the engineering giant from 1955 to 1965.

In the early 1940s he took a job as art director of *Air Tech* and *Air News,* with total control of the format and illustrations. What for many designers would have been a nightmare of designing charts and graphs about aerodynamics, for Nitsche was heavenly. He relished designing technical data for such things as hydraulic systems. "I loved the beauty of it," he once said. "There is so much logic in all that stuff. It's so very Swiss."

At that time Nitsche was developing two approaches that would eventually merge into one signature. The first involved minimal and abstract drawing, including random and geometric scribblings, apparently influenced by Paul Klee, used for record albums and some advertising work. The second was rooted in minimal and elegant typography, which combined a line or two of gothic type, like Akidenz Grotesque (and later Helvetica), with a classic serif face, like Garamond or Didot. Nitsche rejected the *Neue Grafik,* or Swiss International Style, referring to it as "a little too cold for our uses," and stayed "pretty much with the classical typefaces."

In 1950 he took on the General Dynamics account. If destiny does intercede in people's lives, this is definitely when it took over Nitsche's. The advertisements that he created for this growing multinational conglomerate transformed Nitsche from a boutique designer into one of the world's most effective and innovative corporate designers.

General Dynamics was incorporated in 1953 as the parent for ten different manufacturing firms (among them Electric Boat, Canadair Limited, Electro Dynamic, General Atomic, Convair, and Stromberg-Carlson), which at that time were administering to the defense needs of the United States. Its products ranged from atomic-powered submarines to electric motors for destroyers to the B-58 supersonic jet bomber and the commercial 880 jet transport. The company was also working in the areas of electronics, astronautics, aero- and hydrodynamics, and nuclear physics.

The world in the early 1950s was in the deep freeze of the Cold War, and the nuclear arms race was the topic of the day. Yet the spin on nuclear power was also that it heralded peace and progress. General Dynamics' president, John Jay Hopkins, strongly held that his corporation should be positioned in the public's mind as a purveyor of peace. General Dynamics

GENERAL DYNAMICS

was in a position to benefit mankind through scientific research. He further understood that presenting a good public face was endemic to this goal. Nitsche's ads for them stood out like gems, using an abstract drawing style to give a modern aura that at once hinted at General Dynamic's often top-secret products as well as its progressive aspirations.

As builders of the first atomic submarine, the Nautilus (with contracts for three more), and with commitments to produce the first atomic-powered airplane, General Dynamics presumably had exceptional showpieces. Yet they had nothing to show. The company was prevented from displaying anything that would compromise their high-security commissions. In fact, only within limits could General Dynamics even discuss its various research projects at all. So in the absence of their so-called "atomic products," symbolic expression of the corporate mission was the only viable option. Nitsche's first job was to develop a graphic means to present peaceful uses for the atom. The first task he set for himself as the centerpiece of the Geneva exhibit was creating six (35 × 50 inch [88.9 × 127 cm]) posters. He intuited that in Switzerland (what he calls "the nation of posters") posters would appeal to the largely European audience.

Nitsche developed a graphic premise united by the headline "Atoms for Peace." The corporate clarion was a series of six multilingual posters—in English, Russian, German, French, Hindi, and Japanese—featuring both abstract or symbolic imagery and including the biblical text from Isaiah: "They shall beat swords into plowshares, and their spears into pruning hooks: nation shall not lift up sword against nation, neither shall they learn war anymore." Isaiah's testament stood dramatically, albeit ironically, as a backdrop to a model of the hull of the Nautilus submarine. To explain away the irony of juxtaposing a message of peace with the world's most powerful warship, Nitsche added an even more ironic quotation from an Easter message given by Pope Pius XII to the effect that the Nautilus was at last putting nuclear force to the *service* and not the *destruction* of men.

Each poster identified a particular aspect of General Dynamics' research. The most well known of the series, representing "hydrodynamics," was a painting of a nautilus shell, a rendering of Earth in its center with the artist's conception of the Nautilus submarine shooting out of its chamber. It was an indelible logo in its day. Set against a gradated grayish-blue background, the shell was a virtual cornucopia of progress. The submarine was not seen as a killing machine, but rather as the offspring of technological progress poised to help the world. Other posters were much less controversial by today's standards, but no less exquisite by graphic standards. One particularly Klee-inspired poster with a somewhat enigmatic subtitle, "Basic Forces," was an abstract design of the sea (wavy dotted lines), space (dots and dotted lines representing constellations in the sky), and the sun (a white circle with a red center, like an eye) set against a gradated background. In addition to his artistic inspirations, Nitsche derived much of his imagery from science itself, such as the abstracted symbols for isotopes used in his poster for "nucleodynamics."

The first series of six posters established a tone for all future General Dynamics graphics, as well as a paradigm, of sorts, for how the marriage of science and engineering would be visualized by kindred companies. Indeed, Nitsche's brand of artful futurism was copied by many others at the time and might be seen today as representative of the so-called atomic style

/ 56 / i heart design

that emerged in the mid- to late-1950s. Hopkins was genuinely pleased with the initial result and ordered more posters to promote the company with, as he put it, "the spirit of discovery that motivates the corporation's diverse developments." There were a total of four different series in all, including another six posters for Atoms for Peace, six for Exploring the Universe, and eleven divisional posters related to the different subcompanies.

Steven Heller is the cochair of the MFA Designer as Author Program at the School of Visual Arts in New York City. He is the editor of *Voice: AIGA Journal for Design* and he writes the "Visuals" column for the *New York Times Book Review*.

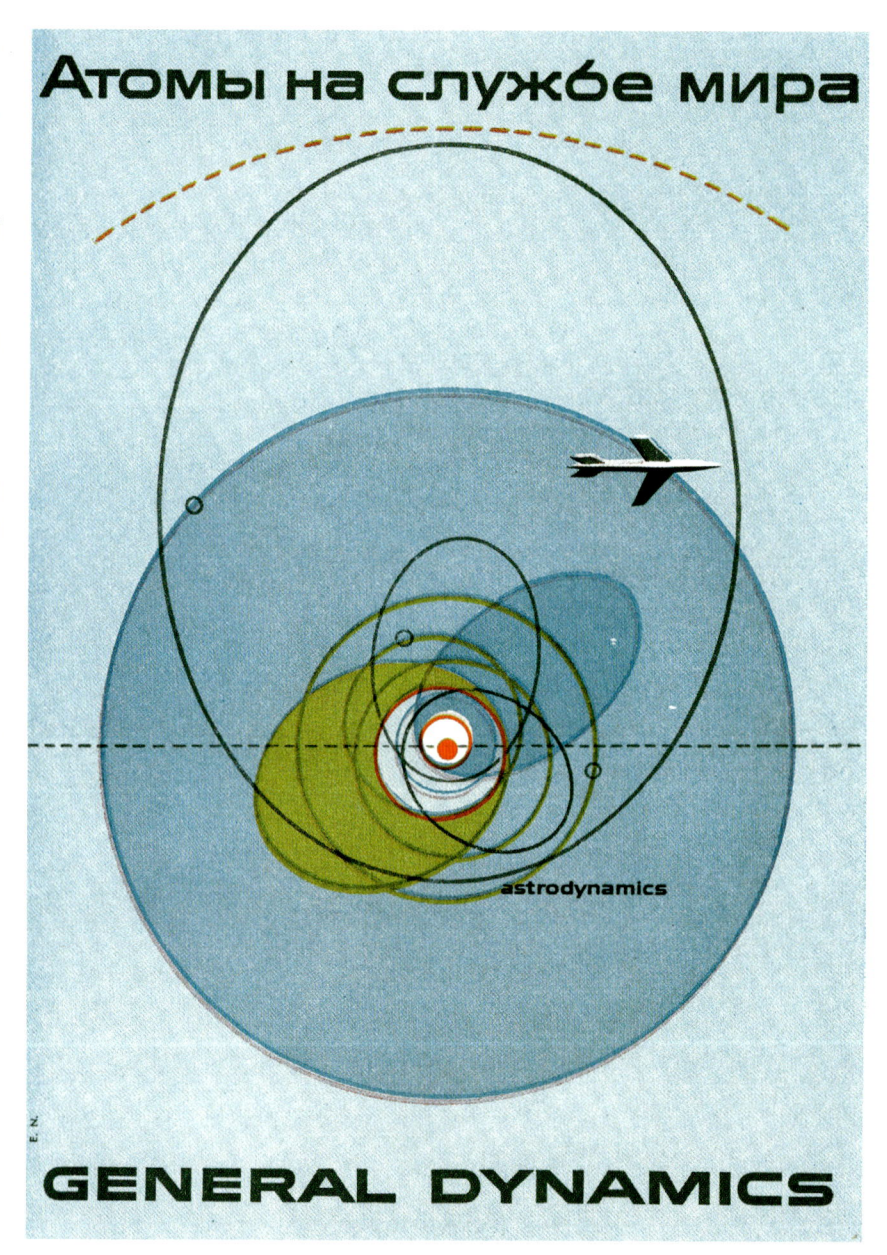

20 no.

SELECTED BY GERRIT TERSTIEGE | **VALENTINE/OLIVETTI POSTER** | **DESIGNED BY HERBERT SPENCER**

It rarely happens that you have to descend deep into the ancient world of myths in order to understand how a graphic motif came about. In the case of my favorite poster, which promotes Olivetti's Valentine portable typewriter, journeying into the past is a trip worthwhile. Indeed, Milton Glaser, who created the poster in 1969, conceals the mythological context of the subject from us by only showing the right-hand edge— or about a quarter of the whole composition. The panorama Glaser cites here (*The Death of Procris*) was originally painted in 1495 by Renaissance artist Piero di Cosimo and now hangs in London's National Gallery. It depicts a shocking scene that we find described in *Metamorphoses* by Roman author Ovid. To make it short: Convinced he is having an affair, the nymph Procris secretly follows her husband, Cephalus, only to discover him out hunting with his dog, Laelaps.

Alarmed at the sound of rustling in the bush his wife is hiding in, Cephalus throws his spear and inadvertently slays the beautiful Procris, whose sandaled feet we see in Glaser's poster. So far, so bad. But what on Earth made Glaser choose this particular subject as a surreal setting for the red plastic typewriter in the first place? Let us not call the gods, they are dead, let's call Milton Glaser in his New York studio!

He remembers the poster's genesis vividly: "I still find it amazing that Olivetti accepted this design from me. The man who made it possible in the first place was Giorgio Soavi, Olivetti's creative director at the time—a poet, writer, and simply this very mundane, sophisticated guy. I had lived in Bologna in the early 1950s, and began to work for Olivetti in the early 1960s. No doubt about it: Everyone who lives in Italy for a while gets quite crazy about the country's art that you see on every corner. When I got the assignment to design a series of posters for the Valentine, I thought it would be quite charming to design each motif as a paraphrase of works from Italian art history. And I particularly loved this painting by di Cosimo, above all because of the sorrowful dog in this magnificent, metaphysical landscape. It reminded me a little of the dog on the RCA Victor logo, listening to its master's voice."

Gerrit Terstiege, born 1968, has been editor in chief of *form* magazine since 2006 (www.form.de). After studying at Köln International School of Design, he joined the editorial team of *form* magazine in 1997. He is the editor of *Three D—Graphic Spaces* and *The Making of Design* (both published by Birkhäuser Basel). Terstiege is currently working on a monograph about the legendary designer and illustrator Heinz Edelmann.

VALENTINE OLIVETTI

no. **21**

THE ROLLING STONES STICKY FINGERS ALBUM COVER

SELECTED BY STEFAN SAGMEISTER | **DESIGNED BY ANDY WARHOL & CRAIG BROWN**

I remember being very impressed with those bulging pants and the actual, real zipper that was featured on this 1971 *Sticky Fingers* Rolling Stones album. I was touched by the unexpectedness as well as the obvious commitment of the designer and the record label to go through such a production nightmare. It raised interesting questions: "Will we see Mr. Jagger naked upon opening?" and "Was the fact that the zipper scratches the cover next to it designed deliberately?"

However, not everybody was impressed by the cover in the same way. When we got a chance to design the latest Stones album, I actually met Mick Jagger and Charlie Watts. I asked Jagger about his favorite Stones covers from the past and he mentioned without hesitation: *Exile on Main St.*, *Some Girls*, and *Sticky Fingers*. I said that these were my favorites as well, only in a different order: *Sticky Fingers*, *Some Girls*, and *Exile on Main St.* So Charlie Watts (in lowered voice) leans over to Jagger and asks, "What's on *Sticky Fingers*?" to which Mick replies, "Oh, you know, Charlie, the one with the zipper that Andy did."

A native of Austria, **Stefan Sagmeister** received his MFA from the University of Applied Arts in Vienna and, as a Fulbright Scholar, a master's degree from Pratt Institute in New York. Sagmeister formed the New York–based Sagmeister Inc. in 1993 and has since designed for clients as diverse as the Rolling Stones, HBO, and the Guggenheim Museum. Having been nominated five times for a Grammy Award, he finally won one for the Talking Heads boxed set. He also earned practically every important international design award. In 2008, a comprehensive book titled *Things I Have Learned in My Life So Far* was published by Abrams. He teaches in the graduate department of the School of Visual Arts in New York City and lectures extensively on all continents.

THE ROLLING STONES
STICKY FINGERS

ROLLING STONES RECORDS TM 1841 Broadway, New York, N.Y. 10023
DISTRIBUTED BY ATCO RECORDS, DIVISION OF ATLANTIC RECORDING CORPORATION

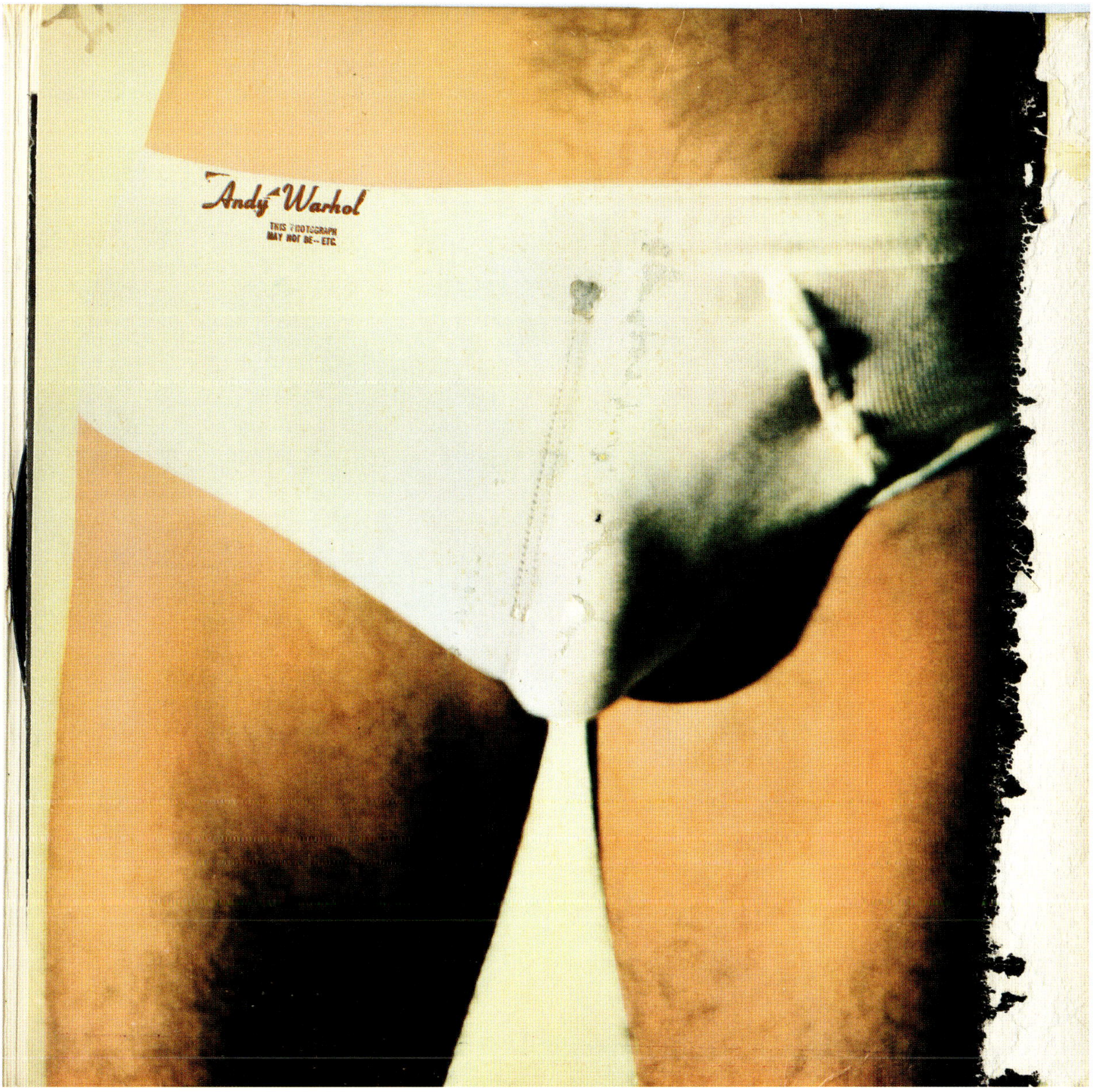
Andy Warhol
THIS PHOTOGRAPH
MAY NOT BE-- ETC.

no. 22

SELECTED BY WARREN LEHRER | APARTHEID MUSEUM | DESIGNED BY VARIOUS DESIGNERS

Approaching the entrance to the Apartheid Museum in Johannesburg, my wife, our friend Mike Premo, and I are faced with choices. Two signs hang above two prisonlike steel entryways. One says Blankes/Whites. The other, Nie-Blankes/Non-Whites. Judith and I enter through Whites and are given laminated cards that also say White. Mike, who is black, walks through Non-Whites. We can see each other through a chain-linked fence. Mike walks under a row of signs forbidding access to Blacks, Coloreds, and Non-Europeans. On both sides hang large-scale reproductions of the hated identity cards and passbooks, which contain photographs, names, addresses, and designation of race and ethnicity, appropriate to the side. Judith and I continue along the corridor of privilege, coming face to face with the vital security data of other whites and information panels that reproduce apartheid's forty years of changing race laws.

| BLANKES | NIE — BLANKES |
| WHITES | NON — WHITES |

We peer through the fence to the other side until we no longer see Mike or any other Non-Whites. The mass uprisings of the '80s and early '90s lead us to a rooftop exhibit. There's Mike! Together, we walk through the twenty-one other exhibition areas that make up the museum.

The entryway to the Apartheid Museum [designed by a multidisciplinary team of curators, historians, museologists, architects, and designers] creates experience, provides choices, and enables visitors to feel a range of emotions from shame and rage to shock and empathy. Some "blacks" and people of color choose to enter through the Whites entryway, knowing full well that they couldn't have made that choice during apartheid. White people can choose to enter through Non-Whites and get a feel for being treated like a subhuman. I love how this work of graphic design creates a conduit for experiencing opposing perspectives and then unites. Through truth comes the possibility of reconciliation.

Here are a few other examples of graphic design[1] that create experience, provide choices, portray multiple perspectives, suggest linkages between seeming opposites, and transform consciousness:

Guillaume Appolinaire's poem "Lettre-Océan" [1916] is an exchange of communication between Appolinaire in Paris and his brother, Albert, in Mexico[2]. Rich with layers of metaphor, the double-page spread mimics the bifurcated format of a postcard, while two word wheels divide the composition into two hemispheres of the globe, bridging the European power with its colonial past. The events of a parade in Paris and spring day in Vera Cruz are broadcast through radio waves emanating from the Eiffel Tower, wireless telegraphic transmissions, and fragments of overheard dialogue. Readers navigate their own way around this spatially dynamic poem that establishes and then crosses the personal and the political, the local and the global, old and new media (of its day), spoken and written word, literature and visual art.

Katherine and Michael McCoy cowrote and designed the book *Cranbrook Design: The New Discourse* about the philosophy, methods, and outcomes of the graduate design programs they headed for twenty-three years. They set their introduction using only typography and the metaphor of the brain's dual hemispheres, so the reader illuminates

from the Tractate Makkoth 10a

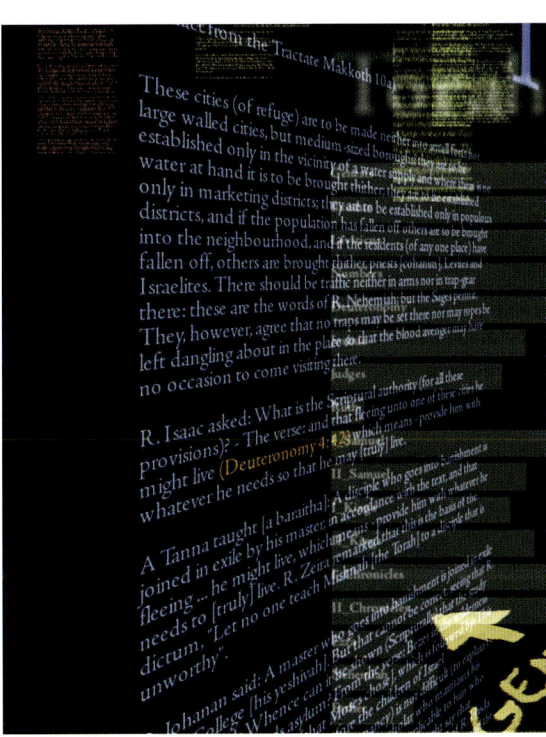

These cities (of refuge) are to be made neither into small forts nor large walled cities, but medium-sized boroughs; they are to be established only in the vicinity of a water supply, and where there is no water at hand it is to be brought thither; they are to be established only in marketing districts; they are to be established only in populous districts, and if the population has fallen off others are to be brought into the neighbourhood, and if the residents [of any one place] have fallen off, others are brought thither, priests [cohanim], Levites and Israelites. There should be traffic neither in arms nor in trap-gear there: these are the words of R. Nehemiah; but the Sages permit. They, however, agree that no traps may be set there nor may ropes be left dangling about in the place so that the blood avenger may have no occasion to come visiting there.

R. Isaac asked: What is the Scriptural authority [for all these provisions]? — The verse: and that fleeing unto one of these cities he might live (Deuteronomy 4:42) which means — provide him with whatever he needs so that he may [truly] live.

A Tanna taught [a baraitha]: A disciple who goes into banishment is joined in exile by his master, in accordance with the text, and that fleeing ... he might live, which means — provide him with whatever he needs to [truly] live. R. Zera remarked that this is the basis of the dictum, "Let no one teach Mishnah [the Torah] to a disciple that is unworthy".

R. Johanan said: A master who goes into banishment — his yeshivah [his College / Whence can it be shown [from the text] that ... asylum ... whoever ...

Whither are they banished? To the three cities situate on the yonder side of the Jordan and three cities situate in the land of Canaan, as ordained, ye shall give three cities beyond the Jordan and three cities in the land of Canaan; They shall be cities of refuge. Not until three cities were selected in the land of Israel did the [first] three cities beyond the Jordan receive fugitives, as ordained, [and of these cities which ye shall give] six cities for refuge shall they be unto you which means that [they did] not [function] until all six could simultaneously afford asylum.

And direct roads were made leading from one to the other, as ordained, thou shalt prepare thee a way and divide the borders of thy land into three parts. And two [ordained] scholar-disciples were delegated to escort the manslayer in case anyone attempted to slay him on the way, and that they might speak to him.

R. Meir says: he may [even] plead his cause himself, as it is ordained, and this is the word of the slayer. R. Jose B. Judah says: to begin with, a slayer is sent in advance to [one of] the cities of refuge, whether he had slain in error or with intent. Then the court sends for him thence. Whoever was ...

Cambodia   Thailand

Tank Ditch

the distinctions and crossovers between science and art as they read across the synaptic gaps of the two abutted columns. Just as soon as you discern the two hemispheres in the page, the writer/designers contradict the logic of the science/art dichotomy through the placement of subheadings that zigzag down the text but don't adhere neatly to the stereotypes of left brain/right brain.

In the late 1970s, thousands of Cambodians crossed into Thailand, fleeing the genocidal Khmer Rouge. Bill Burke's photograph of the border between the two countries cuts through the gutter of this spread from *I Want to Take Picture*, Burke's extraordinary book documenting his travels through Cambodia.

In the graphic design of the Talmud, a passage from the Torah is placed in the middle of a page, surrounded by interpretations by liberal and conservative scholars, commentaries on the commentaries, and hypertextual explanations of particular words and phrases. In contemporary editions of the Talmud, pages give voice to centuries of religious scholars in dialogue and debate about moral choices and the meaning of life.

Appreciating the polyvalent, interactive structure of the Talmud, MIT-trained engineer/designer David Small reinterprets the ancient form of the Talmud for twenty-first-century users. Instead of a finite number of columns and text blocks, Small's interactive digital wall texts rotate and change scale, empowering the reader/user to study amidst a virtual four-dimensional chorus of arguing rabbis.

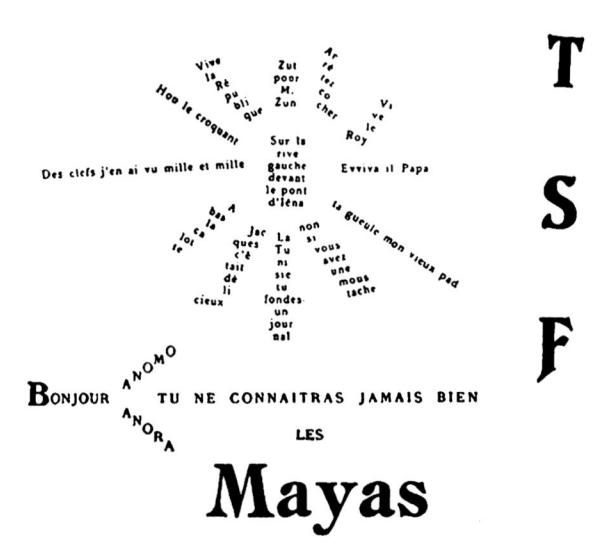

1. Some of the best graphic designs are the products of writers, architects, photographers, engineers, scribes, and occasionally—graphic designers.
2. Johanna Drucker, *The Visible Word: Experimental Typography and Modern Art*, University of Chicago Press, 1997.

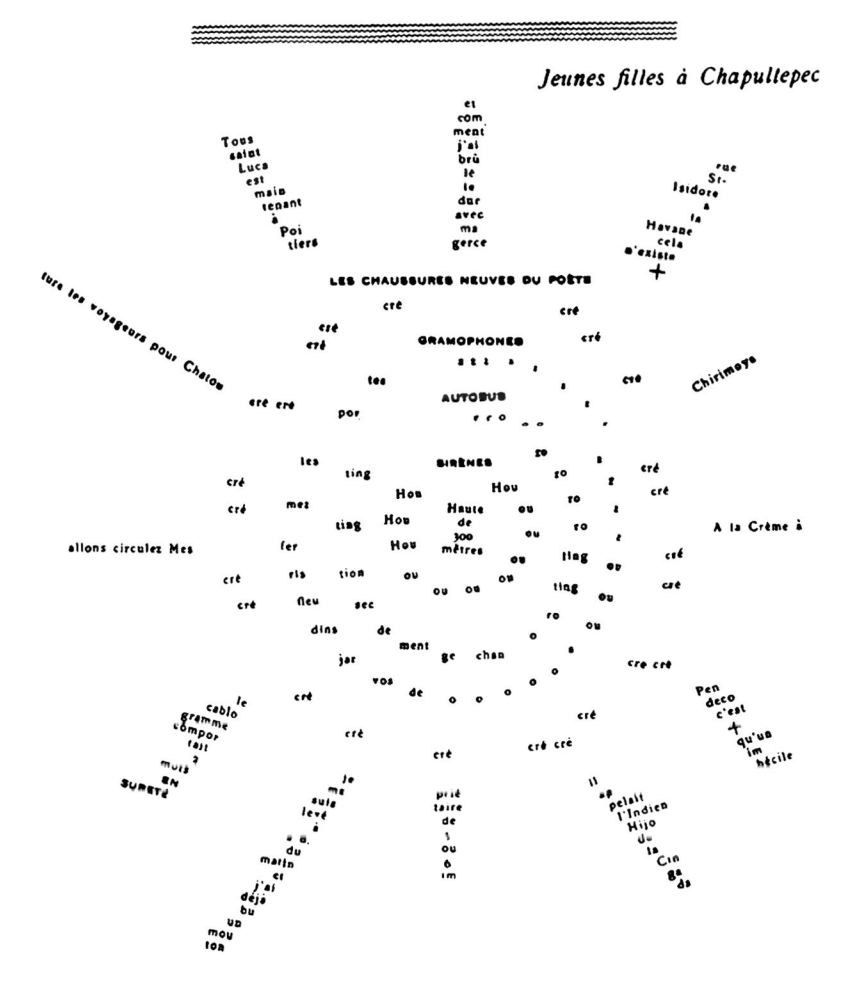

Warren Lehrer is a writer and artist/designer known internationally as a pioneer in the fields of visual literature and design authorship. His work explores the vagaries and luminescence of character, the relationships between social structures and the individual, and the pathos and absurdity of life. His books include *Crossing the BLVD: Strangers, Neighbors, Aliens in a New America* (W. W. Norton) with Judith Sloan; *The Portrait Series: A Quartet of Men* (four-book series, Bay Press); *GRRRHHHHH: A Study of Social Patterns* (Center for Editions); and more. Lehrer is the Leff Distinguished Professor in the School of Art+Design at Purchase College, SUNY, and he is a founding faculty member of the Designer as Author graduate program at the School of Visual Arts in New York City. Together with his wife, Judith Sloan, Lehrer founded EarSay, a nonprofit arts organization dedicated to uncovering and portraying the lives of the uncelebrated in print, on stage, on radio, in exhibitions, and in electronic media.

no. 23

SELECTED BY CHRISTOPH NIEMANN | HISTORY OF RUSSIA | ILLUSTRATIONS & TEXT BY GUSTAV DORE

A friend gave me Doré's *History of Holy Russia* when I was twenty-five. I wish I had gotten it a lot earlier. First of all, it is incredibly well drawn (no surprise given its creator, Gustav Doré). Much more amazing, however, is the humor that reveals itself not only through the language or the skillful caricatures. I have to admit that before I had seen that book, I had considered Wilhelm Busch and Saul Steinberg to be the inventors of 80 percent of the visual humor vocabulary that is used today.

It's so hard to come up with something truly original, so it was a relief to see that even Steinberg sometimes had to rely on the visual inventions of a giant before him (for example, the renderings of huge armies by drawing one detailed soldier in the foreground and then repeating the silhouette hundreds of times in the distance).

Doré is known as an outstanding draftsman of realistic imagery, and there are plenty of incredibly ornate drawings in this book. But my favorite parts are when he starts messing with the conventions of how to handle comic panels, way before there are even proper conventions established. For somebody to invent all-black or all-white panels in the mid-1800s and, most importantly, mix them with such beautiful deadpan text is astounding. As far as I know, there is no version of the book in print right now, but everyone who is interested in the art of visual storytelling should get their hands on this book.

Christoph Niemann (born 1970 in Waiblingen, Germany) is an illustrator, graphic designer, and coauthor of several books. After his studies in Germany, he moved to New York City in 1997. His work has appeared on the covers of the *New Yorker*, *Atlantic Monthly*, the *New York Times Magazine*, and *American Illustration* and has won awards from AIGA, the Art Directors Club, and American Illustration. After eleven years in New York City, he moved to Berlin. Niemann is author and illustrator of the whimsical *Abstract City*, a *New York Times* blog.

HISTORIE

VOM

HEILIGEN RUSSLAND

O rus, quando te aspiciam!
HORAZ

Qui les meut? qui les poinct? qui les conduict? qui les ha ainsi conseillé
Ho, ho, ho, ho! Mon Dieu, mon saulveur, aide-moi, inspire-moi, conseille-moi
RABELAIS

CONFUCIUS

Der Anfang der Geschichte Rußlands verliert sich im finstersten Altertum.

Erst gegen das 4. Jahrhundert beginnen ihre ersten Umrisse sich abzuzeichnen.

Aber der Anbeginn dieser Epoche bietet nicht viel Interessantes.

no. 24

SELECTED BY RALPH CAPLAN | EVERLAST LOGO | DESIGNED BY JACOB GOLOMB

Nearly a century before the Michael Phelps swimsuit controversy, a seventeen-year-old Bronx swimmer named Jacob Golomb set out to improve swimsuit technology. He didn't, but his new sporting goods company, Everlast, produced the gloves that Jack Dempsey wore in 1919 when he won the heavyweight championship of the world.

In 1925, Golomb designed elastic-waist trunks to replace the leather-belted ones then worn by boxers, an innovation quickly adapted by the men's underwear industry. Dempsey wore the trunks with the elastic band prominently featuring the concave logo. The label has been almost synonymous with boxing gear ever since. The logo had a pseudo ubiquity. You didn't actually see it everywhere; in fact you didn't see it anywhere except on the trunks worn by both pro and amateur boxers. But to fans, that was everywhere. Everlast so dominated the field, that it was possible to be a boxing fan without even suspecting that there were any competing manufacturers.

Although I had no known interest in design or marketing, my childhood fantasy was to become lightweight champion of the world, so I was aware of Everlast and fascinated by the manufacturer's audacity in displaying the company name on the *outside* of apparel. Everlast was thus the harbinger of branding strategies that were unthinkable until a culture evolved in which consumers *wanted* to advertise the companies that sold them things, because in that way they could advertise themselves. Gucci, Louis Vuitton, Abercrombie, Tommy Hilfiger, and the Gap were decades behind. The consumers that Everlast reached, however, were consumers of jabs, crosses, and uppercuts. The buying, or even watching, public was not accessible until television brought boxing into the living room on Friday nights.

Raymond Loewy's design of the Lucky Strike cigarette package was praised for assuring that the product name was visible, even after the package had been crumpled and thrown into the gutter. Everlast did better than that. It was not uncommon for both fighters to be wearing Everlast, although it was not always seen by anyone not in a ringside seat. But the advent of television meant that the logo was on camera at all times; thus the brand could be displayed on the trunks and glove cuffs of both the poor stiff lying flat on his back on the canvas and the one, standing in a neutral corner, who had put him there. Talk about product placement!

Ralph Caplan did not become lightweight boxing champion of the world. For most of his adult life, he has masked his disappointment by writing and lecturing about design and consulting with corporations on design issues.

no. 25

SELECTED BY RUDY VANDERLANS | TYPOGRAPHY AS DISCOURSE | DESIGNED BY ALLEN HORI

In my estimation, one can trace much of the experimental typographic expressionism during the early '90s to the work created at Cranbrook Academy of Art in Michigan, where Allen Hori's work was my personal favorite. Hori mixed the precision of Swiss design with the spatial freedom of, for instance, Hard Werken, the famous Dutch design studio where he later worked as an intern. Hori was the bridge.

He tied all these experiments together. He abandoned traditional typographic hierarchy and demanded from the reader a fair amount of involvement in order to decipher the message. Hori was also not too shy to include personal messages in his work, both visual and verbal. These functioned on a secondary level and were not meant to be immediately obvious to the reader. Their mystery drew the reader in.

Hori's work defied what most of us had learned in school about typography: Typography was meant to aid the reader, not put the reader to work. But his posters were never a prescription for anything. They were posters that answered their brief fairly well. If a theory ever accompanied the work, it was to justify his particular design: It was descriptive, not prescriptive. The fact that these mannerisms were widely copied proved that designers recognized the formal beauty of the work and were hungry to expand their typographic palettes.

While Allen Hori has remained a relatively obscure graphic designer, his work—and in particular that poster—provided a typographic breakthrough that showed graphic designers new ways to sculpt their messages.

Rudy VanderLans (born 1955, Voorburg, Holland) is a Dutch type and graphic designer and the cofounder of Emigre, an independent type foundry. VanderLans studied at the Royal Academy of Art in the Hague. Later he moved to California and studied photography at the University of California, Berkeley. In 1984, VanderLans, with his wife, Zuzana Licko, founded Emigre and began to publish *Emigre* magazine, a journal for experimental graphic design.

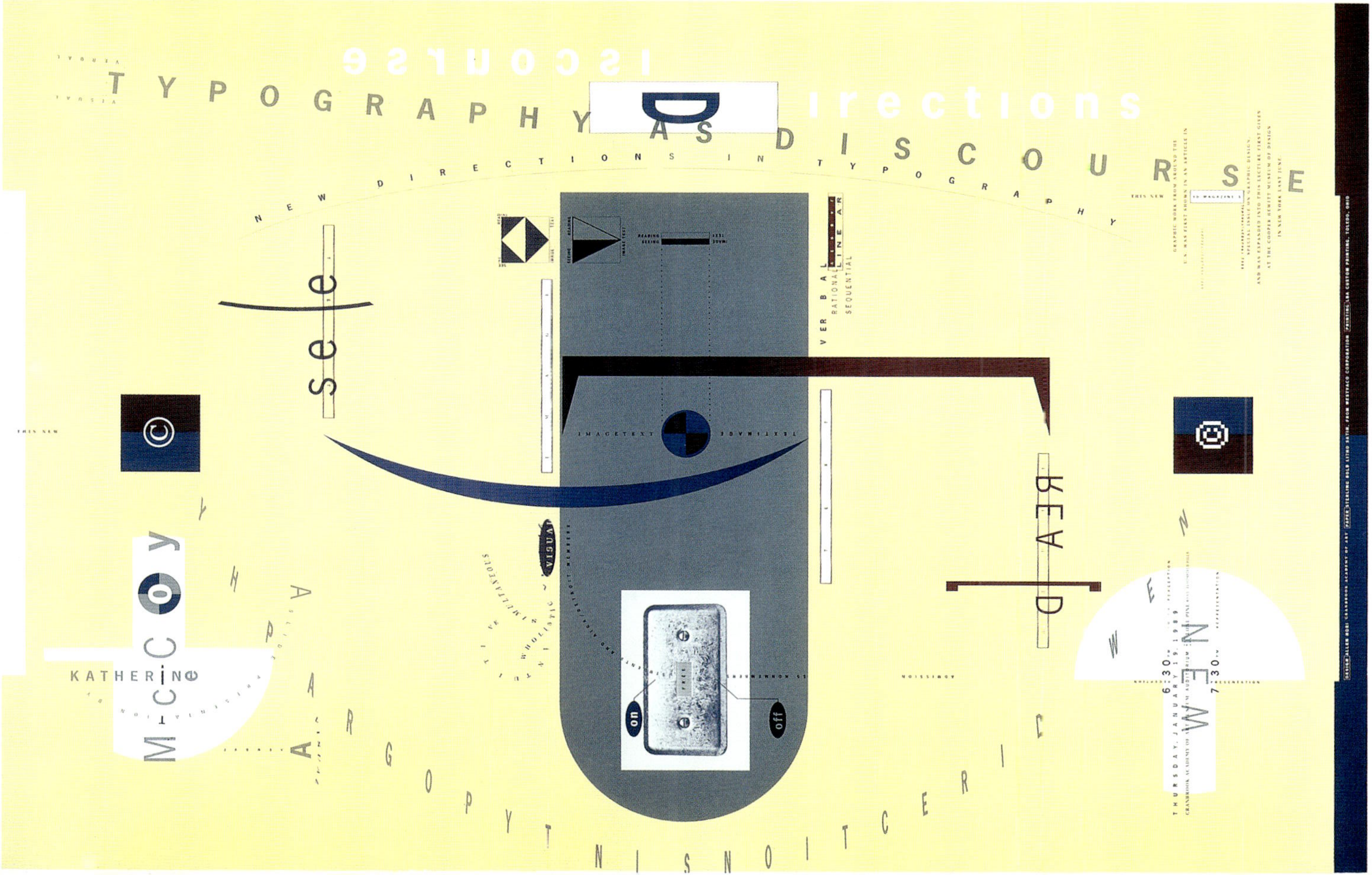
TYPOGRAPHY AS DISCOURSE
Directions
New Directions in Typography
Katherine McCoy
Visual
Verbal
Rational
Linear
Sequential
Image
Text
Imagetext
Textimage
Seeing
Reading
Wholistic
Simultaneous
on
off
Read
New
Thursday, January 19, 1989
6:30
7:30

no. 26

SELECTED BY ADRIAN SHAUGHNESSY | STEDELIJK CATALOGS | DESIGNED BY WILLEM SANDBERG

Is it possible for a piece of graphic design to worm its way into our hearts and become an object of infatuation? It seems hardly likely—after all, most graphic design is ephemeral and ends up as discarded junk. Yet if human beings can become infatuated with jewelry, coins, and rodents (I know people who are smitten with each of these phenomena), it must surely be possible to fall in love with a piece of graphic design.

I should know; it happens to me regularly. But rarely with the impact with which this little book hit me. It was lent to me by my friend the designer and collector Tony Brook and contains the work of the Dutch graphic designer Willem Sandberg. I was aware of Sandberg as an important figure in Dutch design history. He studied psychology in the Freudian hothouse of pre–World War II Vienna. During the Nazi invasion of Holland, he worked for the resistance movement creating fake ID cards. Later, he became the director of the Stedelijk. But before seeing—and holding—this little bibliographic gem, if you'd asked me to name my favorite Dutch designers, I wouldn't have included him. I'd have named van Doesburg, Schuitema, Crouwel, Wissing, van Toorn, Martens, and any number of bright-eyed current practitioners.

Today, Sandberg is top of my list. Odd really, because he doesn't even do the sort of rectilinear, hard-edged, graphically explicit work that I normally like. Yet there's something primal and atavistic in his expressionistic use of type and image that makes me swoon. I get a sense of form-making coming straight from Sandberg's unconscious: the same primordial sense you get from the work of Picasso, African art, and Mayan sculpture. And like a great movie, which hangs around in your head long after you've left the theater, Sandberg's work imprints itself on the soft tissue of memory and refuses to budge.

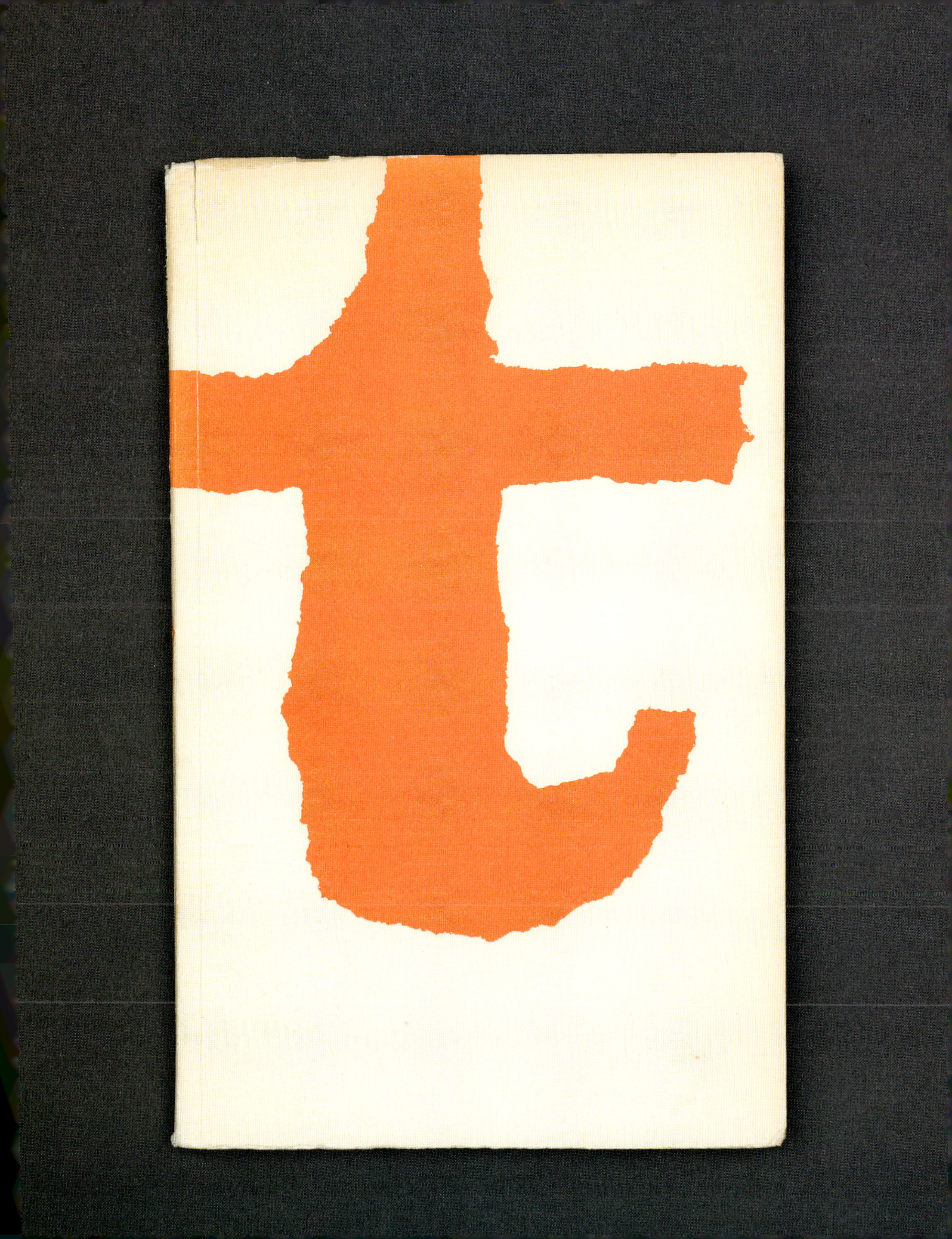

/ 78 / i heart design

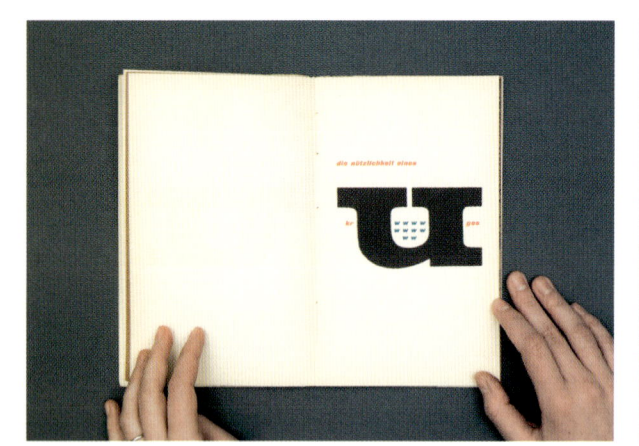

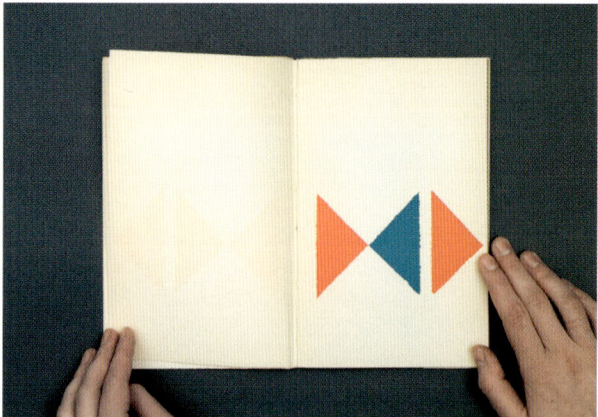

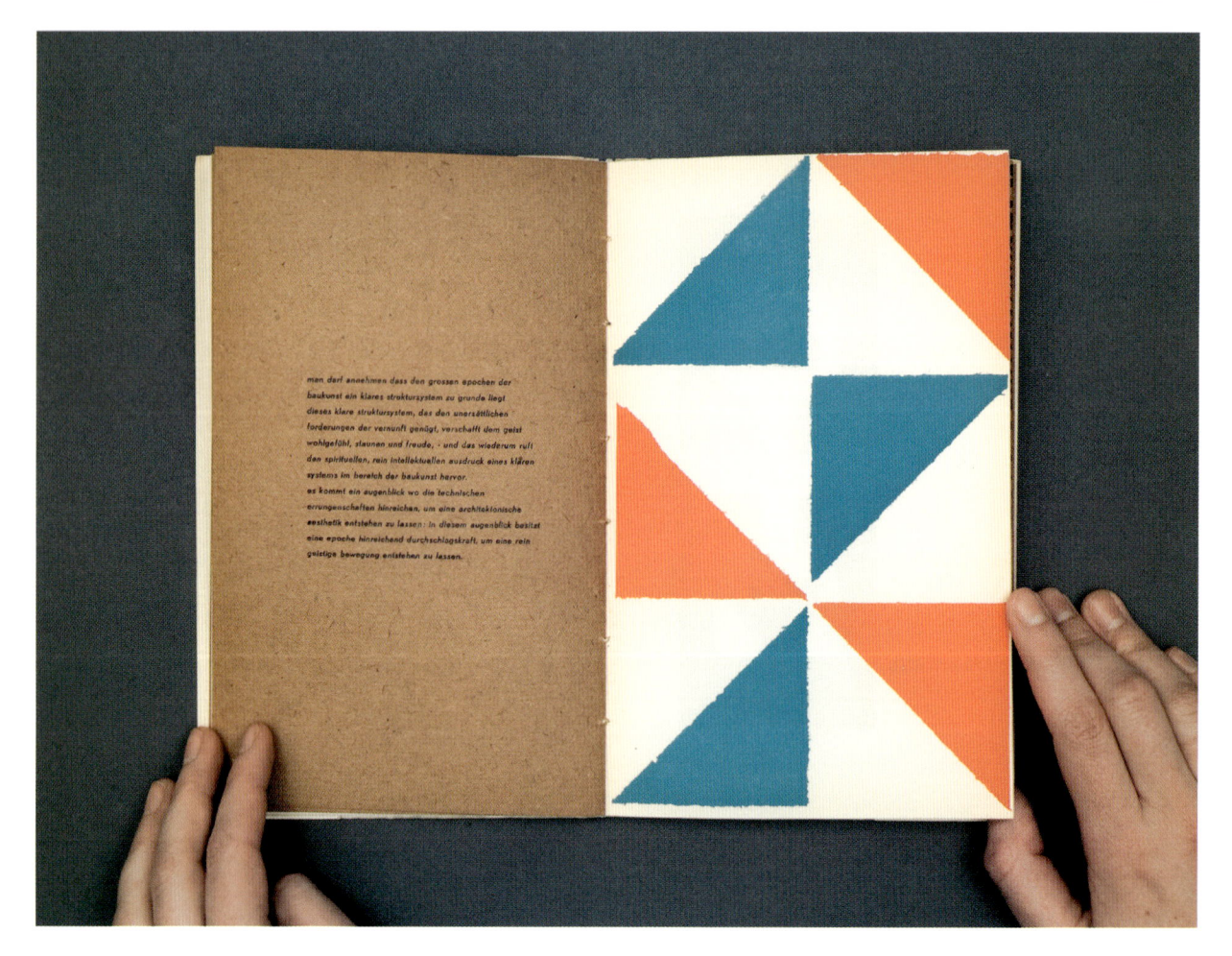

sandberg

/ 80 / i heart design

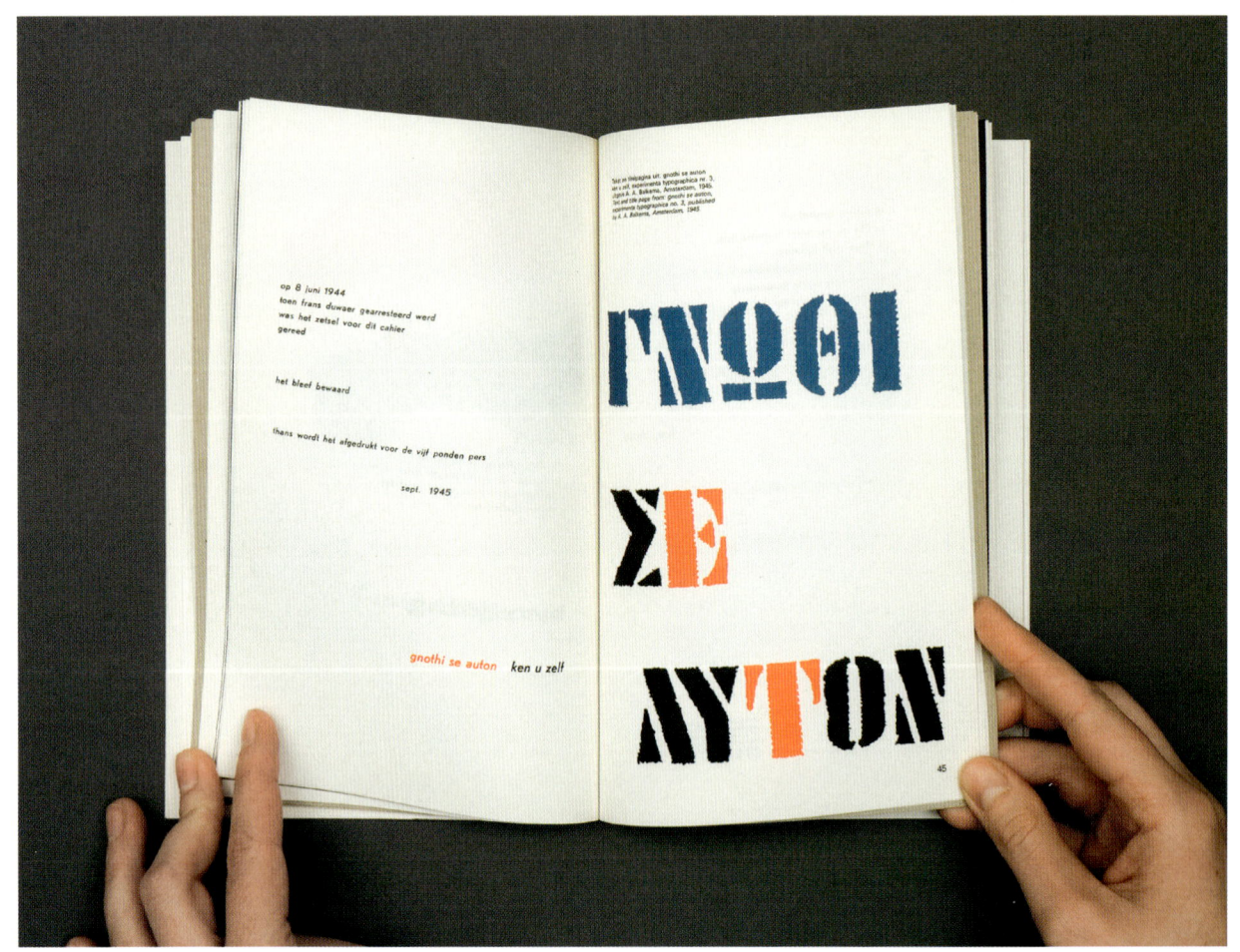

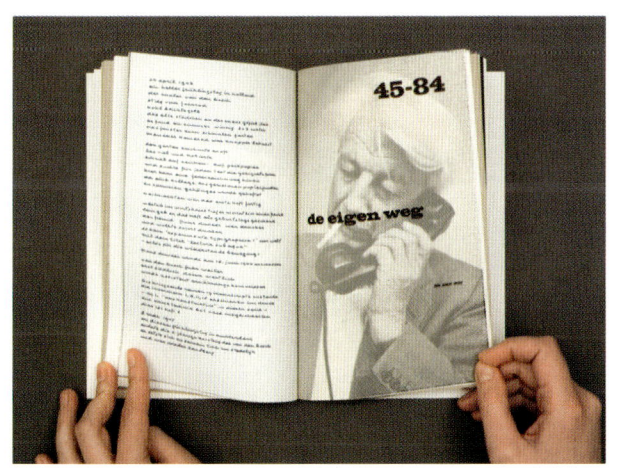

Adrian Shaughnessy is a graphic designer and writer based in London. He runs ShaughnessyWorks, a consultancy combining design and editorial direction. He is a founding partner in the publishing company Unit Editions. Shaughnessy has written and art directed numerous books on design. His latest is *Graphic Design: A User's Manual* (Laurence King Publishers). He writes for *Eye*, *Creative Review*, *Design Observer*, *The Wire*, and has a monthly column in *Design Week*. He was formerly editor of *Varoom*, a publication devoted to illustration. Shaughnessy lectures extensively and hosts a radio show called *Graphic Design on the Radio*.

№ 27

SELECTED BY LIZ DANZICO | EBERHARD FABER MONGOL 482 PENCIL | DESIGNED BY EBERHARD FABER

Like a paintbrush, a musical instrument, a keyboard—objects that give textual or visual form to idea—the pencil holds enormous potential. And yet, for an object so powerful, it's incredibly simple.

The pencil is intuitive. Its form so familiar, it's invisible in our everyday experience. In grammar school, we're taught the proper way to hold a pencil, but its directions for use are otherwise unspoken. There are no user manuals, no instructions for care, no troubleshooting guides. The pencil, with its potential to visualize our most intimate creative thoughts, has no barrier to use, directly linking thought to medium to audience.

The Eberhard Faber Mongol—the first pencil to boast the now ubiquitous yellow—represented a superior-quality writing instrument. At the time it was introduced in the mid-nineteenth century, Siberia had the best pencil companies, and their pencils happened to be yellow. Mongol mimicked that at a time when most other pencils were dark in color.

In 1861, Eberhard Faber opened the first lead-pencil factory in America in New York City, bringing German pencil-making techniques to the United States. After moving to Brooklyn, it became one of Brooklyn's most important factories, employing hundreds of workers, who were mostly women. Teachers once required the No. 2 Mongol.

A pencil's job is structural transparency. Too ostentatious, and it's gotten in the way of the very concepts one intends to sketch or write. Too weak, and it bends to will, forcing the user to turn to a pen for a stronger character and more determined line. For most jobs of note, only a pencil will do. The pencil exists to honor an idea. But clearly, the pencil itself has made a point.

Liz Danzico is equal parts designer, educator, and editor. She cofounded (with Steven Heller) and is chair of the MFA in Interaction Design Program at the School of Visual Arts in New York City. She is an independent user-experience consultant, a columnist for *Interactions* magazine, and is on the editorial board for Rosenfeld Media and advisory board for Design Ignites Change. She has been managing editor for *Voice: AIGA Journal for Design*, and editor in chief for *Boxes and Arrows*.

EE MONGOL 482   2   1S

no. 28

ALBERTUS (1935) / THE PRISIONER (1967–1968)

SELECTED BY | **DESIGNED BY**
KERRY WILLIAM PURCELL | **BERTHOLD WOLPE**

The designs that matter to us often inspire and shape our opinions surreptitiously. Slipping under our critical radar, it is only years later that we become aware of their enduring influence on our choices and obsessions. In retrospect, my Proustian moment was the 1960s program *The Prisoner*, or more specifically, the typeface used throughout "the village" as a kind of totalitarian identity.

For those unaware of this cult classic, the program follows an ex secret agent (played by Patrick McGoohan) who is held captive in a secret coastal village. Upon arrival, all the individuals in the village are given a number, with the main character appointed Number 6. In each episode, the authorities devise various means by which to discover why Number 6 resigned from his job. As noted, beyond the narrative's absorbing twists and turns, what is most striking about this show is the use of a bastardized version of Berthold Wolpe's 1935 typeface, Albertus.

Originally released by Monotype, Albertus was used most extensively by Wolpe himself in his book designs for Faber & Faber. It was possibly something about the traditionalism of that institution that first appealed to McGoohan (who was a major influence on the look of all seventeen episodes) to use it as the voice of authority in *The Prisoner*. Throughout the village, posters, maps, street signs, food labeling, and even newspapers are all set in this classical, but also curiously modern, typeface. In each instance, the typeface is applied to designs that are reduced to their bare essence. Whether it is neutral colors on tins of peas or objective imagery in electoral posters, all merely serve to enforce the sense of insidious authoritarianism that pervades the village.

The Prisoner's visual identity remains an oft-ignored but highly influential work in the history of design.

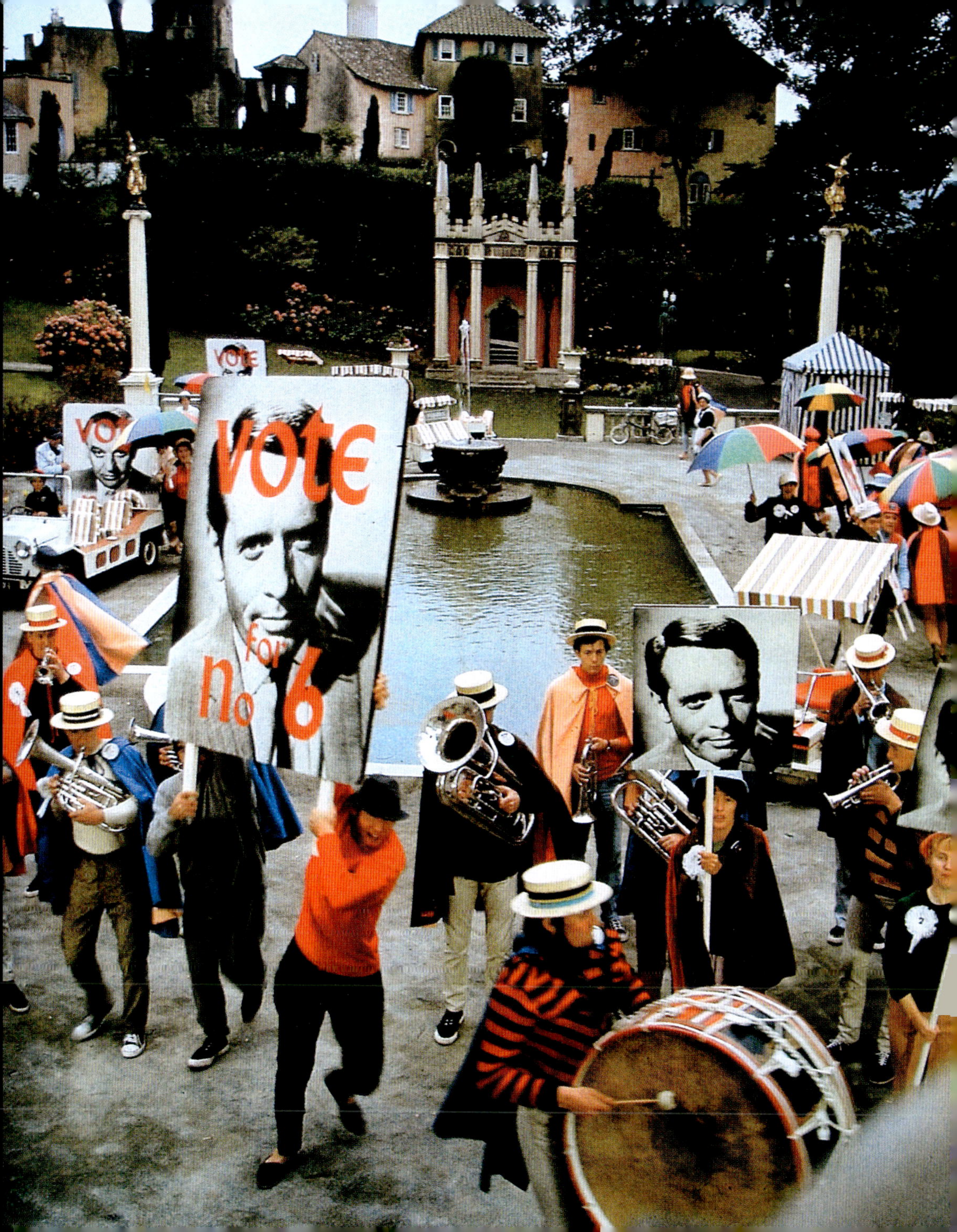
VOTE
VOTE for No 6
VOTE

/ 86 / i heart design

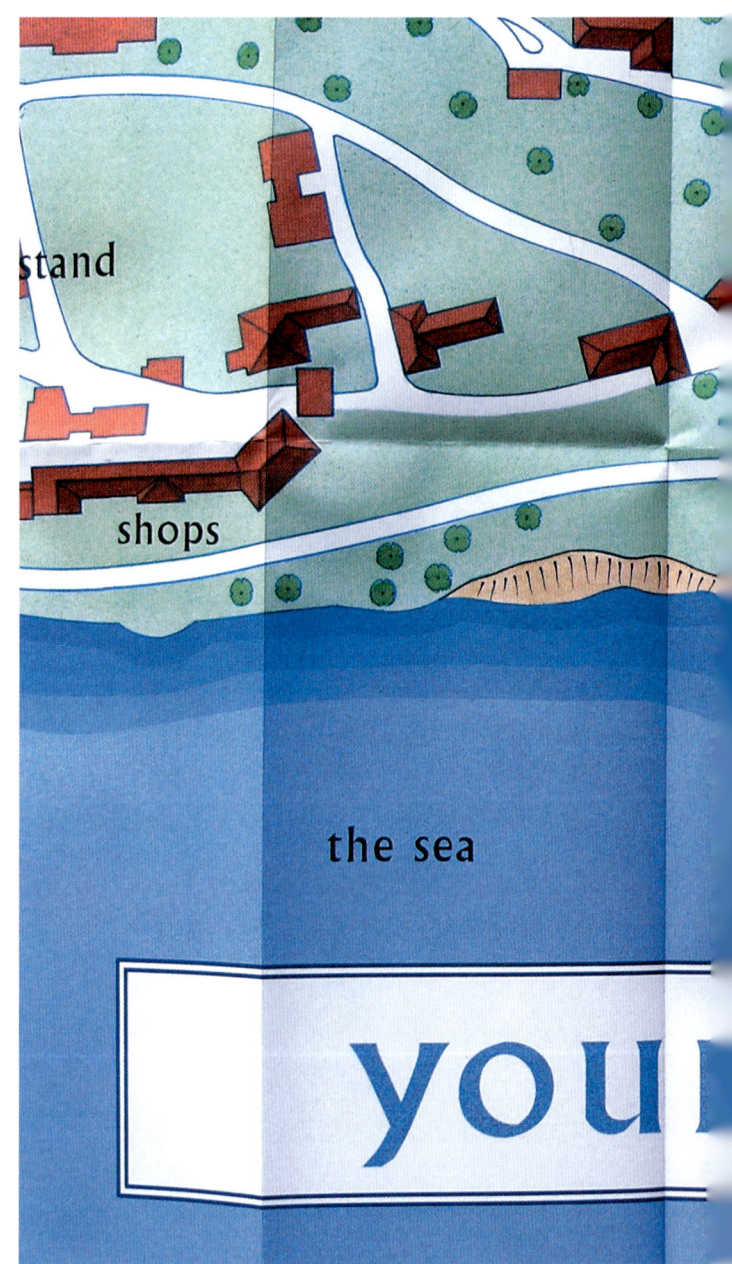

Kerry William Purcell is a writer, critic, and historian. His study of the celebrated art director and designer Alexey Brodovitch was published by Phaidon Press in 2002. This has been followed by his concise biography on the New York photographer Weegee (Phaidon, London, 2004); his comprehensive study of the Swiss graphic designer Josef Müller-Brockmann (Phaidon, London, 2006); and a book on the work of Magnum photographer Steve McCurry titled *In the Shadow of the Mountains* (2007). Most recently, he has coedited the *Phaidon Archive of Graphic Design* (2010).

№ 29

SELECTED BY R. ROGER REMINGTON | THE NATIONAL PARKS SERVICE | DESIGNED BY MASSIMO VIGNELLI

When speaking about his design methodology, Massimo Vignelli said, "Design without structure is anarchy." This quote is a particularly relevant introduction to my favorite Vignelli graphic design, the programfor the United States National Parks Service (NPS), developed in 1977.

Its purpose was to unify the information graphics of the NPS into a consistent program that would be appropriate and functional for the informational needs of users at the 391 units of the NPS, of which fifty-eight are designated national parks.

The "unigrid" is the central element of the program. It solves two primary problems in planning the information folders that are distributed at the entrance to each national park. First, it organizes the editorial and other visual components with a fixed format and graphic standards. Additionally it helps determine how a folder will be printed—the inks, paper, and the sheet size. From this basic grid, all print formats can be imposed on printing sheets with minimal waste. These graphic standards open the way for graphic improvements, the elimination of production inefficiencies, and the overall effectiveness of NPS publications.

R. Roger Remington considers himself primarily a teacher who has critical interests in design studies (graphic design history, theory, and methods); research; writing; and graphic design practice. He has cochaired two major symposia on graphic design history and written a book, *Nine Pioneers in American Graphic Design*, for the MIT Press. His second book, *Lester Beall: Trailblazer of American Graphic Design* was published in July of 1996 by W. W. Norton. *The Graphic Design Archive* at RIT, which he developed, involves preserving and interpreting the original source materials of sixteen design pioneers such as Lester Beall, Will Burtin, Cipe Pineles, William Golden, and Alvin Lustig, among others.

Site Bulletins
Supplementary Graphics Systems
Unigrid
Design Specifications
National Park Service Informational Folder Program
Moultrie
Fort Sumter National Monument
National Park Service U.S. Department of the Interior
JNEM
Jefferson National Expansion Memorial
St Louis Missouri
Park Name
National Historical Park Seattle, Washington
National Park Service U.S. Department of the Interior
Navy Yard
Crater Lake
Denali
Cabrillo
North Cascades
Big Bend
The Rise of Salem
Part 1
Birthplace of the Nation
The History

no. 30

SELECTED BY JASON GODFREY | LIGHTNIN'! | DESIGNED BY MILTON GLASER

Objects are defined by their dimensions, a fact Milton Glaser, the maestro of American graphic design, took advantage of with the design of the LP sleeve for the 1969 LP, *Lightnin'!*

The work is illustrated in his classic monograph *Milton Glaser: Graphic Design* as an example of "dealing with two sides of a surface." Printed in monochrome, the front and back are shown on sequential pages of the book, the turning of the page mimicking the effect of rotating the actual album.

Whilst the graphic sleight of hand is undoubtedly clever, it is the artwork on the original album that dominates. The front of the sleeve is an unrestrained and gutsy portrait of the Texan bluesman Lightnin'. Sam Hopkins—a faux wood engraving drawn in heavily crosshatched ink and filled with a palette of electric colors. A repeated halo and starburst motif gives a nod to the graphic style of the West Coast psychedelic poster artists working at the time. It is a prime example of Glaser's superb image-making skills. The back is simply the reverse view, showing Hopkins's shoulders, the back of his trilby hat, and the tip of his cigarette.

Pictured here are covers from the U.K. release of *Lightnin'!*, published as two separate volumes and both purchased secondhand from Honest Jon's on the Portobello Road during extended lunch hours of vinyl hunting in the early 1990s. The U.S. issue would presumably have been a double LP with gatefold, giving validity to Glaser's concept of a two-sided object. These editions must stand on their own merits and allow for the slightly preposterous notion that somebody coming across Volume 2 would be faced with only the back of Hopkins's head.

Jason Godfrey is a designer and author whose book *Bibliographic* on classic graphic design books was published by Laurence King in 2009. He worked as a designer in London, New York, and Texas before returning to London to set up Godfrey Design in 2002. His clients include the Royal Mail, Dorling Kindersley Publishers, and the illustration agency, Heart.

Lightnin'! Volume 1

Lightnin'! Volume 2

no. 31

SELECTED BY ARTEM DUPLESSIS | **VIBE COVERS** | **DESIGNED BY** GARY KOEPKE & RICHARD BAKER

It's funny how one little thing can change your entire life, or at least a portion of it. When I was a graduate student at Pratt Institute, way back in the day (1994), a friend and fellow student showed me a book that helped give me some guidance. (I desperately needed it.) This book was the Society of Publication Designers' *29th Best Magazine Design* annual. What stood out in this little treasure chest of design (for me) was the work that *Vibe* magazine was producing. It was beautiful, and it spoke to me on a personal level. It was the first magazine of its kind to feature, on a consistent basis, young people of many different ethnicities representing the youth culture.

Led by a remarkable team—creative director Gary Koepke, art director Richard Baker, and director of photography George Pitts—*Vibe* was close to magazine perfection: Clean, simple design, with subtle twists to elevate a message paired with some of the most beautiful photography in the business. The Mail page, which looked like something out of the Talmud, with paragraphs of type wrapping around bolder paragraphs of type, was simply amazing. *Vibe* would invite readers to submit pictures, and the best ones ran in the Mail section above a simple title that read "Drive-By Shooting." The feature well was dynamic and extremely elegant. One of my favorite spreads was

VIBe

WESLEY SNIPES

The Vibe Q: Bald Ambition by Danyel Smith

de la soul

krs-one

buju banton

tony toni toné

robin s

efua

souls of mischief

rage

$2.50   October 1993

PLUS: FLORIDA'S DRAG-QUEEN MAFIA • CONFESSIONS OF A VIDEO BIMBO • FREAKS

/ 94 / i heart design

a story on Wesley Snipes. Partnered with a beautiful Dan Winters photograph of Snipes covered in dried mud against a simple headline, set in all caps, highlighting the key word TROUBLE, this layout is the perfect example of restraint at its highest level.

Vibe invented the rules. The design was not layered and dense like some of the trends of that era dictated; it was simple and pure. The work was mesmerizing, and it meant something to me. This was my culture, and I related to every page.

Arem Duplessis is currently the design director of the *New York Times Magazine* division (the Sunday magazine, *Key*, and *T*.) He has held design director and art director positions at various titles, including the *New York Times Magazine*, *Spin*, *GQ*, and *Blaze* magazines. His work has been recognized by organizations like the Society of Publication Designers, where he most recently won both the Members Choice Award for best magazine, and the prestigious Magazine of the Year Award for work done at the *New York Times Magazine*.

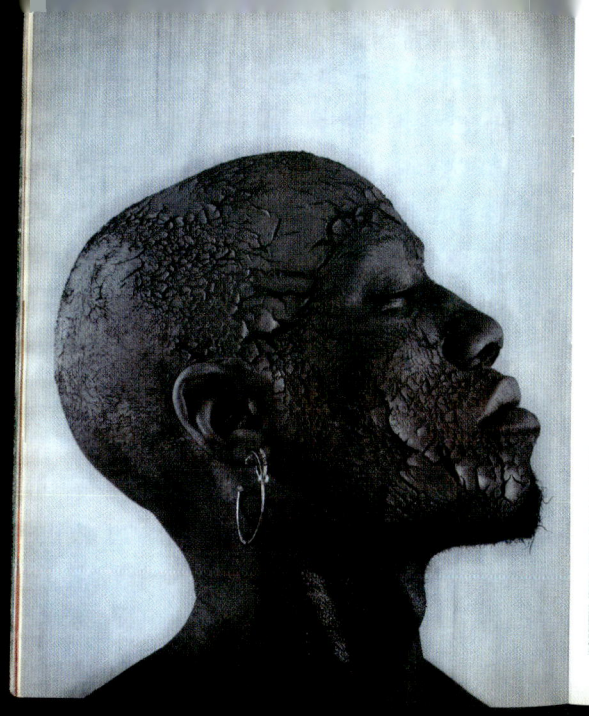

The Vibe Q

THE TROUBLE WITH WESLEY

Wesley Snipes crashes motorcycles, packs a semiautomatic, and beats up the bad guys. Onscreen and off. Danyel Smith catches the first black action hero on his day off from living the life of a Hollywood bad boy.

Photographs by Dan Winters

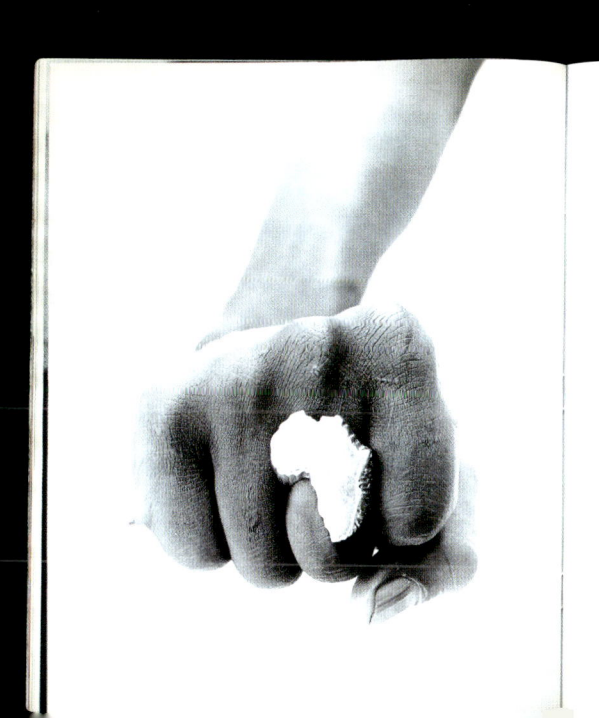

no. 32

SELECTED BY KEN CARBONE | PEACE POSTER | DESIGNED BY ROBERT BROWNJOHN

There are iconic works of graphic design whose timeless quality transcends stylistic fashion. In rare cases, some achieve a mythical aura. One such example is a peace poster designed by Robert Brownjohn in 1969. It was a radical departure from the peace posters of the time. Absent the Day-Glo colors, acid-trip type, and hippie imagery, it is oddly haunting and potent.

Brownjohn, known to his friends as BJ, was a founding member of Brownjohn, Chermayeff & Geismar. In 1959, he moved to London, where he became renowned as the creator of title sequences for classic James Bond films including the audaciously sexy *Goldfinger*.

I was fortunate to work for Chermayeff & Geismar after graduating college in 1973. It was my first job. This poster hung in the office, and I saw it on a daily basis. Unaware of Brownjohn's notoriety, I was initially puzzled by the poster's cryptic symbolism, but when I finally put the pieces together, it was an epiphany. Uncovering the message embedded in the visual code was revelatory and deeply impressionable to me.

Despite its simplicity and apparent immediacy, I see this poster as a very refined design and continue to find meaning in the image. However, I want to believe it was created in minutes. It is fast, fierce, and transforms the ordinary into the extraordinary. I often try this in my own work but rarely execute it at this level.

This is purported to be the last design by Brownjohn before his untimely death at 44, perhaps from complications related to drug addiction. This adds even deeper mystery to the poster. Why the ace of spades, a symbol of death, and not hearts? Was he questioning the futility of achieving world peace? Or was it BJ's final quest for peace?

Ken Carbone is a designer, artist, musician, author, teacher, and featured blogger. He is the cofounder and chief creative director of the Carbone Smolan Agency in New York City. Their client list includes W Hotels, Morgan Stanley, Canon, the Chicago Symphony Orchestra, Nonesuch Records, Corbis Images, *Architectural Record* magazine, Mandarin Oriental Hotel Group, and the Musée du Louvre. The agency's work is widely published and is recognized for excellence worldwide. However, he says he would give it all up for the chance to play guitar on tour with Tina Turner.

PE ♠ ?

Love - Bj.

no. 33

SELECTED BY TIM HOSSLER | COCA-COLA BOTTLE | DESIGNED BY EARL R. DEAN

This humble bottle is a souvenir from my father's trip to Egypt in the early 1980s. I like its strangeness and history, as it is familiar yet exotic, ordinary but slightly off. The almost unbreakable glass container is a relic from the Cold War era. Containing a sugary syrup drink, this coca pod–shaped vessel was intended to spread democracy and goodwill. Even as a prop, it is a movie star as instantly recognizable and meaningful as James Dean. The bottle transcends its functional role, standing for the good, the bad, and the ugly of the country that created it. Whether labeled in a Roman, Cyrillic, or Arabic font, this bottle will always symbolize U.S. culture and capitalism. It is poetically American.

Growing up in the historic town of Dodge City, Kansas, **Tim Hossler** developed a love of American myth and pop history. Iconic actor Dennis Hopper hailed from the same town, which has always been a source of pride. He moved from the Midwest to New York City, where as a designer he worked with photographer Annie Leibovitz. Her work strengthened Hossler's vision of referencing the past. He currently holds the position of art director for the Wolfsonian-Florida International University in Miami Beach, Florida.

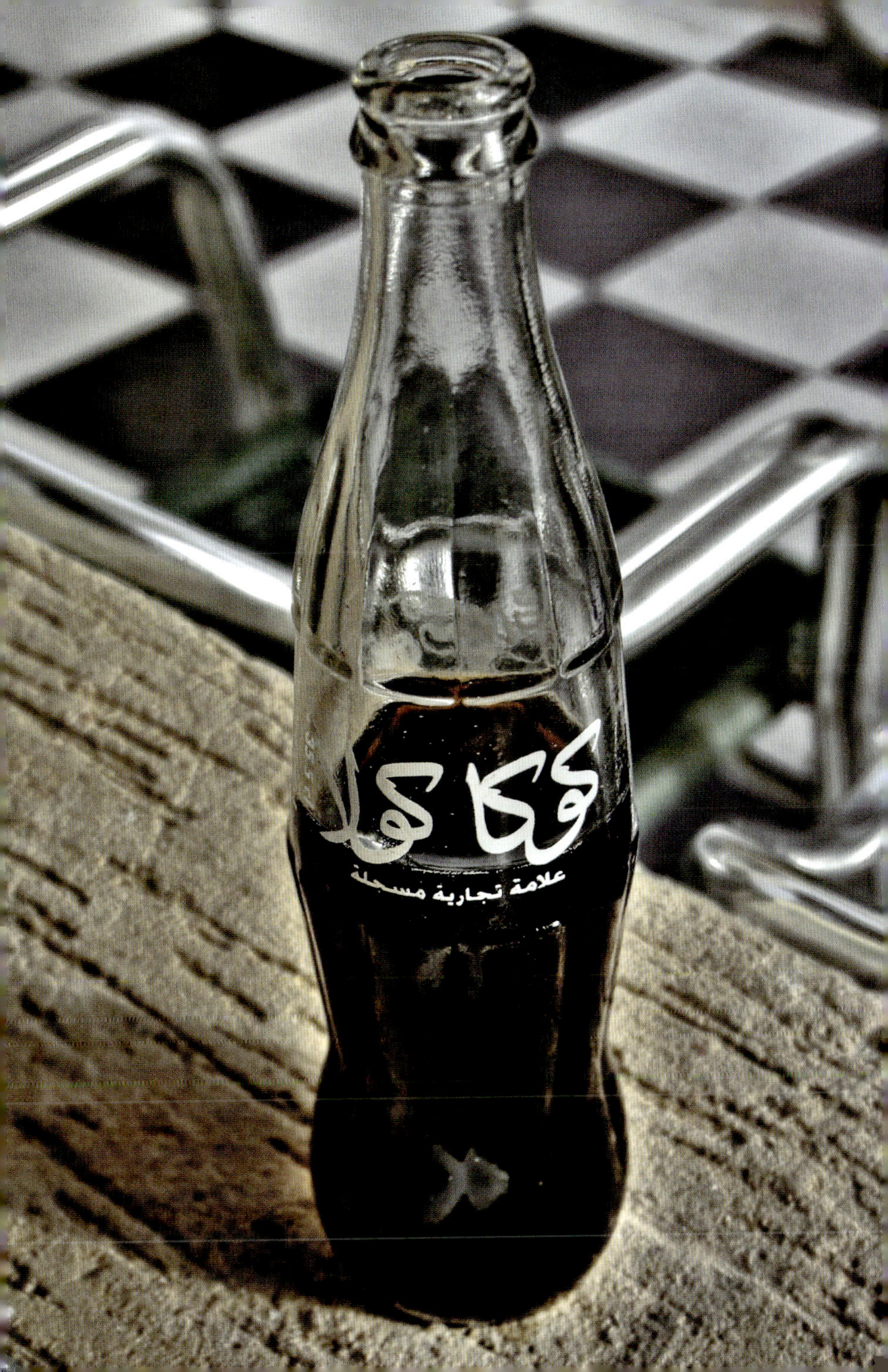
كوكا كولا
علامة تجارية مسجلة

no. 34

SELECTED BY ALLEN HORI | THE EQUIVALENT SERIES | PHOTOGRAPHED BY ALFRED STIEGLITZ

The Equivalent Series by Alfred Stieglitz is ostensibly a collection of photographs of clouds and sky intended as abstract images conveying the photographer's emotive and philosophical summation of his life's work. The images in the series are mostly without any traditional reference points and transcend literal interpretation of evidence of nature; they are destabilized evocations equally dependent on the perceptions of the viewer as well as each image's inherent formal qualities.

This series was, and continues to be, an important representation of how I regard the power and poetic rationale in graphic design. It set the foundation for me to actively engage with the highly influential see/read/image/text continuum proposed by Katherine McCoy at Cranbrook Academy of Art. The significant overlaps include abstract references, variant meanings and readings, intentions untethered of literal depiction, the use of metaphor to construct poetic bridges through image and text, and interpretation of messages necessarily activated by both the maker and viewer. These ideas continue to inform my approach, process, and execution of almost all the work the studio produces; an active measure of equivalence that apparently self-adjusts, providing a moving target of clarity and intention.

Allen Hori is a designer dedicated to the poetics of graphic design who willingly and pragmatically pursues the incongruities and surprising tangents of fancy found in studio practice. His experience covers a diverse range of clients from corporate, fashion, music, culture, art, and the publishing industries. As principal of Bates Hori, he focuses the studio's process of extensive research and exploration while critically balancing the relationship between words and images, and the fluid conceit of design and photography as practice and play. Hori is on the graduate faculty in graphic design at Yale University School of Art and a past Frank Stanton Chair in Graphic Design at the Cooper Union School of Art. He holds a BFA in photography from the University of Hawaii and an MFA in design from Cranbrook Academy of Art.

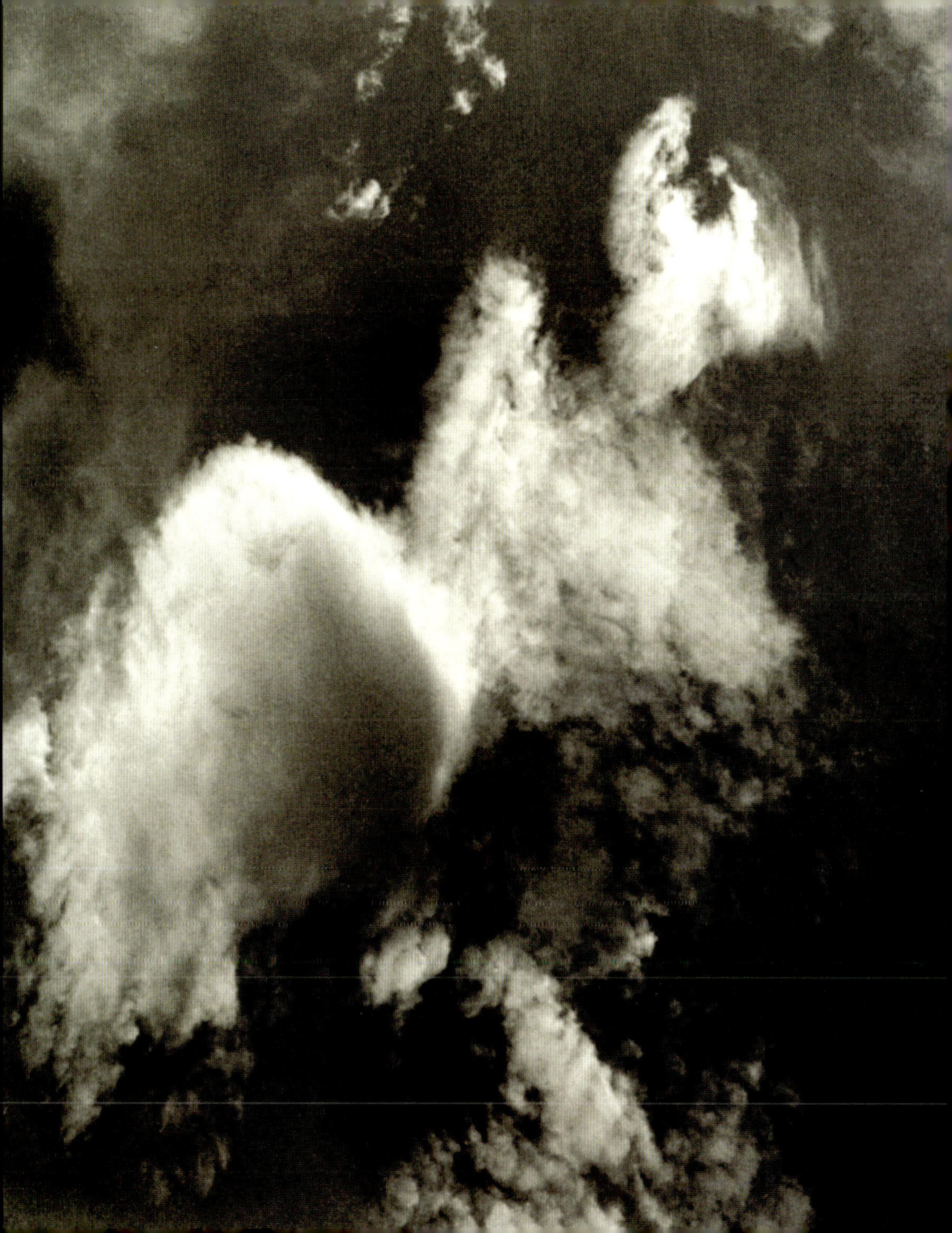

no. 35

SELECTED BY CHARLES SPENCER ANDERSON | **AD CUTS FROM A–Z** | **DESIGNED BY** CHARLES SPENCER ANDERSON

The *Ad Cuts from A–Z* book was published by the French Paper Company in 1989 and is a classic example of design from that time. Our work for French today is very different, and our approach to design continues to evolve. The A–Z book is important because it was influential when it was released and helped popularize the use of uncoated, recycled paper and vernacular line art illustration, in direct contrast to most corporate, generic design at the time, which relied largely on photography and slick, shiny paper. The *Ad Cuts from A–Z* book added a decidedly American low-brow pop culture component to the postmodern continuum.

Even more significantly, the A–Z book began to alter our own perception of the design process and made us realize that we could expand our scope of influence beyond designing specific projects to creating images and design elements for others to use. Later, the Web expanded this idea, making our images accessible to designers worldwide and transforming our design company from a service provider to corporations to a self-sustaining creator and licensor of digital products, providing us a new way forward in the constantly changing design profession.

Today, we view csaimages.com as a digital museum of art for commerce, an eclectic and tightly curated design resource of images, elements, patterns, and

OLD
Advertising
CUTS
FROM
A-Z
Over
222
PAGES
AD CUTS
Fresh
From FRIENDLY
FOLKS
SWELL STUFF
OK
Rely on
Amazing
LOW Price
$19.95
complete
OK
COMPILED BY CHARLES S. ANDERSON
OLD ADVERTISING CUTS FROM A-Z / ANDERSON

type developed over the past three decades. CSA Images is stylistically diverse and both timely and timeless because it takes its inspiration from the entire history of design and illustration as well as the highs and lows of visual pop culture. CSA Images licenses unique visual content across a number of different media types including print, online, products, mobile, and TV.

Charles Spencer Anderson established the Charles S. Anderson Design Company in 1989 after spending time at Duffy Design in Minneapolis. The company has produced design for French Paper, Nike, Target, Pottery Barn, and Coca-Cola, among others. As an offshoot, Anderson founded CSA Images, which harvests vintage graphics and repurposes them for contemporary usage.

/ 105 /

no. 36

POSTER FOR THE 50TH ANNIVERSARY OF THE UNION INTERNATIONALE DE LA MARIONETTE, 1978

SELECTED BY JAMES VICTORE | **DESIGNED BY HENRYK TOMASZEWSKI**

No design history would be complete without mention of the "Polish poster school," in general, and Henryk Tomaszewski, in particular.

I have always felt that Henryk's work presented a small rift in the design continuum, a break from the European-centric styles of Art Deco and artists like Cassandre and a proposal for a more modern type of poster art. One possible example of any knowledge or homage to design history would be the simplicity and reductivist attitude of Lucien Bernhard's commercial poster work.

What I respond to in his work is the simplicity, the clumsy typography, the lack of what we generally perceive as "rules," as well as the thinking present in all his work. This one example for puppet theater completely avoids the set responses or clichés generally seen, such as strings, cross supports, and doll heads. Instead, Tomaszewski talks of emotions—the relationship of the puppet to the master—then, to mess us up even further, he invokes the relationship of the warm, human leg to the leg of the chair. *A ménage à trois*, if you will.

The influence of Tomaszewski's work can be found through the students who flocked to him at the Academy in Warsaw, notably the French designers who spread his message outside of Poland. Designers like Pierre Bernard, Gerard Paris-Clavel, and Alain Le Quernec, who learned at his knee, then inspired younger studios such as the French M/M and Swiss Cornel Windlin, even trickling down to an American like me.

James Victore is a graphic designer whose clients include Moët & Chandon, Target, Amnesty International, the Shakespeare Project, the *New York Times*, MTV, the Lower East Side Tenement Museum, and Portfolio Center. He has been awarded an Emmy for television animation, a gold medal from the Broadcast Designers Association, the Grand Prix from the Brno Biennele (Czech Republic), and gold and silver medals from the New York Art Directors Club. Victore's posters are in the permanent collections of the Palais du Louvre, the Library of Congress, and the Museum für Gestaltung, among others.

50-ème Anniversaire de l'Union Internationale
de la Marionnette

no. 37

SELECTED BY SAGI HAVIV | THE CBS EYE LOGO | DESIGNED BY WILLIAM GOLDEN

As a designer in the modernist tradition, I value simplicity and originality above all. In trademark design, this often means creating a mark out of elementary shapes to achieve universality and timelessness, but configuring those shapes in a way that is original and distinctive. There is no better exemplar of this than the CBS eye. Designed by CBS's art director William Golden and first appearing on the air in 1951, the logo takes simple, elementary shapes—two circles, two arcs—and configures them into an original form—a pictographic eye. It's been in use, unchanged, for sixty years. It's so distinctive it can stand on its own without the name of the company attached to it. Its power has only grown over time. The remarkable success of the CBS eye demonstrates why designers follow modernist principles in the first place. In today's graphic tornado of complex, busy, and often disposable trademarks, the CBS eye stands like a beacon not only for the modernist ideal, but in my opinion, for good design.

As much as it is a beacon, especially for designers such as myself who came of age in the twenty-first century, it is also, in its own way, a barrier. The CBS eye was created just when modernism was entering the mainstream of corporate design culture. Like my partner Tom Geismar's logo design for Chase Bank a few years later, the CBS eye was one of the very first. But there are, by definition, a finite number of simple forms. In the decades since 1951, modernism swept graphic design, resulting in countless modernist-inspired marks and a crowded visual field. Simplicity has always been hard enough to achieve, but today originality is perhaps even harder.

When I'm designing a trademark, my job is to travel the continuum between simplicity and originality—to discover just how unique you can make a mark while maintaining its elemental forms. To make something new, creative professionals are told to "think outside the box." The challenge for modernist trademark designers is that the ultimate "box" is precisely the set of universal formal parameters that make our creations powerful, iconic, and timeless. You have to find the new thing in the box ... and pray nobody else found it first.

Sagi Haviv is a partner and designer at Chermayeff & Geismar. Among his projects for the firm are the logo designs and identity systems for the Library of Congress, National Parks of New York Harbor, Radio Free Europe, the John D. and Catherine T. MacArthur Foundation, and the fashion brand Armani Exchange. Haviv designed the award-winning animation *Logomotion*, a ten-minute tribute to the firm's famous trademarks. Haviv's other motion graphics work includes the opening sequence for the celebrated PBS documentary series *Carrier*.

38 no.

SELECTED BY WOODY PIRTLE | THE CBS EYE LOGO | DESIGNED BY WILLIAM GOLDEN

The CBS symbol, designed by William Golden in 1951, is a modern classic that after decades of exposure to tens of millions of viewers every day, has proven to be one of the most enduring symbols in the history of graphic design.

Inspired by the illustration of an eye in an article on Shaker design by Alexey Brodovitch, Golden created the stylized icon just as television was emerging as the dominant medium of communication in America.

The symbol's majestic simplicity and its ability to immediately connect the network with its audience has given CBS an identity that is as powerful and appropriate today as it was when it was designed almost sixty years ago.

In my view, it is unlikely to ever become dated because its reductive quality allows for infinite flexibility when applied across multiple mediums.

The Golden eye and its accompanying Didot logotype, which was hand-drawn by staff designers George Lois and Kurt Weihs, has established a benchmark of quality for all of us who create symbols, logotypes, and identity programs to aspire to. For me, this is the symbol and logotype that always comes to mind when I ask myself if I have created a design that is simple, appropriate, and timeless.

Woody Pirtle established Pirtle Design in Dallas, Texas, in 1978. In 1988, he became a partner of Pentagram. For eighteen years Pirtle was a partner in the New York office. In 2005, he reestablished Pirtle Design. His work has been exhibited worldwide and is in the permanent collections of the Museum of Modern Art and Cooper-Hewitt Museum in New York, the Victoria & Albert Museum in London, the Neue Sammlung Museum in Munich, the Zurich Poster Museum, and others. In 2003, he was awarded the prestigious AIGA Medal for his career contribution to the design profession.

no. 39

SELECTED BY GEOFF McFETRIDGE | STP & MOONEYES LOGOS | DESIGNER UNKNOWN

Like anyone, my history is a history of both experiences and images. I find it hard to place a value on the things that have influenced me visually. Looking back, I see a muddy concoction of things from my youth, things from yesterday, and images passing by in a blur as if seen from a car window, all appearing with an apparent equal value.

Images always meant a lot to me. Visuals affected me; they made me feel good. I could glance at the *Fantastic 5* on TV, close my eyes, and soak in the colors and lines. *Tintin* and *Judge Dredd* comics would ring in my head like church bells. My history is a visual history. Since I was a child, I dedicated myself to being affected by what I saw—it was my primary source of navigation, thus it is difficult to determine what thing affected me most. So my thoughts go back to some of the first things—maybe not the most important—that really affected me.

When I was around seven or eight, my father would take me to the stock car races. I was born in 1971, so this was the late '70s. We were living in St. Albert, Alberta, Canada, a small town outside of Edmonton. The stock car races were of the "homespun" variety. There were a couple of main races, and a demolition derby. It was loud, dirty, and awesome. I remember the rough crowd, the haze of unmuffled exhaust, and rusty clunkers with their doors filled with concrete...and stickers, cars covered in stickers.

At home, my dad would draw a stock car in profile. I would then draw all the stickers, numbers, and logos on it. I loved drawing the numbers and the logos, but it was pretty hard, as I had to draw them quite small. Of course the best logos were STP and MoonEYES. Most cars would have STP drawn on them so many times that even NASCAR would cringe. MoonEYES was always carefully placed near the wheel wells at the bottom of the car.

Did VonDutch design the MoonEYES logo? I am not sure. But that logo made a real impression on me.

When I was older, I got into skateboarding, which in the '80s was similar to stock car racing—bright colors and boards covered with stickers. From there I started making my own stickers, T-shirts, and logos.

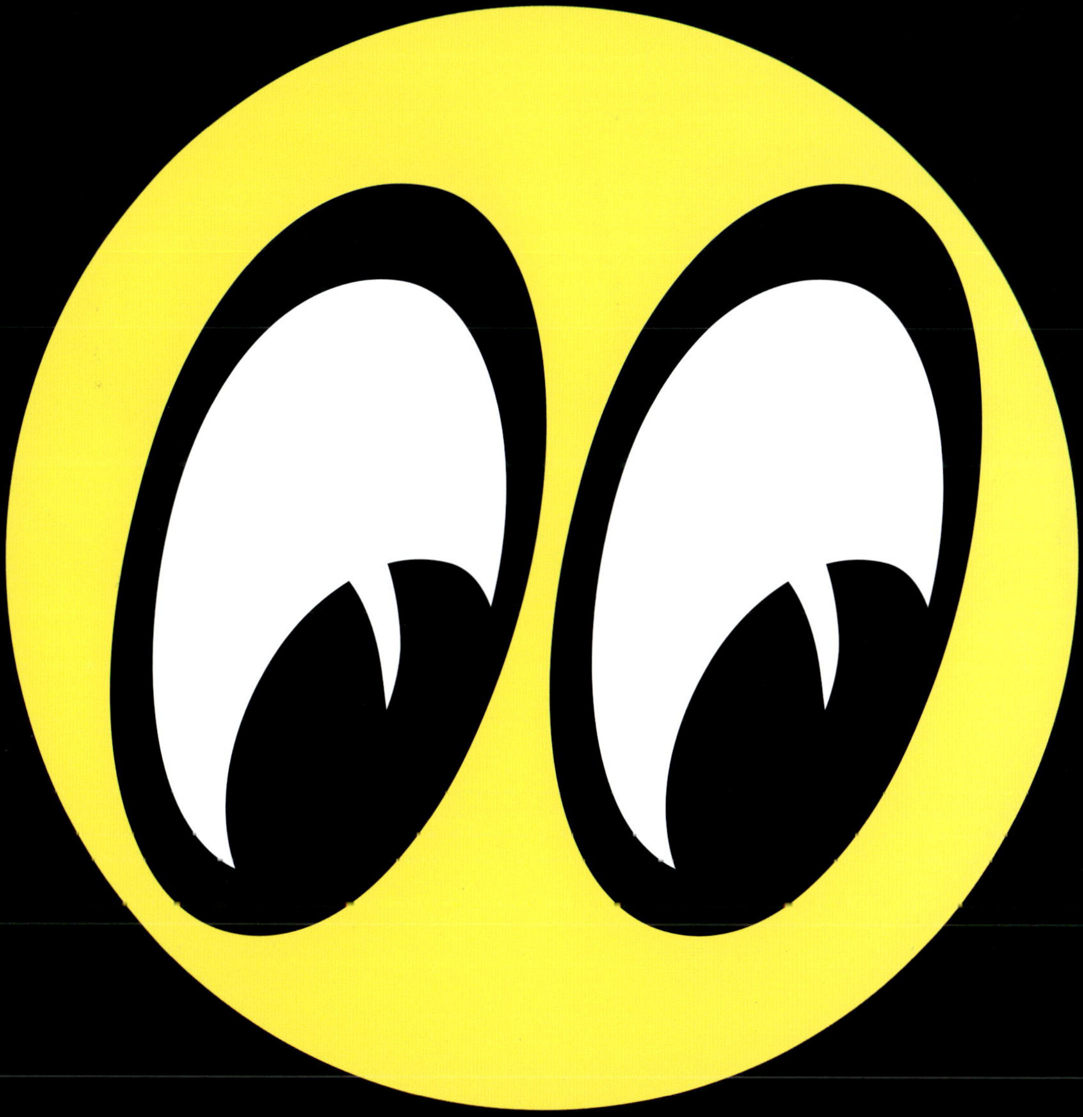

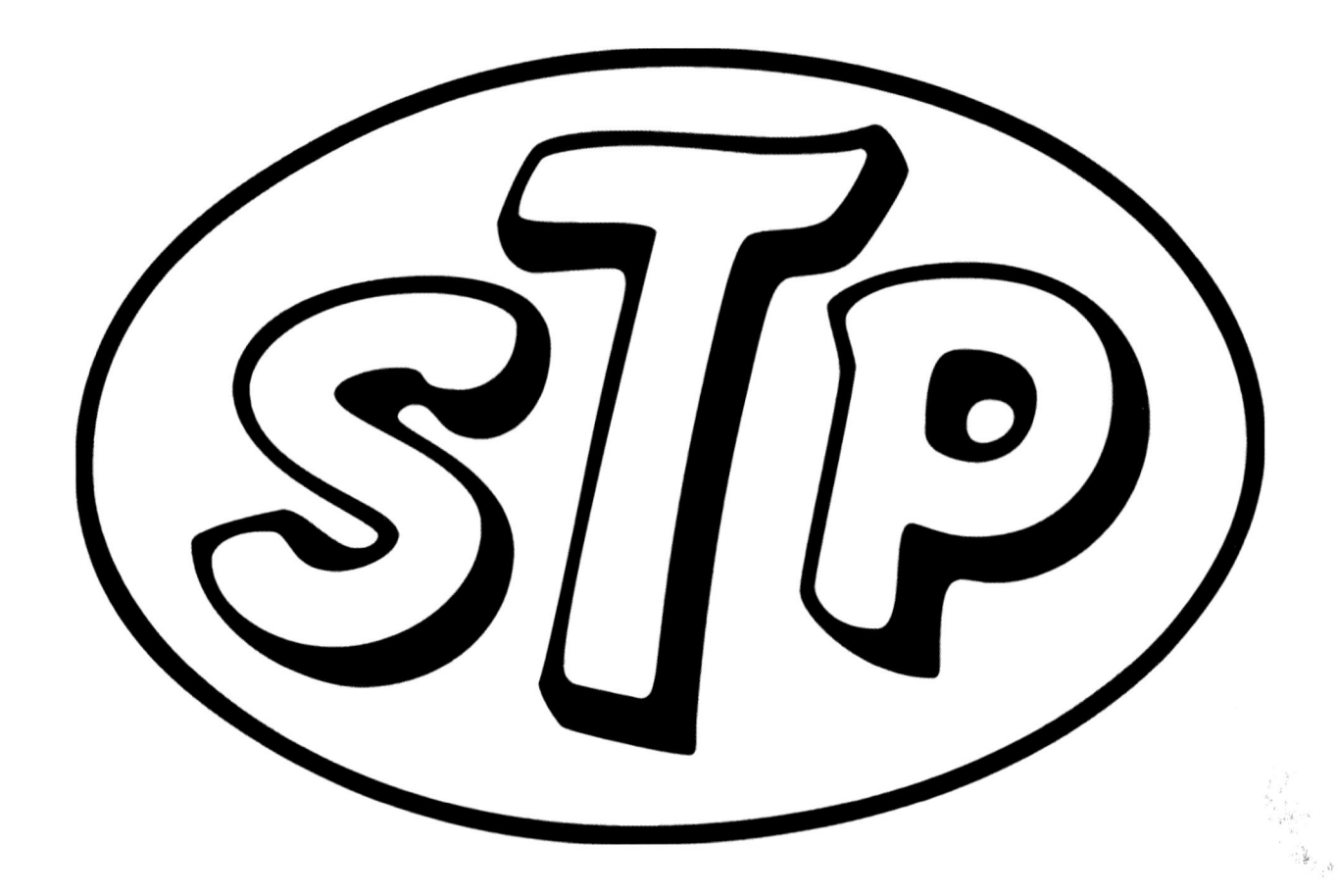

Looking back, I see a seamless evolution from being a kid and absorbing the things around me to being a grownup and reflecting all these influences and images back to the world in my own work.

I never knew what STP or Moon did as companies ... but that was not the point. As images, they stood alone, they captured the spirit of the races. To this day, I am trying to have that depth, the connective power that those simple icons had, in my own work.

Geoff McFetridge is a graphic designer, visual artist, and design entrepreneur based in Los Angeles. He was born in Calgary, Canada, and received his BFA from the local Alberta College of Design. He continued his education at California Institute of the Arts in Los Angeles, receiving his MFA in 1995. In 1996, McFetridge established Champion Graphics in Atwater, California.

no. 40

SELECTED BY ROSS MacDONALD | MY BOOK HOUSE | DESIGNED BY OLIVE BEAUPRE MILLER

Olive Beaupre Miller was thirty-seven in 1920 when her newly founded publishing company released the first edition of the *My Book House* set. In it, Miller had collected and edited (and in some cases, written) the best in children's stories and poems from around the world. It was the first time anyone had published a collection of stories that grew with a child's developing abilities and needs. It's an amazingly diverse and sensitive sampler of children's literature, remarkably free of much of the prejudice of the time, and one that still holds up today. In fact, it's still in print. A true innovator—Miller was an early proponent of sex education for children, and her publishing company was staffed mostly by women—her influence on the world of children's publishing is unjustly overlooked.

Not just great literature, the books are beautiful as well. The original set of six books was sold in a little red wooden house bookshelf. It was expanded to twelve volumes in 1937. Beautifully designed—the first two volumes are set in Monotype Centaur and Arrighi—the books were full of thousands of illustrations by some of the top children's illustrators of the day. One of my favorites—Miriam Story Hurford—went on to illustrate one of the classic Dick and Jane books a couple of years later.

Like me, untold thousands of children learned to read with *My Book House*. We had hardly any other books when I was growing up, but I didn't need any others. Battered and rife with tears and stains and the crayon chicken scratches that were our early attempts at writing and drawing, the well-worn pages testify to the many happy hours we spent with these books.

I believe they're the reason I'm an illustrator and designer today.

I'll always be grateful to the anonymous traveling salesman who managed to talk my mother into buying this twelve-volume set in 1950.

Ross MacDonald is an illustrator, autodidact, former egg candler, and onetime rugged Canadian boy currently residing in New York City. His rogue to riches story is common currency. Little is known of MacDonald, and less is spoken. His doodles have stained the pages of most magazines and sullied movies and Broadway plays, but he finds peace in his happy home life.

The Green Bus*

WAIT a minute,
Green bus!
Slow down!
Stop!

I will climb
Your winding stair
And ride
On top.

Along
The busy river,
Down
The avenue,

Any day
I like to take
A trip
With you.
—James S. Tippett

The Police Cop Man**

I'M the police cop man, I am, I am.
   Cars can't go till I say they can.
I stand in the middle of the street, I do,
And tell them to go when I want them to.
Whizzing taxis and automobiles,
Trotting horses and clattering wheels,
And rumbling, grumbling, huge big trucks,
And even the lazy old trolley car,
Can't go very far
   When up goes my hand
                                    and

"Traffic stop,"
   Says the traffic cop,
Then many little children's feet
Go hippity across the street.
—Margaret Morrison

* "The Green Bus" is from I Go A-Traveling, by James S. Tippett. By permission of Harper and Brothers, publishers.
** "The Police Cop Man" is reprinted from Streets, Cooperating School Pamphlet No. 2, by permission of the Bureau of Educational Experiments, 69 Bank Street, New York, and the John Day Company.

173

no. 41

SELECTED BY JAN WILKER | VH PLAKATE | DESIGNED BY OTL AICHER

I grew up in Ulm, the little city in the South of Germany that used to be the home of the *hfg ulm*, an influential design school internationally known as the Ulm School of Design. After World War II, with the help of the United States, it was founded by Inge Scholl together with her husband, Otl Aicher, and Max Bill, amongst others. Opened in 1953, it was seen as the beginning of a new era for Germany and its cultural and political future, where rational thought and science would be the basis of the design education. The school had to close a mere fifteen years later, in 1968. I wouldn't be born for another four years.

In the late '70s, we would very often visit my father at his workplace in the former *hfg* building, which quickly had been taken over by the University of Ulm, where he was conducting research with autistic children. At home, we had the *stackable ashtray* and the Ulm *hocker*. Posters showed lowercase typography and geometrical shapes. I grew up thinking this was the norm. And although I grew up there long after the school ceased to exist, its spirit must have still lived on. In hindsight, I want to convince myself that I was influenced by it—I'm sure I couldn't prove it scientifically. I chose four random posters from hundreds designed by Otl Aicher starting in 1948 for the *vh Ulm* (the city's adult education center).

Jan Wilker, of karlssonwilker inc. in New York City, was raised in Ulm, Germany, and later graduated from the State Academy of Art and Design in Stuttgart. In 2000, he and Icelander Hjalti Karlsson founded karlssonwilker inc., a design studio located in the heart of Manhattan. The two of them work on all sorts of projects for an eclectic mix of cultural and commercial clients, from local nonprofits to global corporations. Wilker frequently lectures and gives workshops on design on all continents (except Antarctica).

Kurs

Du und die Sterne

**dienstags
ab 14. September**

no. 42

SELECTED BY KIM ELAM | L'INTRANSIGÉANT POSTER | DESIGNED BY A. M. CASSANDRE

Good posters communicate thoughts and ideas at a glance. Great posters tell stories. The *L'Intrans* poster tells a story of dynamic communication—the news of the day flows from the telegraph wires into the ear, and is being screamed out through the newspaper, *L'Intrans*!

The angles and repetition of the telegraph wires pull the eye to the stylized head and wide-open mouth. There is no embellishment or clutter. The poster is pure, simple, and geometric. Every single line and object on the poster has purpose and meaning. Nothing can be taken away. The only type on the poster is the newspaper masthead, *L'Intrans*. Geometric circles, angles, and shapes speak to the fine art Cubist influences that are melded into the imagery. The woman's head is symbolic of Marianne, an allegorical figure who is, "the voice of France." The construction of the poster and proportion of the elements were not the result of a fortuitous accident. Everything was carefully planned, thoughtfully considered, and the original construction diagrams still exist. The poster is the result of a powerful concept and plan that were fused in the design of the poster.

The designer, Adolphe Mouron, created posters under the pseudonym, A. M. Cassandre, so as to shield his own name for a later time when he envisioned a return to fine art painting. The appearance of Cubist influences in his posters in the 1920s was intensely criticized by architect Le Corbusier and fine artist Ozenfant as, "...a formula purloined and massacred by a dauber." In spite of the criticism, *L'Intrans* signaled a philosophical change for Cassandre from creating fine art paintings for the elite to creating poster art for the masses. It also signaled a change in visual culture and the emergence of graphic design.

Kimberly Elam is a writer, educator, and graphic designer. She is currently the chair of the graphic and interactive communication department at the Ringling School of Art and Design, Sarasota, Florida. Her published books include: *Expressive Typography—Word As Image*, *Geometry of Design—Studies in Proportion and Composition*, *Grid Systems—Principles of Organizing Type*, *Graphic Translation*, and *Typographic Systems—Rules for Organizing Type*. Her current work focuses on the development of a series of e-books and print-on-demand books for design education on the website, StudioResourceInc.com.

LE PLUS FORT
L'INTRANS
AMCASSANDRE
1925
HACHARD & Cie
8, PLACE DE LA MADELEINE PARIS

no. 43

SELECTED BY ALLAN CHOCHINOV | **BLUE, JONI MITCHELL** | **PHOTOGRAPHED BY** TIM CONSIDINE | **DESIGNED BY** GARY BURDEN

Gary Burden designed so many iconic record covers—for Crosby, Stills, Nash & Young and the Doors to the Eagles and Jackson Browne. But Joni Mitchell's *Blue* (cover photo by Tim Considine) is the one that speaks most personally to me. I wouldn't say that growing up in Canada I took pride in listening to Joni; I didn't have nationalistic listening habits. But Joni Mitchell was a huge influence on my guitar playing, and *Blue* was one of the most hauntingly beautiful records I owned.

As it turned out, a few years ago I was in Aspen, Colorado, for a design conference, and one of the evening activities was a book-launch party for Burden himself. All of the attendees were given a copy of a slim, FSC-certified monograph—the evening was sponsored by the Domtar sustainable paper company—and Gary was there with Sharpie in hand. I waited patiently in line, my finger tucked into the Joni Mitchell *Blue* page, and as I approached him, opened it up, offered it to him, and told him how much I loved the album and all that it had meant. He looked at me with what can only be described as a combination of outrage and near disgust. "I'm not going to write on her cover!" he declared, "and if you loved her as much as I do you'd understand that, man." I recoiled, bewildered, then embarrassed: He had felt that his signature would be defacing the art, and offered to sign the inside cover of the book instead.

The next person in line moved forward, and I slunk out of there...yup, blue.

Allan Chochinov is a partner of Core77, a New York–based design network serving a global community of designers and design enthusiasts. He is the editor in chief of Core77.com, Coroflot.com design job and portfolio site, and DesignDirectory.com design firm database. He has been named on numerous design and utility patents and has received awards from *Communication Arts*, the Art Directors Club, *I.D.* magazine, and the One Club. He teaches in the graduate departments of Pratt Institute and the School of Visual Arts in New York City and writes and lectures widely on the impact of design on contemporary culture.

JONI MITCHELL

no. 44

SELECTED BY ANDREA RAUCH | DYLAN POSTER | DESIGNED BY MILTON GLASER

Milton Glaser's "Dylan" poster was perhaps the most influential graphic object of my formative years, the early '70s, when I just got out of school. "Dylan" was full of the spirit of the time, and if on one hand it described in a perfect manner a singer, author, and poet of great charm and success, on the other hand it was having a deep dialogue with the artistic culture of the 20th (it is known that the first inspiration for Glaser came from the famous black-and-white silhouette of Marcel Duchamp).

The poster also brings about a wonderful synthesis between the world of image and the world of type, transforming the two parts of the project in a totally inextricable unit, exceeding also the apparent aridity of design, typical of European and Italian rationalism dominant at that time. Fifty years later, Glaser's poster retains all of its topicality and freshness. It doesn't seem to be a historical object, but one could say it was produced today by a contemporary designer. For my work, it was the source of admiration, amazement, reflection, and emulation. When I found myself working with Glaser on a show in Italy, I couldn't help myself to paraphrase it, changing only the hair that "is blowing in the wind" in color and actual pixel (my poster is from 2000); in a book dedicated to revisiting the myth of the Beatles, drawn to recall the great pop graphic of the sixties, the portrait of Dylan, the way Milton had wanted it, is talking with Ringo Starr.

Andrea Rauch lives and works near Florence at his studio, Rauch Design. He has drawn for many public institutions and for political and opinion movements such as Greenpeace and UNICEF. His posters are part of many important collections in the world, such as the New York Museum of Modern Art and the Musée de la Publicitè of Louvre, Paris. Until 2002 he was a teacher of graphic design at Siena University.

DYLAN

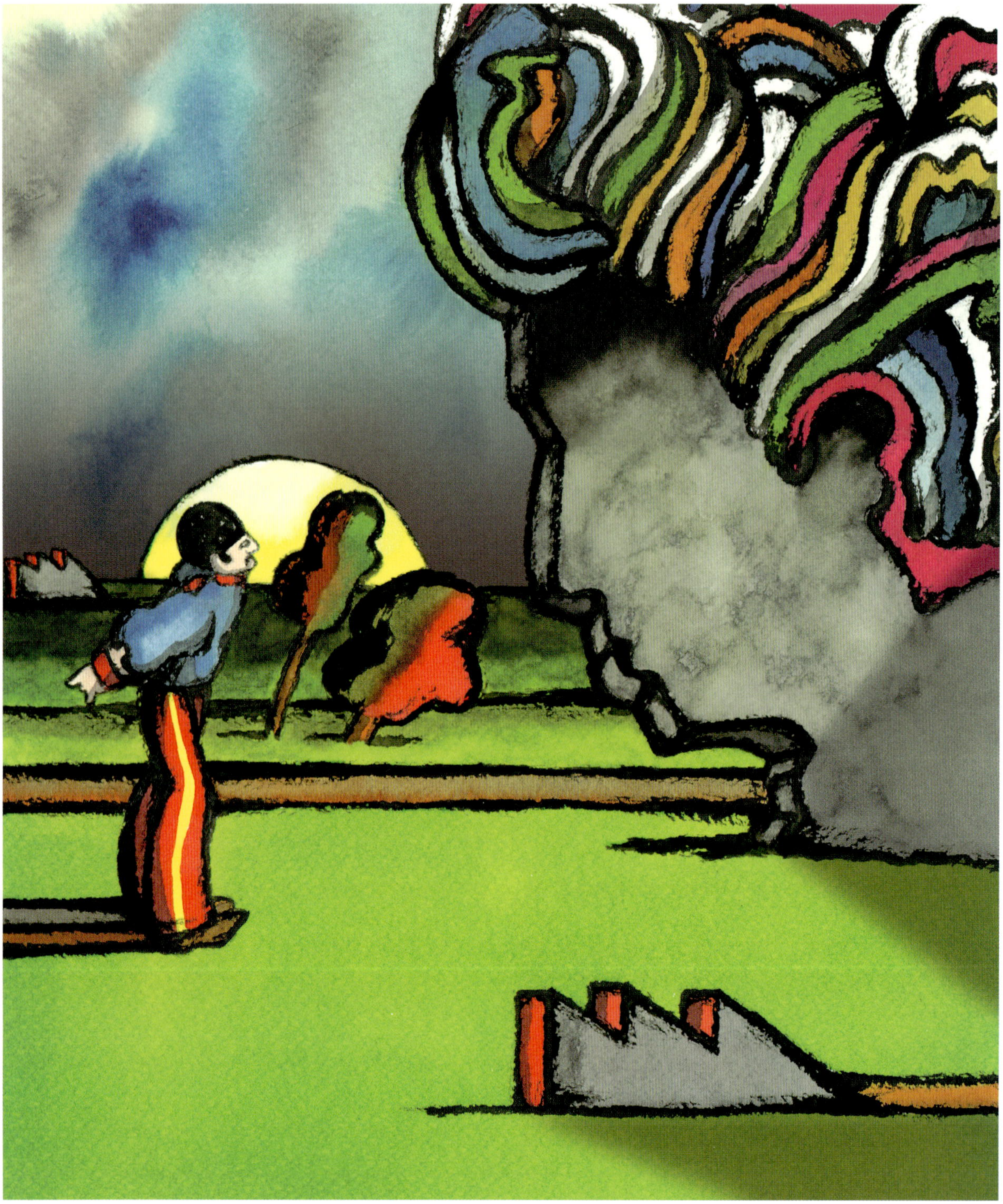

/ 127 /

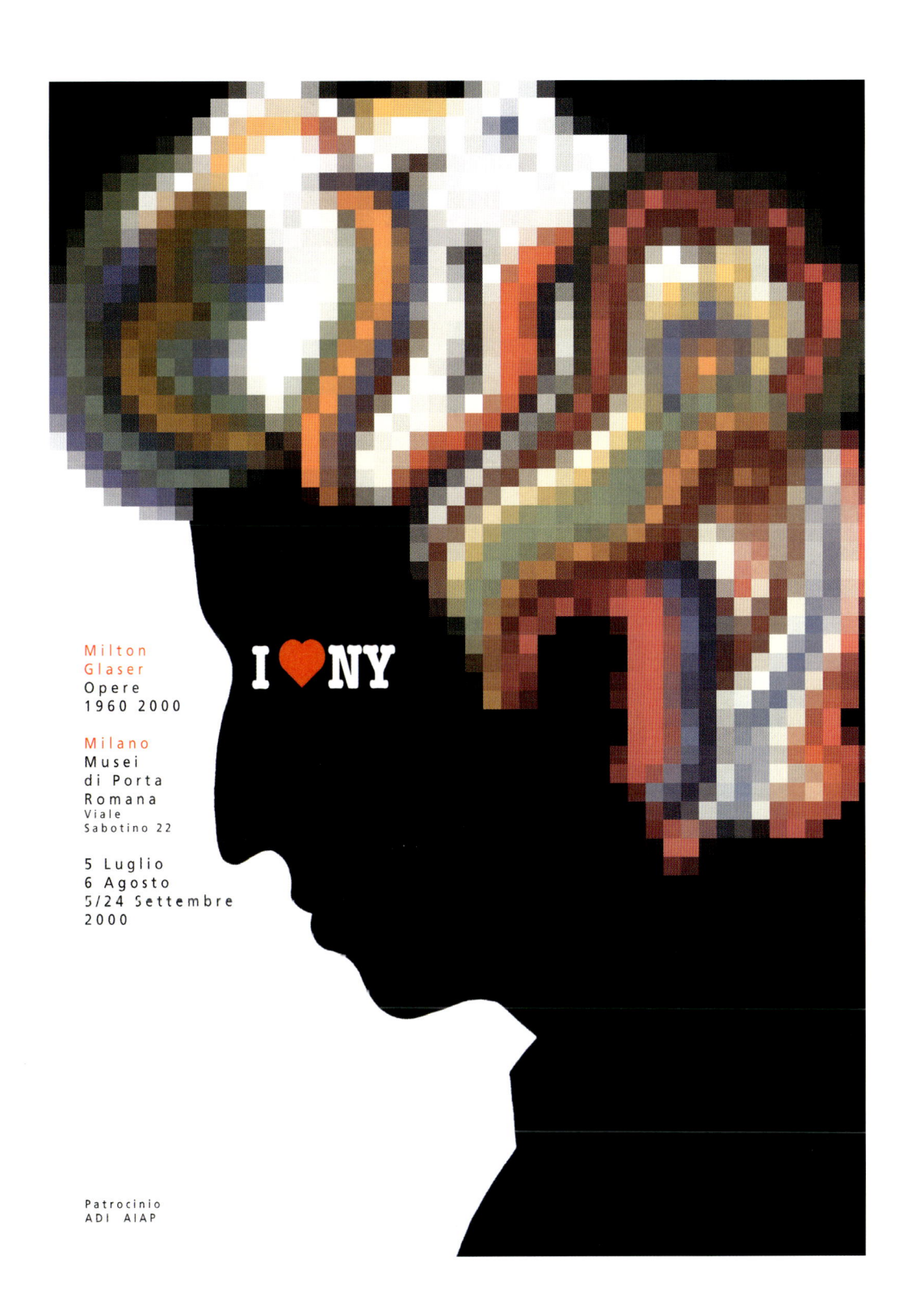

**Milton
Glaser**
Opere
1960 2000

Milano
Musei
di Porta
Romana
Viale
Sabotino 22

5 Luglio
6 Agosto
5/24 Settembre
2000

I ♥ NY

Patrocinio
ADI AIAP

no. 45

SELECTED BY MARK LAMSTER | JOHN M. WARD BASEBALL CARD, 1887 | DESIGNER UNKNOWN

Like so many boys, my first prolonged exposure to a piece of graphic design came in the form of baseball cards. These nonfunctional objects are pure works of design, and even in my adolescent years, I had a tendency to evaluate them as such. While I always put a premium on acquiring star players from my favorite Yankees, I also went out of the way to pick up cards and sets that I found visually compelling, immersing myself for hour after hour in their every typographic and compositional detail.

A few years ago, after writing a book on the early history of the sport, I picked up a facsimile of the first great baseball card, an 1887 John M. Ward, one of ten baseball players in Allen & Ginter's "World Champions." Allen & Ginter made a newfangled product called cigarettes and stuck the cards in the packs to push sales. Only much later were they sold with gum. Ward was a particularly compelling figure. The star shortstop of the New York Giants, he was a tabloid fixture on the order of Derek Jeter. He was also a lawyer, trained at Columbia University, who founded the first baseball players union. In 1889, he led the players in that union to form their own upstart league, the Players' League, in competition with the established National League. That was a failure, but he continued to play professionally. He is now in the Hall of Fame.

Mark Lamster writes about architecture and design. His first book, *Spalding's World Tour* (PublicAffairs, 2006), tells the story of America's first cultural diplomats, an intrepid group of professional baseball players, John Ward among them, who fully circumnavigated the globe in the nineteenth century.

JOHN M. WARD.
ALLEN & GINTER'S
RICHMOND. Cigarettes. VIRGINIA.

THE WORLD'S CHAMPIONS
ONE PACKED IN EACH BOX OF
TEN CIGARETTES

BASE BALL PLAYERS.
CHAS. W. BENNETT.
JOHN M. WARD.
MIKE KELLY.
JOHN CLARKSON.
TIMOTHY KEEFE.
JOSEPH MULVEY.
ADRIAN C. ANSON.
CAPT. JACK GLASSCOCK.
R. L. CARUTHERS.
CHARLES COMISKEY.

OARSMEN.
WM. BEACH.
JOHN TEEMER.
E. A. TRICKETT.
ED. HANLAN.
WALLACE ROSS.
JACOB GAUDAUR.
GEO H. HOSMER.
ALBERT HAMM.
JOHN MCKAY.
GEO. BUBEAR.

WRESTLERS.
JOE ACTON.
WM. MULDOON.
THEO. BAUER.
MATSADA SORAKICHI.
J. H. MCLAUGHLIN.
JOHN MCMAHON.
YOUNG BIBBY. (Geo Mehling).

PUGILISTS.
JOHN L. SULLIVAN.
JAKE KILRAIN.
JEM SMITH.
CHARLIE MITCHELL.
JIMMY CARNEY.
JACK DEMPSEY.
IKE WEIR.
JACK MCAULIFFE.
JOE LANNON.
JIMMY CARROLL.

RIFLE SHOOTERS.
CAPT. A. H. BOGARDUS.
DR. W. F. CARVER.
HON. W. F. CODY (Buffalo Bill)
MISS ANNIE OAKLEY.

BILLIARD PLAYERS.
WM. SEXTON.
M. VIGNAUX.
J. SCHAEFER.
JOS. DION.
MAURICE DALY.
GEO. F. SLOSSON.
YANK ADAMS.

POOL PLAYERS.
ALBERT FREY.
J. L. MALONE.

LINDNER, EDDY & CLAUSS, LITH. N.Y.

no. 46

SELECTED BY CHRISTIAN ANNYAS | THE MAN WITH THE GOLDEN ARM | DESIGNED BY SAUL BASS

Before the mid-1950s, most Hollywood movie title cards and opening credits were typographically static. Projectionists only pulled back the curtains to reveal the screen once they'd finished. Then Saul Bass came along with his expressionistic animated title sequences.

His design for *The Man with the Golden Arm* (1955) has become a landmark in title design and set the bar for what has become an essential popular art. These movies within movies are sometimes as memorable as the films themselves. And designers have been paying homage to—and building on—them ever since.

So novel was this sequence, when the reels of film for *The Man with the Golden Arm* arrived at U.S. movie theaters in 1955, a note was stuck on the cans: "Projectionists—pull curtain before titles."

"My initial thoughts about what a title can do was to set mood and the prime underlying core of the film's story, to express the story in some metaphorical way," Bass said about his rationale. "I saw the title as a way of conditioning the audience, so that when the film actually began, viewers would already have an emotional resonance with it."

The influence of the groundbreaking design work of Bass continues today, whether it's the controversial "homage" in the poster for the Spike Lee film *Clockers* (1995), the opening titles of Spielberg's *Catch Me If You Can* (2002), or the more recent torrent of Bass-inspired posters for movies like *Before the Devil Knows You're Dead* (2007), *Burn after Reading* (2008), *The Men Who Stare at Goats* (2009), and *Precious* (2009).

Christian Annyas is a Web designer based in the Netherlands. He studied photography for two years, then switched to graphic design and finished his study at the Academy of Modern Arts in 's-Hertogenbosch, the Netherlands. His passion for film title design led to the creation of the Movie Title Stills Collection, which contains hundreds of screen shots of movie title stills from feature films and trailers.

OTTO PREMINGER PRESENTS

FRANK SINATRA ELEANOR PARKER KIM NOVAK

THE
MAN WITH
THE GOLDEN
ARM

with ARNOLD STANG
DARREN McGAVIN
ROBERT STRAUSS
JOHN CONTE
DORO MERANDE

GEORGE E. STONE
GEORGE MATHEWS
LEONID KINSKEY
EMILE MEYER

screenplay by WALTER NEWMAN and LEWIS MELTZER

from the novel by NELSON ALGREN

music ELMER BERNSTEIN

film editor LOUIS R. LOEFFLER music editor LEON BIRNBAUM

assistant to producer MAXIMILIAN SLATER

costume supervisor
MARY ANN NYBERG

sound engineer
JACK SOLOMON

director of photography SAM LEAVITT, A.S.C.

production manager
JACK McEDWARD
assistant directors
HORACE HOUGH
JAMES BRIBIR
script supervisor
KATHLEEN FAGAN
men's wardrobe JOE KING
women's wardrobe
ADELE PARMENTER
camera operator
ALBERT MYERS

makeup JACK STONE
BERNARD PONEDEL
BEN LANE
hairstyles HELENE PARRISH
HAZEL KEATS
lighting technician
JAMES ALMOND
head grip MORRIS ROSEN

titles designed by
SAUL BASS

produced and directed by OTTO PREMINGER

THE END

no. 47

SELECTED BY LAURA GUIDO-CLARK | DR. SEUSS | DESIGNED BY DR. SEUSS

Books uninspired, the classrooms were bored.
Illiterate children created a war.
Until one man, a doctor, referred to as Seuss
stood up to the challenge and called it a truce.

Armed with his pencils he thought he would try
to begin with blank paper and a question called "Why?"
Unleashing the powers of his imaginative mind
he created a wonder, a new paradigm.

Rendering his characters in round droopy form
and elaborate machines that were out of the norm
he took 50 small words and a creature named Sam
to a best-selling reader named *Green Eggs and Ham*.

No longer a drudgery, no longer deplored
voracious new readers were clamoring for more.
And still I remember the school library nook
where I pulled out the cover and read the whole book.

I laughed as I traveled to a new far-fetched land
I vowed to eliminate boring and bland.
Flipping life on its side, understanding what's fun
he taught me the power of what could become…
If you stopped the expected and felt with your heart
then all journeys and roads would succeed from the start.

Laura Guido-Clark is an experience consultant focused on engaging consumers with more rewarding experiences. Guido-Clark has spent her life studying human nature and sensorial mediums expressed through color, materials, pattern, and finish. Through her trademarked process, Climatology, she researches and tracks relevant changes on the social, political, economic, and emotional fronts. Her multiple-disciplinary design studio collaborates with Fortune 500 companies as well as start-ups across multidisciplinary industries such as automotive, consumer electronics, and home furnishings.

Green Eggs and Ham
By Dr. Seuss

THE CAT
Green Eggs and Ham
By Dr. Seuss

no. **48**

SELECTED BY GAIL ANDERSON | TYPE SCULPTURE | DESIGNED BY JUNE CORLEY

I first saw June Corley's type sculptures as I was leaving TypeCon last summer and made a very spontaneous purchase about ten minutes before I left for the airport. About a week later, an intricate, lovingly packaged box arrived at the office containing a large, smiling type man with a head made out of a DC voltmeter. He's lived on the bookcase across from me since then, occasionally sporting a baseball cap. He's everything I love; type as signage, and reclaimed objects (meaning junk)—all on a pedestal. He is found art.

And like tramp art and outsider art, there's just something unpretentious and homey about him, like he has a story to tell.

I like reusing found type in my work, and am always on the lookout for materials to hoard. I now imagine June Corley as a kindred spirit—with more room for storage, and actual power tools. She is my new hero.

Gail Anderson is the creative director of design at SpotCo. From 1987 to early 2002, she served as senior art director at *Rolling Stone* magazine. Anderson's work, which has received numerous awards, is in the permanent collections of the Cooper-Hewitt Design Museum and the Library of Congress. She is co-author, with Steven Heller, of six design books, including *New Ornamental Type* (Thames & Hudson). Anderson teaches in the School of Visual Arts MFA and undergraduate design programs in New York City.

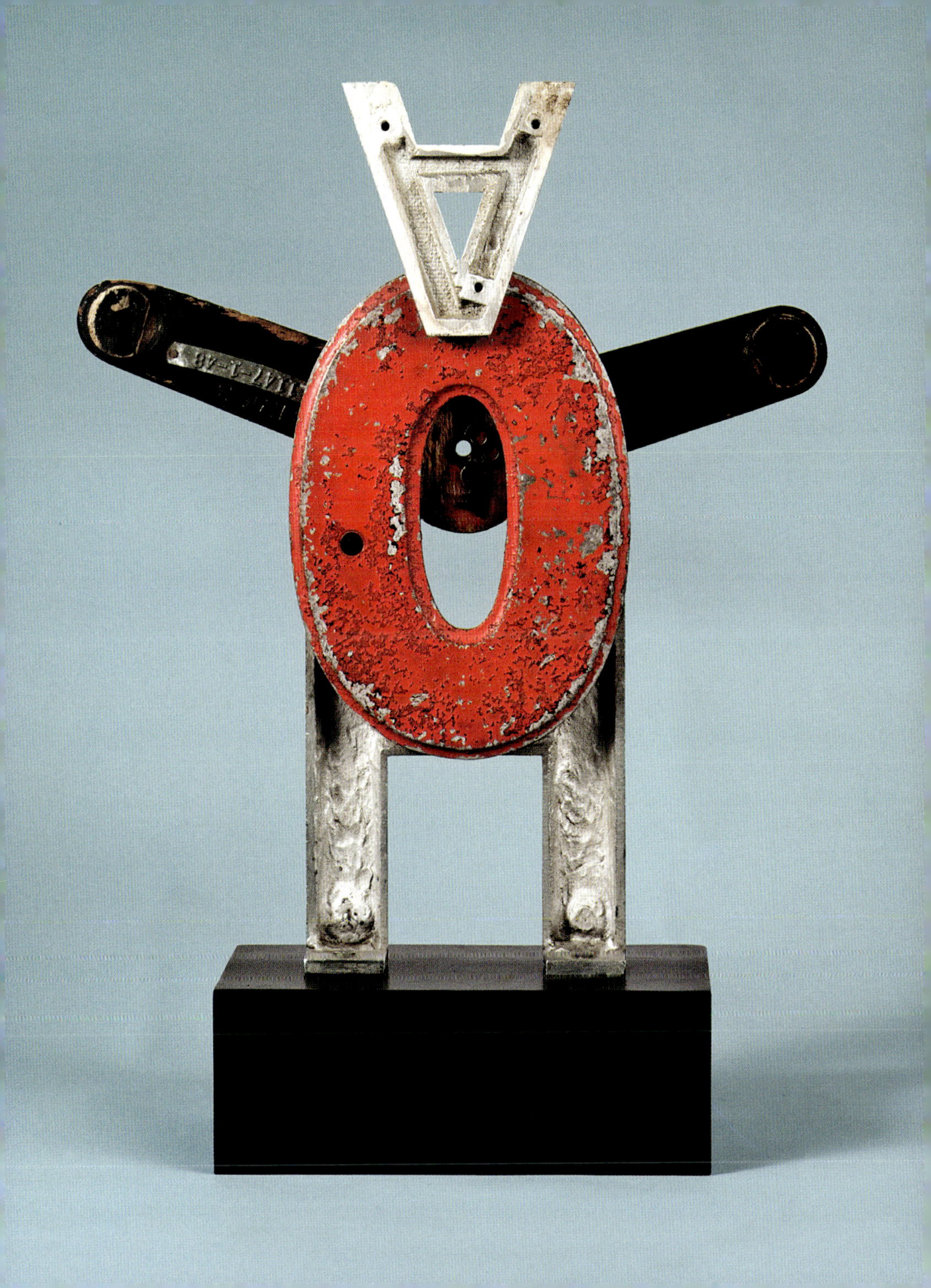

no. 49

SELECTED BY MONTE BEAUCHAMP | THE CHROMOLITHOGRAPHIC POSTCARD | DESIGNER UNKNOWN

Austria debuted the first government-sanctioned postcard in the autumn of 1869. Dubbed the Correspondenz-Karte, the rudimentary paper novelty sold over nine million units the first year. Soon after, sales avalanched into numbers far greater.

In 1890, government relinquished control over the lucrative card-stock creation, granting publishing licenses to private industries. Unhampered, the postcard began to flourish artistically. Application of a resplendent printing technique born from lithography, known as chromolithography, evolved it much further.

The postcard's vibrant new look enthralled not only consumers but publishers as well. Imprints abroad dramatically improved the look of their own line by diverting production to key chromolithographic centers such as Munich, Frankfurt, Dresden, and Berlin.

At the dawn of the twentieth century, German presses churned out spectacular examples, accelerating postcard mailing and collecting into a full-blown mania worldwide. In 1907, European postcards accounted for 75 percent of annual sales in the United States alone, with an estimated 677.7 million of them being mailed by 1908.

A category I place at the pinnacle of all cards ever produced are those of the Krampus. Not only because they sprung forth from precision German presses, but also because their imaginary content sprang forth from uncanny German minds.

Krampus was St. Nikolaus's dark servant: a hairy, horned, tongue-swaggering beast that terrorized bad children until they promised to be good. Each Christmas, both young and old "oohed" and "ahhed" over the season's new offerings of Krampus cards—an enthralling pleasure forever shattered by the arrival of World War I.

The boycott of Germany caused postcard sales to plummet, bringing a swift end to its Golden Age. What makes this chapter in design history particularly unique is that it clearly demonstrates that when commerce allows craftsmanship to thrive, prosperity can rise to a zenith.

BLAB! founder **Monte Beauchamp** is an award-winning art director/graphic designer whose work has appeared in *Graphis, Communication Arts*, SPDA, *Print, American Illustration*, and the *Society of Illustrators Annual*. He is the founder and editor of the graphics illustration comics annual *BLAB!* His books include *The Life and Times of R. Crumb* (St. Martin's Press), *Striking Images: Vintage Matchbook Cover* Art (Chronicle Books), *The Devil in Design: The Krampus Postcards*, and *New and Used BLAB!* (Chronicle Books).

Gruss vom Krampus

Gelukkig Nieuwjaar.

Pozdrav od čerta!

Gruss vom Krampus

no. 50

SELECTED BY JONNY HANNAH | **THE HIP** | **DESIGNED BY DAVID STONE MARTIN**

When I first flicked through *The Hip* by Roy Carr, as a student, I was introduced to the wonderful work of David Stone Martin. It's graphic, yet painterly; humorous, but not daft. And it oozed music—the music of improvisation. It seemed his brush and pen could work wonders with simplicity. He could tell a story with the bare minimum. I then picked up a few of his actual covers—this one included. It's beautiful, for a beautiful man. Two colors say it all. I like to think DSM could draw absolutely anything, and only he could get away with drawing Pres as this mysterious caped crusader.

Jonny Hannah draws, paints, and prints. Sometimes his images go through Photoshop. It depends. If he's not busy with a client, be it the *Sunday Telegraph* or the *New York Times*, he's busy with his own primitive publishing empire, the Cakes and Ale Press, farming out his various prints, posters, T-shirts, and books to galleries, hoping to make ends meet. He reads Bukowski and listens to Lester Young play "Shoe Shine Boy." It all adds up, and makes the next working day a mystery and a joy.

LESTER YOUNG
WITH THE OSCAR PETERSON TRIO
COLUMBIA
LONG PLAYING 33⅓ R.P.M. RECORD
SUPERVISED ... MAN GRANZ
CLEF SERIES

no. 51

SELECTED BY SHEPARD FAIREY | **PINNACLE HENDRIX POSTER** | **DESIGNED BY** JOHN VAN HAMERSVELD

What makes a "perfect" image? One that couldn't be improved by rendering it differently, that needs nothing added or subtracted. Not only is a perfect image difficult to imagine any other way than it is, it's impossible to forget. The term "instant classic" is used far too loosely, but it does truly apply to a perfect image. Many people recognize a perfect image when they see one, at least subconsciously if not deliberately. A perfect image has the power to seep into people's minds and become the exemplar for the thing it depicts. When I think "banana," I picture Warhol's banana cover for the *Velvet Underground* and *Nico*; when I think of Jimi Hendrix, it's John Van Hamersveld's *Pinnacle Hendrix* poster that comes to mind.

PINNACLE CONCERTS SAT FEB 10
JIMI HENDRIX
& THE SOFT MACHINE WITH
THE ELECTRIC FLAG
AND BLUE CHEER

SHRINE AUDITORIUM 8:30 PM
RESERVED SEATS NOW AVAILABLE AT ALL
WALLICH'S MUSIC CITY STORES AND ALL MUTUAL AGENCIES
VISUALS BY THOMAS EDISON LIGHTS & ACME CINEMA

Before discovering the *Pinnacle Hendrix* poster, I had never thought consciously about what constituted, or how to make, a perfect image. John's iconic image gave me an epiphany that sharpened my focus as an artist. The Hendrix poster fit all of the aforementioned criteria. It's an illustration with the perfect balance of designed restraint and idiosyncratic, organic style. The image also, though highly stylized, conveys the essence of Jimi Hendrix.

However, it goes beyond style. Through abstraction, the black-and-white image achieves something similar to a Rorschach inkblot test: it takes on the different interpretations projected by each viewer. I immediately saw a connection to Beethoven in John's rendering of Hendrix. I made the analogy of Hendrix's Afro to Beethoven's wig and Hendrix's ascot to Beethoven's frilly frock. I've since seen this interpretation from other sources, and my assumption was that Hendrix was being put on a pedestal as a musician and cultural icon on the scale of Beethoven. When I spoke to John about the *Pinnacle Hendrix* image years later, he explained that the ascot was not inspired by Beethoven, but by Eric Clapton and Cream, who Hendrix admired for their music and fashion. However, the Beethoven comparison had inspired John to illustrate a fantastic series of classical composers.

Great images have the power to inspire consciously and subconsciously, creating a dialogue and cycle of inspiration between artist and viewer. When I decided in the early '90s to make mash-ups of my Andre the Giant image with famous images from pop culture, I didn't think twice about where to start. He was no Jimi, but I must say Andre took to that psychedelic Afro like a natural.

Frank Shepard Fairey was born on February 15, 1970, in Charleston, South Carolina. In 1992, while still an illustration student at Rhode Island School of Design, Fairey started his first business venture, Alternate Graphics. He created stickers, T-shirts, skateboards, and posters, which were all available via black-and-white mail-order catalogs that he distributed. He also did small commercial printing jobs for clients to help cover some of his expenses. In 1994, Helen Stickler created a documentary film, *Andre the Giant Has a Posse*, that focused on Fairey and the growing phenomenon of his subversive stickers and posters. By 1995, he also created a small sister brand, Subliminal Projects, with Blaize Blouin, and released several skateboard and poster designs. In 2008, he created the Obama Hope poster.

no. 52

TOMATO: SOMETHING UNUSUAL IS GOING ON HERE, 1978
FROM POPPY WITH LOVE, 1968

SELECTED BY BETH KLEBER | **DESIGNED BY MILTON GLASER**

In 1966, Milton Glaser met Kevin Eggers, an Irish music entrepreneur who was just starting up the Poppy label. Glaser designed the company's logo as well as all of its album covers and promotional materials. Poppy became Utopia, then Atlantic Deluxe, and ultimately Tomato Records, and Glaser continued his long and creatively satisfying relationship with the label. Tomato released the work of artists as distinguished and diverse as Bach, Dave Brubeck, Townes Van Zandt, John Cage, Philip Glass, Ray Charles, and Albert King.

To me, the Tomato Records poster typifies everything that makes Glaser so remarkable. He has always had a special affinity for design and illustration for music, even before his iconic Dylan poster for Columbia Records in 1966. Although this 1978 poster was done four years after Glaser departed Push Pin Studios to start his own firm, it certainly represents a continuation of the lush, eclectic, and conceptual style he and Seymour Chwast pioneered at Push Pin, leading a break away from the spare, modernist approach that had dominated the design world. Glaser is passionate about the painters of the Italian Renaissance and baroque architecture, and that expressiveness and technical mastery are evident here, though in a tongue-in-cheek sort of way. (Ten years earlier, Glaser did a poster of a flower growing out of a concrete block for Poppy Records expressing much the same idea—that music turns up and flourishes in unexpected places.) But the bottom line is, the Tomato poster never fails to make me smile. I've never seen the point of design without a sense of humor, and there's something so sublimely silly about that big, ripe tomato in such a formal and dignified setting, as if she's inviting you to join her for a snifter of brandy and then, who knows?

Beth Kleber is the archivist at the Milton Glaser Design Study and Archives and the School of Visual Arts Archives, where she has the massive good fortune to be surrounded by great design every day. She helped found the Glaser Archives in 2003 and has since added collections from distinguished designers and illustrators including Ivan Chermayeff, Tom Geismar, Henry Wolf, Seymour Chwast, James McMullan, Heinz Edelmann, George Tscherny, and Tony Palladino.

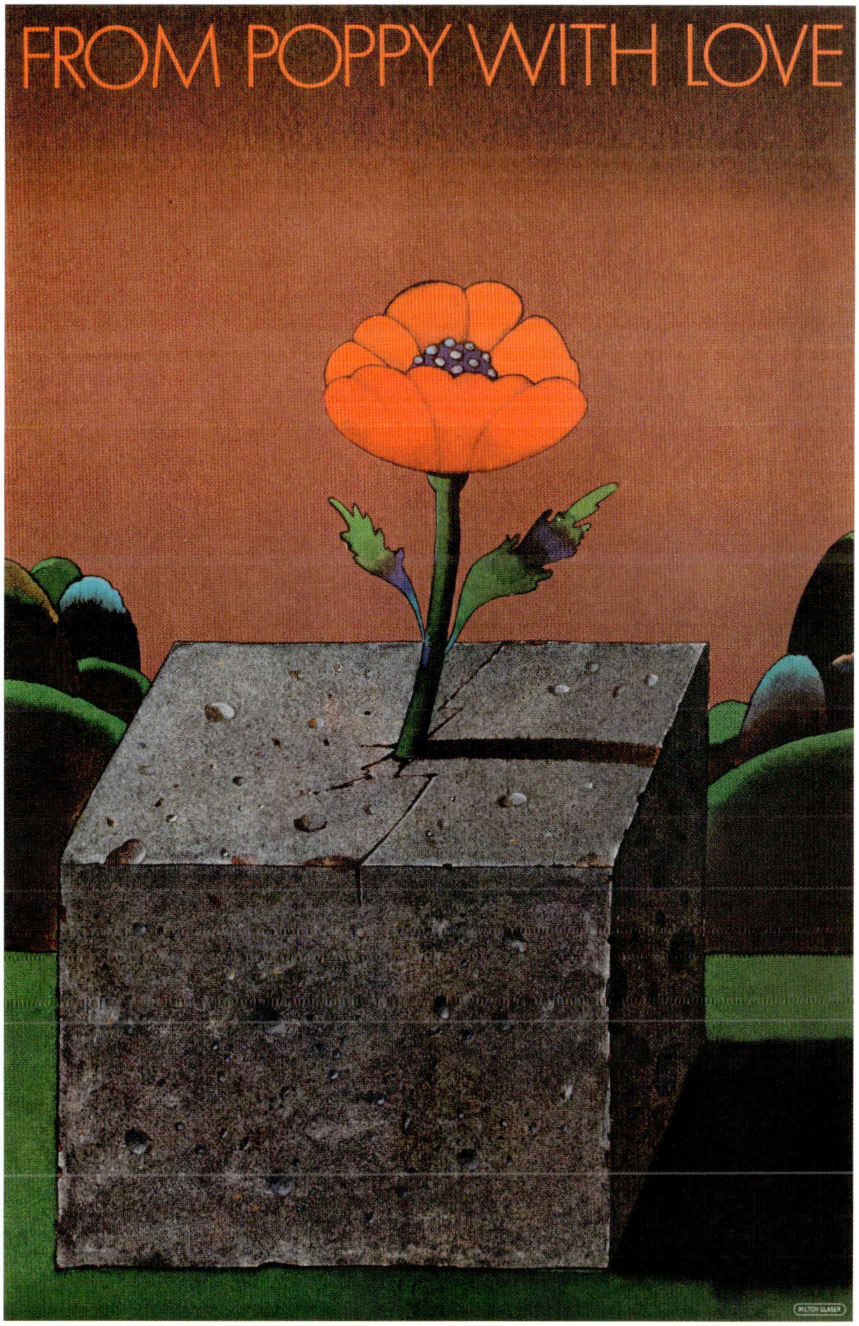
FROM POPPY WITH LOVE
MILTON GLASER

no. **53**

SELECTED BY | KODACHROME II | DESIGNER
JEFF SCHER | | UNKNOWN

It's hard to separate my lust for the contents of this box from the design of it. This film was one of Kodak's greatest achievements. Kodachrome was the motion picture stock of choice when I began making films. It was very expensive to buy and to process, but the colors and contrast it delivered were so stunning, it rivaled Technicolor. This box contained a 100-foot (30.5 m) spool of the film, about two and a half minutes. It was in a plain shiny metal can, sealed with tape. It was heavy when you picked it up. Having it in your hand was like being passed the Olympic torch. It was your moment. You were holding a box of raw cinema, and anything was possible.

While I don't know who designed this box, I still get a chill looking at it. The very uncluttered Bauhaus-flavored design of the box gave it an industrial and professional look. The spacing of the type and the simplicity of the labeling tell you they don't have to sell it, the product speaks for itself. All you need to know is what's inside. The Kodak logo is integrated into the name of the product, and was perhaps even synonymous with it. This was the last evolution of this type logo, having changed little since its introduction in 1935. I appreciated the continuity with Kodak and movie history. The big red *K* in a box replaced this logo in 1971. That logo always seemed mass market-oriented and a little overdesigned. I also very much liked the prominence of the arrowhead pointing to "For Daylight." It answered your first question about what type of film it was, which was important.

Sadly, Kodachrome is no longer manufactured. I consider myself fortunate to have had it as a tool for the time I did. Now that movies are being primarily recorded on various digital media, there is little romance with the recording medium and its packaging, but back in the day, this yellow box contained all the magic you could ask for.

Jeff Scher is a painter who makes experimental films and an experimental filmmaker who paints. His work is in the permanent collection of the Museum of Modern Art and the Hirshhorn Museum and has been screened at the Guggenheim Museum, the Pompidou Center in Paris, the San Francisco Museum of Modern Art, and at many film festivals around the world, including opening night at the New York Film Festival. Scher has had two solo shows of his paintings, which have also been included in many group shows in New York galleries. Additionally, he has created commissioned work for HBO, HBO Family, PBS, the Sundance Channel, and more. Scher also writes a blog for the *New York Times* called *The Animated Life*.

№ 54

SELECTED BY BONNIE SIEGLER | NEWSWEEK | DESIGNED BY ALFRED LOWRY

As the death toll of magazines continues to ring, I have become especially romantic about the covers of yesteryear. This particular one of Richard Nixon has been hanging on my wall for the last year, and I am continually engaged by it. I think it's the simplicity and elegance of the solution that gets me. The illustration tool is actually the content itself, and using it as such, the tape literally and figuratively defines the president. I also love how spare it is. There is not one element that is superfluous. And, it's funny.

Bonnie Siegler founded the multidisciplinary design studio Number Seventeen with her partner, Emily Oberman, in the summer of 1993. Their work includes magazine design (like *Newsweek*), logo and Web design (*This American Life*), book design (like *Superfreakonomics*), and design for television (like *Saturday Night Live*).

November 12, 1973 / 50 cents

Newsweek

What Next?

no. **55**

SELECTED BY OMAR VULPINARI | **COLORS MAGAZINE, NO. 1, 1991: "IT'S A BABY"**

EDITORIAL DIRECTOR | **EDITOR IN CHIEF** | **PHOTOGRAPHER (COVER)** | **DESIGNED BY**
OLIVIERO TOSCANI | **TIBOR KALMAN** | **OLIVIERO TOSCANI** | **EMILY OBERMAN**

"The message of this magazine is that your culture (whoever you are) is as important as our culture (whoever we are)." (*Colors*, issue 1, editorial)

The first interesting novelty was that in 1991, *Colors* presented itself as "a magazine about the rest of the world." It was multilingual and distributed globally. The focus of *Colors* was, and still is today after 19 years and 76 issues, about celebrating the similarities and differences of people and societies from all corners of the Earth.

Colors, as it describes itself in the first editorial, is founded on a simple idea—diversity is good—inspired by the Benetton branding campaigns.

Another important feature of the inaugural issue of the magazine was that United Colors of Benetton was the only sponsor. In fact, the second half of this issue included the company's product promotion, while the cover image of the neonatal baby, representing the birth of the magazine, had already been used for a Benetton branding campaign.

Benetton, Tibor Kalman, and Oliviero Toscani gave life to a vital and provocative avenue of discussion regarding the controversial effects springing from this new combination of communication, global social commentary, and commercial enterprise.

This cover, and the context it came from, represents an important shift in my life and my social concerns as a designer/communicator. In the late '80s and early '90s, I was already working extensively for local public utility and cultural commissions in Pesaro, in the Italian region of the Marche, but I was mainly focused on the aesthetic quality of design and not yet totally aware of the designer's enormous social role. When *Colors* and the Benetton campaigns started coming out, I understood how deeply design could catalyze worldwide social debate and change.

Omar Vulpinari is head and creative director of visual communication at Fabrica, the Benetton Group communication research center in Treviso, Italy. He directs advertising and communication design projects for UNWHO, UNICEF, UNESCO, the World Bank, Witness, Amnesty International, Reporters without Borders, Coca-Cola, Porsche, Vespa, the *New Yorker* magazine, and Fox International. Vulpinari teaches communication design at the IUAV University of Venice in San Marino. He is advisor for the United Nations World Health Organization and Regional Ambassador for INDEX: Design to Improve Life Awards.

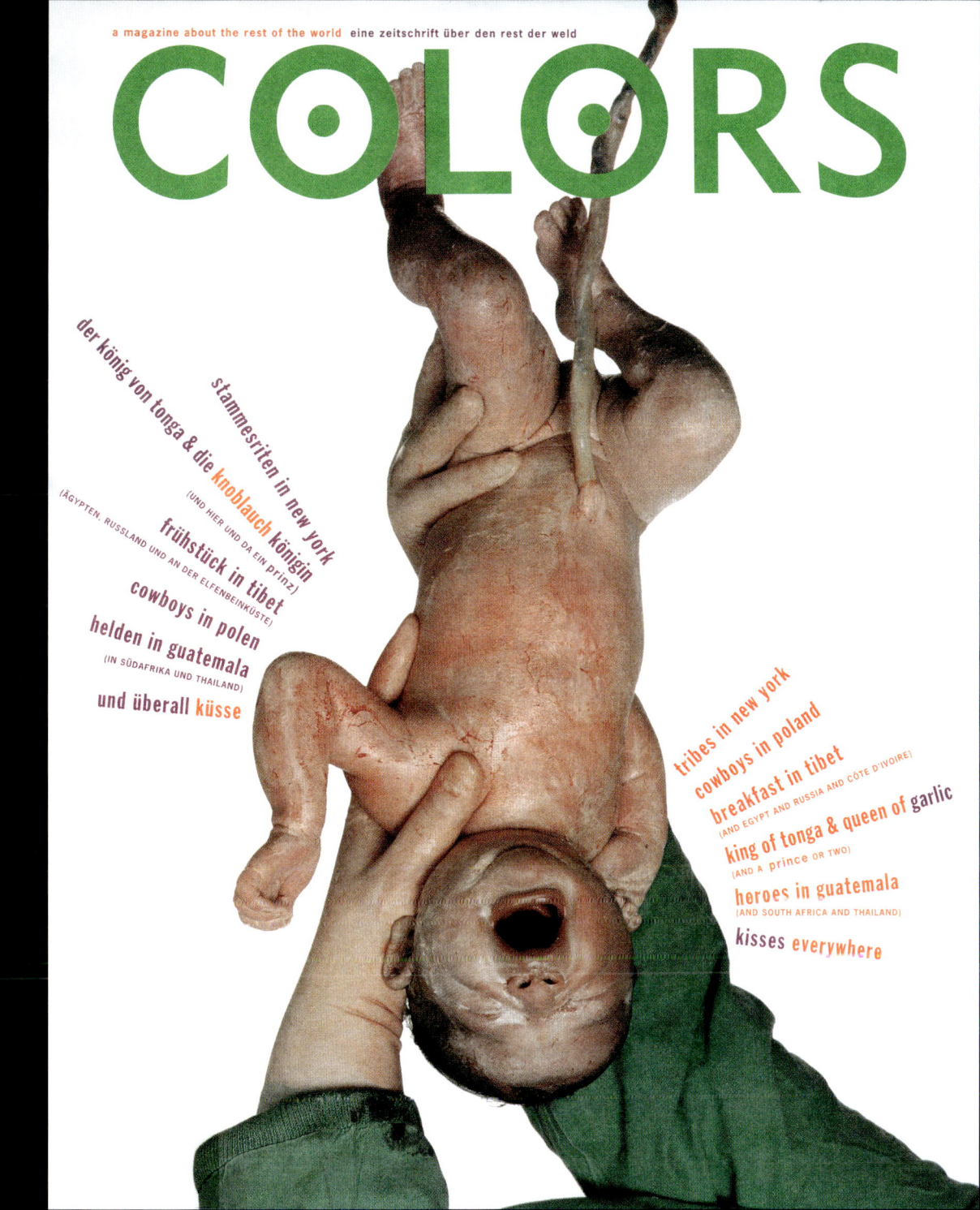

a magazine about the rest of the world   eine zeitschrift über den rest der weld

COLORS

stammesriten in new york
der könig von tonga & die knoblauch königin
(und hier und da ein prinz)
frühstück in tibet
(ägypten, russland und an der elfenbeinküste)
cowboys in polen
helden in guatemala
(in südafrika und thailand)
und überall küsse

tribes in new york
cowboys in poland
breakfast in tibet
(and egypt and russia and côte d'ivoire)
king of tonga & queen of garlic
(and a prince or two)
heroes in guatemala
(and south africa and thailand)
kisses everywhere

no. **56**

"ADOLPH THE SUPERMAN SWALLOWS GOLD AND SPOUTS JUNK" AIZ MAGAZINE, JULY 17, 1932

SELECTED BY ROBBIE CONAL | DESIGNED BY JOHN HEARTFIELD

Everything about this image knocks me out. I'm still overwhelmed by John Heartfield's personal and artistic courage in making, reproducing, and distributing it—considering how, where, and when he did all this. For me, "Adolph the Superman…" is even more than a beloved object.

When I finally got around to making art for nonsanctioned public address in 1986, *graphic design* wasn't even Greek to me, it was Egyptian hieroglyphic writing. A beautiful thing, yes. An exotic cryptic code, more so. "Adolph the Superman…" became my personal graphic design *Rosetta Stone*. Say what? Here's a rough translation:

"Adolf the Superman…" is paradigm example No. 1 in the John Heartfield gallery of my heart—razor-sharp, nonsanctioned (to say the least about the most), satirical public art made to give Hitler indigestion—expressly for reception by an audience of regular people on the streets in Germany, as they went about their daily business, whatever that was. It must have just gotten weirder and weirder, until it got scarier.

This particular photomontage was designed to pierce Hitler's superficial anticapitalist rhetoric and expose his hidden capitalist practices, as he rose to state power in Germany. Though it was featured in a special issue of *AIZ*, I believe it was also produced as a street poster. Whether or not they actually did the deed themselves, it helps me to imagine Heartfield running the late-night streets of Berlin with pals like his brother Wieland and George Grosz, slapping up multiple copies of this image right under Hitler's little lip wig!

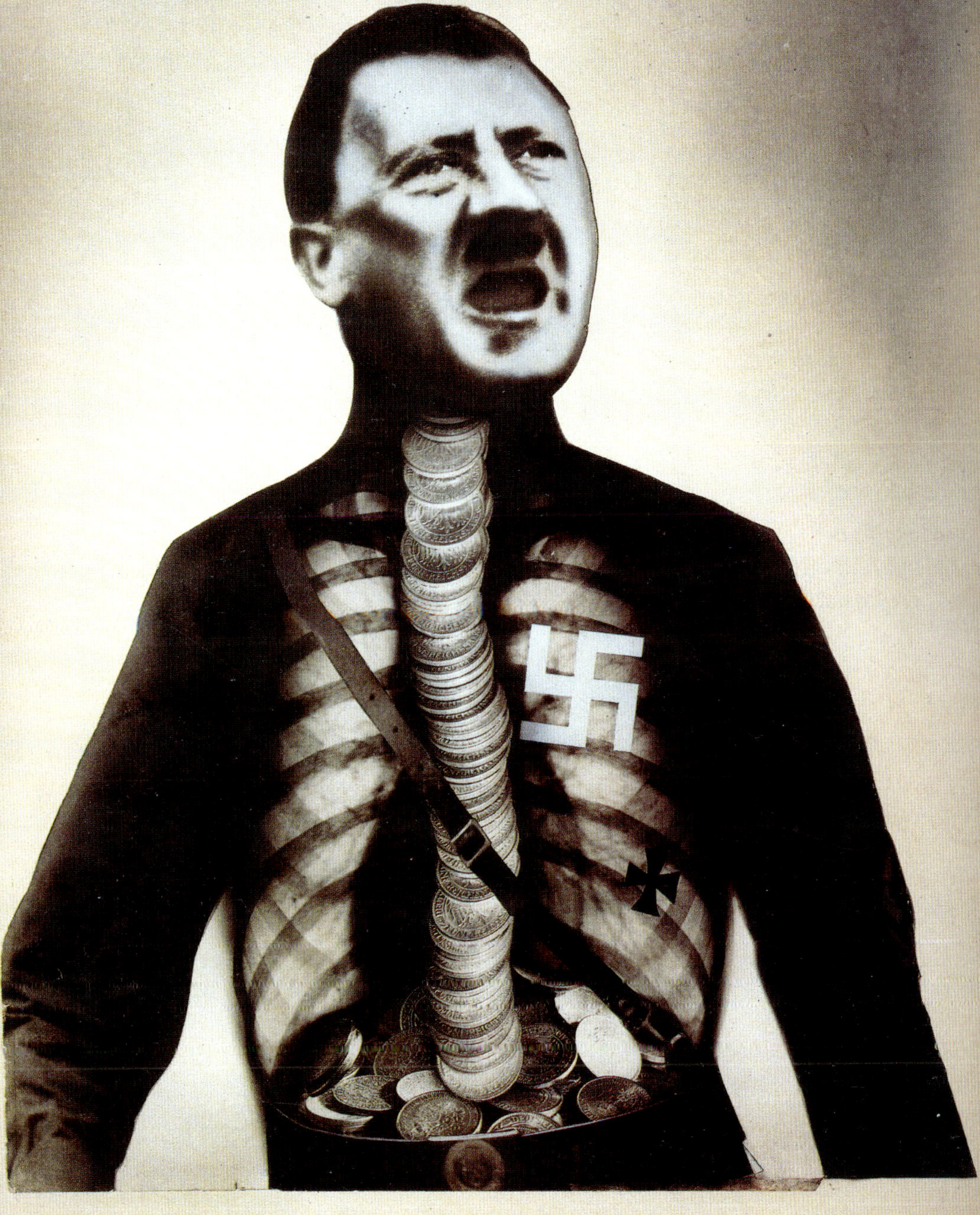

Artistic courage: Heartfield tailored an art form to suit his ideological purpose, expressly designed to take full advantage of the methods of production and distribution available to him at the time. I imagine him furiously carving his way free of the pictorial conventions of European design, by sheer force of will and talent, splicing a streamlined, wicked pictorial slang into dramatic partnership with punning text that was easily understood by ordinary people sneaking furtive glances at illegal 'zines and, occasionally, even looking up at kiosks in the streets of Berlin.

Hitler got it, too:

"On Good Friday [April 14th], 1933, the SS broke at night into my apartment, where I happened to be in the process of packing up my works of art. I managed to escape arrest by jumping from the balcony of my apartment, which was located on the ground floor. At the urging of the [Communist] Party, I emigrated by walking across the Mountains to Czechoslovakia on Easter. In early November 1934, I was expatriated by Hitler's government."

So what's my point? John Heartfield (and the great Leon Golub and Nancy Spero) taught me to be specific—not go all woo-woo about abstractions like freedom, peace, equality, and shit. They're all good, but pointing that artistic poison pencil at the actual perpetrators does more damage. "Adolph the Superman Swallows Gold and Spouts Junk" had a festival of pictorial information crammed into it, but it was basically *Direct*. Hitler was coming directly, it's just that along the way he transformed gold into bullshit.

John Heartfield, 1934.
Masterpieces of Political Art: The Middle Ages and the Third Reich
In the middle ages, prisoners were broken on wheels. Now, the Nazi victim is broken on the swastika.

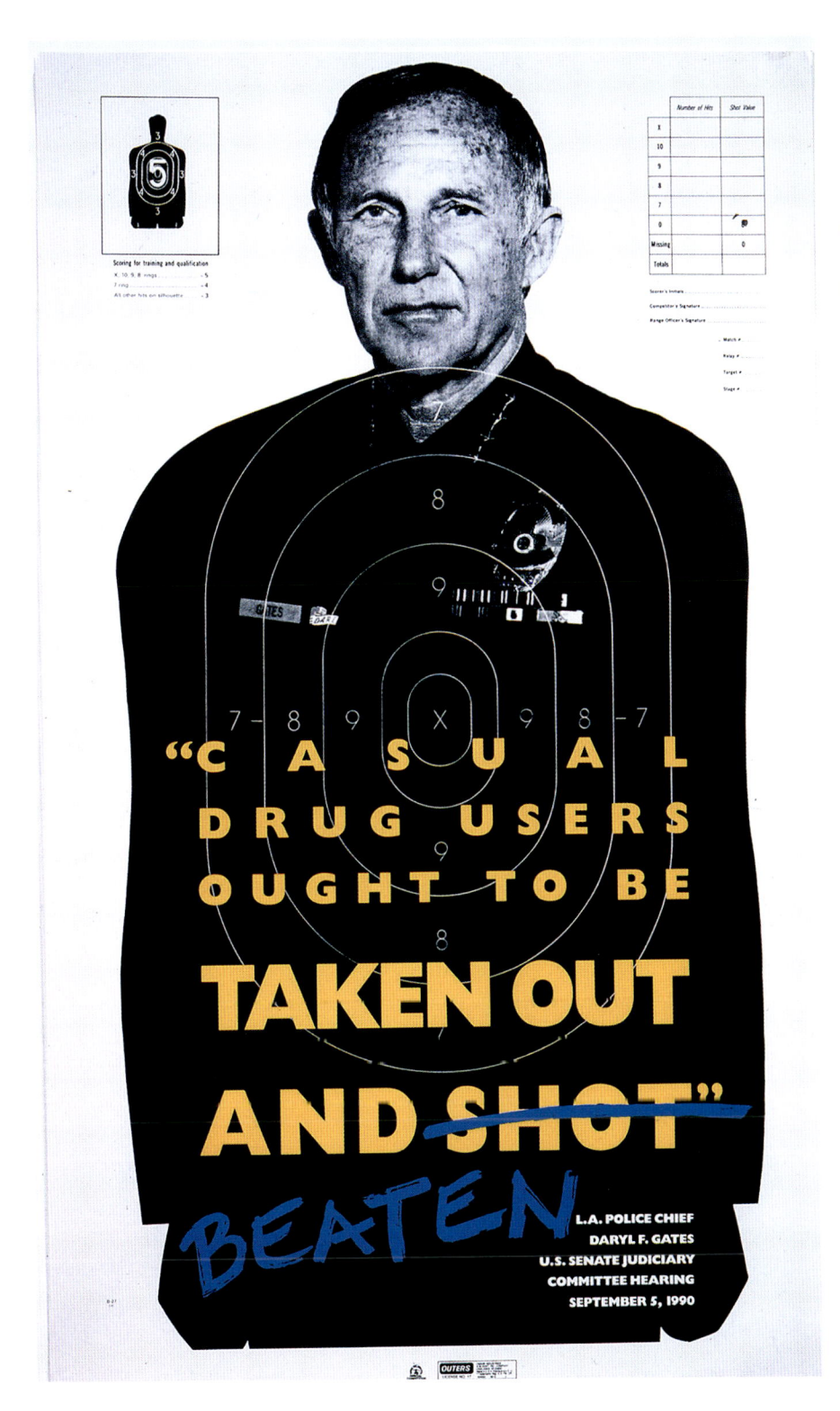

Robbie Conal, 1990.
"Casual drug users ought to be taken out and shot."
—L.A. Police chief, Daryl F. Gates

Robbie Conal grew up in New York, on the upper "left side" of Manhattan in the 1950s. He went to the Art Students' League to draw when he was eight years old and basically went to art school all his life. He received his MFA at Stanford University in 1978 and moved to Los Angeles in 1984, where he started posting his satirical guerrilla street posters such as *Men with No Lips* and *Women with Teeth*. Over the years, he accumulated a very irregular volunteer guerrilla army of lovely people in major cities around the United States.

no. 57

SELECTED BY JESSICA HELFAND | CERTIFICATE OF APPROVAL | DESIGNER UNKNOWN

My father acquired this print (and several more like it) in a collection he bought from the estate of a friend in France: a certificate of approval for a pharmaceutical product, combining official stamps, labels, and signatures—a visual testament to the due diligence of a battalion of government bureaucrats who were, one can only assume, its intended audience.

It is, of course, so much more than this—a composition of stunning modernity, especially given that it was produced at the end of the nineteenth century. The print is dated 1889—the same year that marked the Exposition Universelle in Paris, the inauguration of the Eiffel Tower, and the opening of the Moulin Rouge. (Van Gogh painted *Starry Night* in 1889, too.) A good quarter-century before Saul Steinberg would begin making his mixed-media collages, this stunning piece of graphic design gestures at once to the formality of the past and the uncertainty of its future: Centered and serious, yet marginally askew and surprisingly dynamic, it's both classical and modern. It may just be my favorite thing, ever.

Jessica Helfand is partner with William Drenttel in Jessica Helfand | William Drenttel, a design consultancy that concentrates on editorial design and the development of new models for old and new media. Clients include *Newsweek*, *Businessweek*, *Lingua Franca*, America Online, and Champion International Corporation. Helfand is a visiting lecturer in graphic design at Yale University School of Art and adjunct professor at New York University's graduate program in interactive telecommunications, and has lectured at the Cooper-Hewitt National Design Museum, the Columbia University School of Journalism, and the Netherlands Design Institute, among others.

MARQUES DE FABRIQUE

DÉPOSÉES AU CONSERVATOIRE DES ARTS ET MÉTIERS.

Copie.

Duplicata. Le soussigné, mandataire de M. Eugène Fournier, fabricant de produits pharmaceutiques à Paris, rue de Cléry, 31, déclare déposer au nom de son mandant, comme marque de fabrique, dont il entend se réserver la propriété exclusive pour distinguer un produit de sa préparation, les signes distinctifs suivants: 1° La dénomination "Pilules anti-névralgiques de Deslauriers" indépendamment de toute forme distinctive. 2° l'étiquette A qui s'imprime sur l'enveloppe des flacons renfermant le produit. 3° l'étiquette B qui s'applique sur la panse des susdits flacons. Les étiquettes A et B portent la signature "Deslauriers" en rouge avec paraphe caractéristique. Ces divers signes pris ensemble ou séparément constituent la marque de M. Eugène Fournier.

Greffe du tribunal de Commerce de Paris,
N° 21260.
Dépôt du 7 février 1887 à 10 h 40 du Sr Eugène Fournier, pharmacien, 31, rue de Cléry, à Paris, représenté par le Sr Léon Avy, 28 avenue de l'Opéra, à Paris, ayant charge [illegible] enregistré et annexé.

A

Destiné à un produit pharmaceutique

Signature du déposant, mandataire
Signé: Léon Avy
Signature du Greffier en Chef
Signé: Ad. Glanday

Signature du déposant, mandataire
Signé: Léon Avy
Signature du Greffier en Chef
Signé: Ad. Glanday

Pour copie conforme.
Le Directeur
du Conservatoire Nal des Arts et Métiers

Paris, le 14 avril 1887

no. 58

SELECTED BY JIM HEIMANN | **JIMI HENDRIX** | **DESIGNED BY** RICK GRIFFIN

Rick Griffin was a Southern California high school student smack in the middle of a post–World War II generation weaned on comic books, television, and rock and roll when he took up surfing in the late 1950s. Expressing his youth and emerging lifestyle through the comics he wrote and drew, the self-taught teenaged Griffin would eventually come up with a comic strip and character named Murphy, which was published in *Surfer* magazine. The first time I saw "Murph," I identified instantly with him and later snapped up *Surfer Cartoons,* a compilation of surf-inspired comics at a local newsstand. This booklet and Griffin's later art would become the impetus for my eventual career in the visual arts.

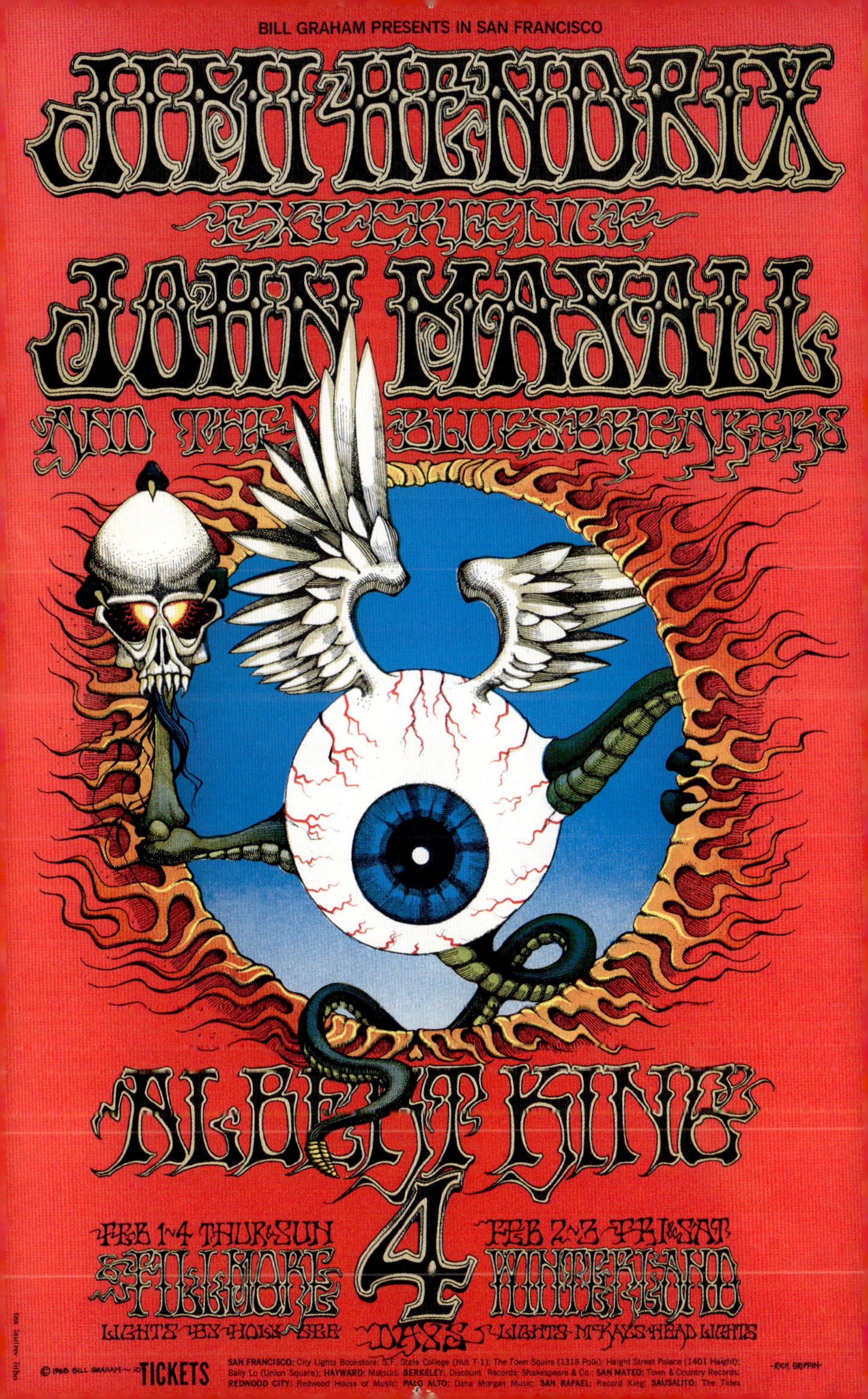
BILL GRAHAM PRESENTS IN SAN FRANCISCO
JIMI HENDRIX
EXPERIENCE
JOHN MAYALL
AND THE BLUESBREAKERS
ALBERT KING
FEB 1-4 THUR-SUN
FILLMORE
LIGHTS BY HOLY SEE
4
DAYS
FEB 2-3 FRI & SAT
WINTERLAND
LIGHTS MCKAYS HEAD LIGHTS
© 1968 BILL GRAHAM ~ 10
TICKETS
SAN FRANCISCO: City Lights Bookstore; S.F. State College (Hut T-1); The Town Squire (1318 Polk); Haight Street Palace (1401 Haight); Bally Lo (Union Square); HAYWARD: Matsuri; BERKELEY: Discount Records; Shakespeare & Co.; SAN MATEO: Town & Country Records; REDWOOD CITY: Redwood House of Music; PALO ALTO: Dana Morgan Music; SAN RAFAEL: Record King; SAUSALITO: The Tides
RICK GRIFFIN
tea lautrec litho

Griffin seemed to disappear for a while in the mid-sixties, but then reemerged in San Francisco, extending his satirical and bizarre imagery to a newly wedded lifestyle that had been forged between musician, artist, and environment. A full-blown hippie, Griffin was creating posters for dance concerts fueled by drugs and a well-tuned imagination.

Griffin and other San Francisco poster artists employed an eclectic borrowing of photographic and illustrated images from the late-nineteenth century through the mid-twentieth century, assimilating them in their art and often incorporating their own typography. Of his many efforts, his poster for Jimi Hendrix coalesced all of the elements of his psychedelic toolbox into a classic of the genre, expressing the zeitgeist of a generation.

Griffin's work and that of his fellow poster artists cemented my commitment to the commercial arts. Although this poster movement was fleeting, it remains a pivotal footnote in design history. As the direct and indirect message of the counterculture ethos, it still resonates today in tangential design statements.

Jim Heimann is a native of Los Angeles who, in addition to his past career as a graphic designer and illustrator, currently serves as the American executive editor of Taschen Publishing LLC. A graduate of California State University at Long Beach, he has been active in the arts field for the past thirty-eight years. In conjunction with his design work, he has authored numerous books, including *California Crazy*; *Out with the Stars*; *Car Hops and Curb Service: A History of the Drive-in Restaurant*; *Sins of the City*; *The Real Los Angeles Noir*; and *Los Angeles, Portrait of a City*. He is a current faculty member of Art Center College of Design, Pasadena.

no. 59

SELECTED BY MARTHA SCOTFORD | **HET BOEK VAN PTT** | **DESIGNED BY** PIET ZWART

Written and designed for children by Piet Zwart, this book describes and illustrates the extensive services of the Dutch postal, telegram, and telegraph service, and how to use them properly. The pages are dense with information in words and pictures. The texts pulse as the sans serif font expands and contracts, changes size and weight; handwriting adds more contrast. The images are a compendium of what European avant-garde design had discovered and explored in typography and photography by the 1930s. And, we must be reminded, the compositions were compiled using film and handmade mechanicals, printed by rotogravure that provides the deep colors that soak into the paper.

Zwart (with illustrations by Dick Elffers) created the images using pen and ink drawing, color illustration, collage, and photomontage. There are straight documentary photographs of citizens at the post office, as well as postal workers and postal facility details; photos of real children combined with studio shots of paper dolls showing how to make a phone call or how letters are delivered; photos to show official documents, proper envelope addressing, and different kinds of packages. Illustrative elements include old printers' pointing hands, and the typographic variety of stamps and official labels.

Zwart employed all forms of information design: maps, diagrams, 3-D models, and proto-international style pictograms. He used common objects (spool of thread, matchbox) to show size and proportion, and hands for counting. There is humor (a monster in a package); there are surreal landscapes of strange proportions and viewpoint. A hand-drawn *X* covers the dog you should not mail; a fragile package of paint ends up spilled with tiny handprints all over the page. Four-color artwork merges into black-and-white photos and duotones; process colors combine and separate; all possible permutations are employed.

Piet Zwart was a prominent designer and teacher in the Netherlands between the world wars—part of an international group that included Lissitzky, Rodchenko, van Doesburg, Schwitters, and Bauhaus faculty, in contact through exhibitions, publications, friendship, and professional visits. He and others worked in the method of "typo-photo," composing corporate, government, and institutional messages by manipulating their own photographs and typography to produce colorful layered compositions that directed your eye to objects, essential facts, and telling details.

For children, Zwart did not hold back. Using all his experience, he brought brilliant color effects, blended images of fact and fancy, an invitation to engage in civic life, and communication to these pages. There is an entry point on every page; the reader/viewer can explore and discover. Like many of the children for whom this was created, many of us enjoy and understand this book without reading a word!

Photographs made with permission from original 1938 book in the Special Collections, D. H. Hill Library, North Carolina State University, Raleigh.

Martha Scotford teaches design and design history at North Carolina State University. Her writings have appeared in American Center for *Design Statements*, *AIGA Journal of Graphic Design*, *Print*, *Design Issues*, *Visible Language*, and *Eye*. She was the recipient of two National Endowment for the Arts grants supporting research on women in design, leading to the publication of her book *Cipe Pineles: A Life of Design* (Norton, 1999). Scotford was a designer and author for the project For the *Voice: Mayakovsky and Lissitzky* (The British Library, 2000). Following four months in India teaching as a Fulbright Lecturer, a visible language article described a multiple-language typography project, and she guest edited an issue of *Design Issues* about Indian design and design education.

no. 60

SELECTED BY GEORGE TSCHERNY | POLAR BEAR (1928) | DESIGNED BY ISAMU NOGUCHI

We are all familiar with the work of Isamu Noguchi (1904–1986): his lamps, gardens, playgrounds, the "amoeba" coffee table, stage sets for Martha Graham, and most of all his sculpture. Therefore, I was startled to encounter this early drawing of a polar bear.

I would have expected Noguchi to use a sculptural approach in his drawings, where line is piled upon line to create volume and bulk. Instead, we have here a king of visual shorthand—the contour of a bear, an eloquent line direct in its pursuit of clarity. A quick gesture that has no time for mannerisms and is devoid of detail.

Needless to say, all art evolves from somewhere. Here, there are links to faces in Matisse, the fashion illustrator Carl (Eric) Erickson—a master at keeping detail to a minimum—and Alexander Calder, a friend and acknowledged influence. Calder's line, however, is more tentative, the consequence of the wire-bending process. Still, that line, too, knows where it is going.

I love that drawing of the bear—I wish I had done it.

George Tscherny has been a designer since 1950. In 1988, he was awarded the AIGA Medal for Lifetime Achievement and in 1997 was inducted into the New York Art Directors Hall of Fame. He is the author of *Changing Faces* (Princeton Architectural Press, 2005) and *Where Would the Button Be, Without the Button Hole?* (RIT Graphic Arts Press, 2008), which celebrated the work of anonymous designers.

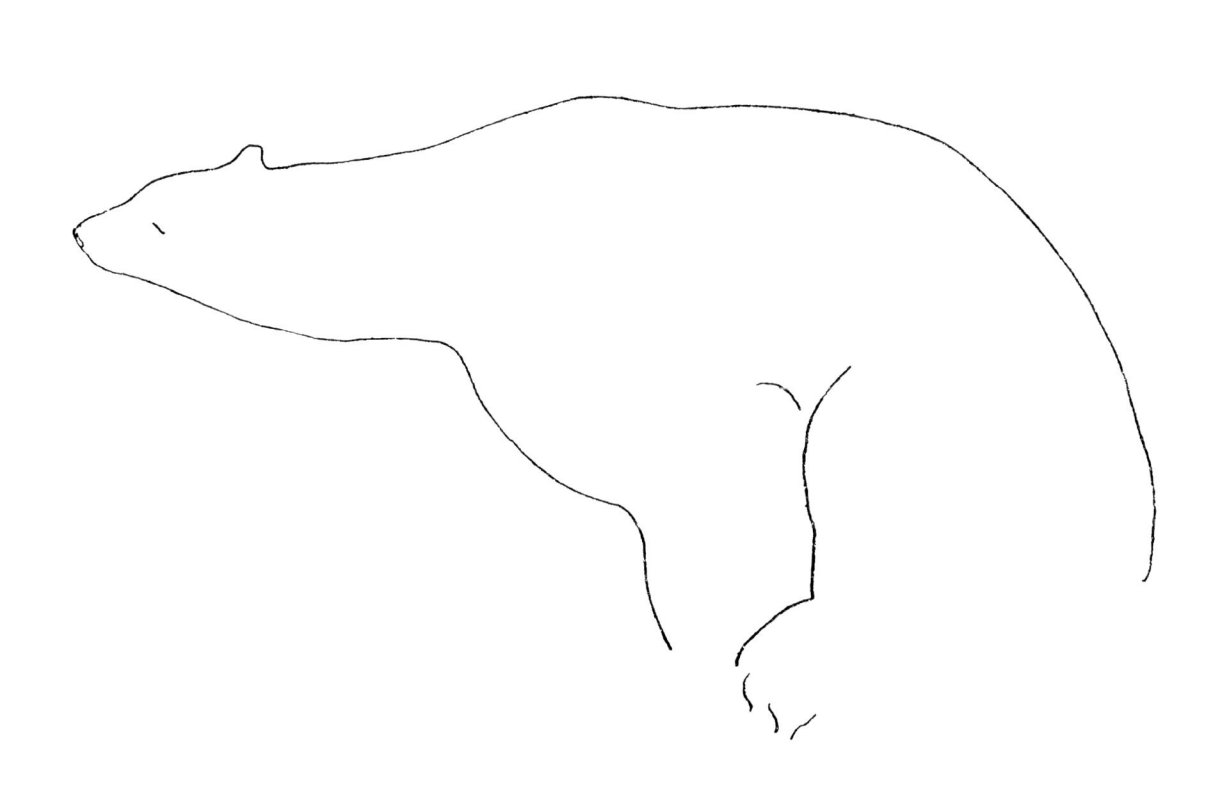

no. 61

SELECTED BY STEVEN HELLER | BIFUR | DESIGNED BY A.M. CASSANDRE

In 1929, Charles Peignot, director of Deberny & Peignot, sponsored A. M. Cassandre's experiment with a new typeface and engraved Bifur. This complex melange of fat and thin lines and crossbars knocked the typographic world on its ear, but not always in positive terms. "There were no new or innovative typefaces which existed at the time. Bifur created a real scandal…at least in the small world of publishing and printing," wrote Peignot. "Engraving this design took considerable effort. Needless to say (however), Bifur was not a financial success, but in those happy days one could afford to take a few risks."

The story of Bifur is as much a testament to Deberny & Peignot as it is one of Cassandre's legacies. It was through his advocacy that type and typography progressed, not only in France, but throughout the West in forward thinking. Peignot, who led the way in pushing the development of phototypography, proudly noted that with Bifur, he brought an era of type to an end, but at the same time proved that "functionalism" pushed graphically to its extreme limit "could not effectively be a source of inspiration for the future of typography."

Although World War II interrupted the progressive work of Deberny & Peignot, Charles Peignot remained committed to the modern movement. After the war, he went even further in his quest to improve on modernity. He hired Adrian Frutiger, then a young apprentice, to design the twenty-one variations of Univers (which, along with Helvetica, has certainly defined the typographic style of the present age). "Univers is not exactly my favorite," admitted Peignot. "It was an excellent treatment of an existing theme, but not really a creation in the true sense of the word; but I knew that it was a good character for the times and that it would be very successful. It was, for me, a commercial venture. In fact, it is with Univers that French typography regained its position in the international market."

DIVERTISS[EMENTS]

*Recueil
d'idées et de modèles
à l'usage des imprimeurs,
éditeurs et publicistes*

TYPOGRAPHIQUES

no. **62**

XIII SECESSION EXHIBITION, VIENNA, 1902 [COLOR LITHOGRAPH]

SELECTED BY DAVID RAIZMAN | DESIGNED BY KOLOMAN MOSER

Koloman Moser's (1868–1918) 1902 poster for the XIII Vienna Secession exhibition demonstrates a designed object's resonance with a particular historical moment that moves beyond descriptions of formal invention or relationships to general tendencies or influences of the period and engages other aspects of the viewer's experience.

It goes almost without saying that Moser's image and lettering are modern for their time, exploring a vocabulary of flattened simplified shapes and experimental letterforms that unify the composition and show broad similarities to contemporary strategies in painting and in printing, moving away from narrative images, illusionistic space, and naturalistic decoration while activating negative space through stronger figure-ground contrasts. It is also clear that Scottish design played a role in ushering in this formal vocabulary, since the work of Charles Rennie Mackintosh and other Glaswegian designers had been displayed at the VIII Secession exhibition in autumn 1900, where an analogous movement away from organic shapes can be observed.

But the story seems to me far richer than that: Posters served many purposes, but the communication of information for the events or products they advertise is certainly part of the decision-making process of designers in that medium. Yet in this case, Moser's letterforms not only ignore traditional variations between thick and thin strokes, but also are, quite obviously, difficult to read, with virtually no spacing between words and similarities among letters (e.g.,

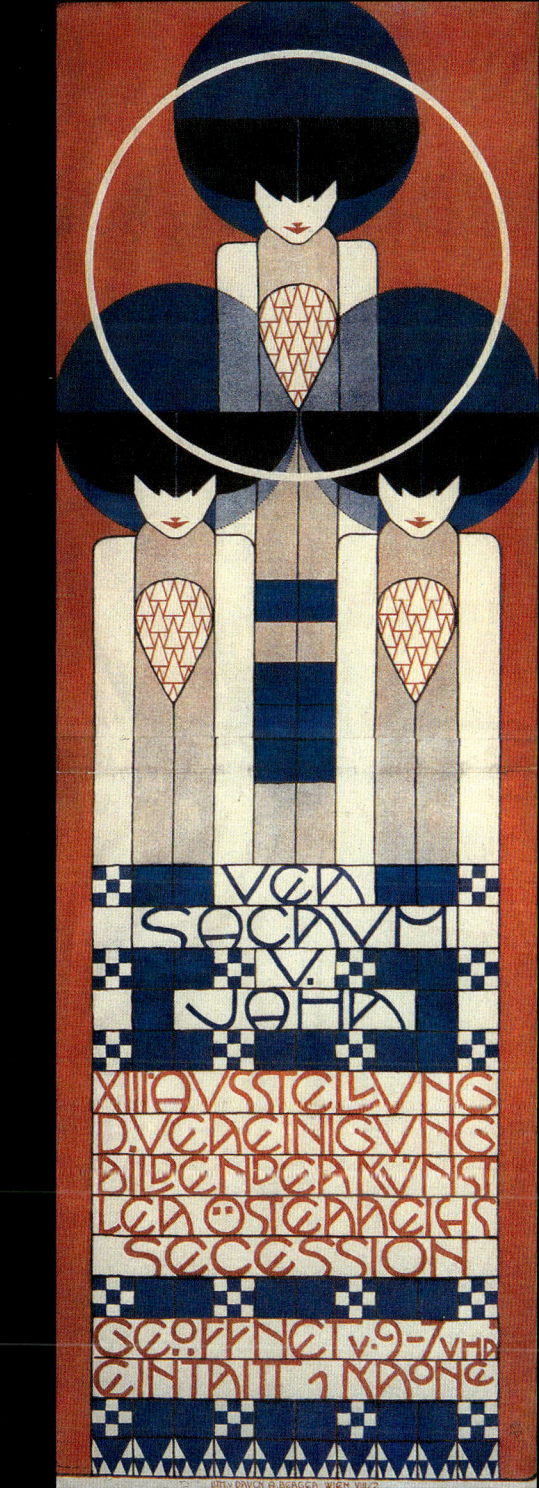

Moser Poster:
(69 × 23 inches [1.75 × 0.6 m])
Museum of Design,
Zurich, Poster Collection;
Photographer: Franz Xaver Jaggy

the difficulty of identifying, let alone distinguishing, between *R* and *A*). Since posters were meant to be seen from a distance by pedestrians rather than examined in galleries, Moser's exhibition poster conflicts with the "immediacy" for which the poster medium in the later nineteenth century is often noted. On this evidence, the poster fails at least in some of its primary functions.

And yet, was Moser so ignorant or dismissive of his audience and his poster's function? Perhaps not. It seems likely he could assume his Viennese public's familiarity with the prominent and distinctive Secession Building designed by architect Josef Olbrich and completed in 1898. The building's oft-quoted motto ("to every time its art, to every art its freedom") announces its modernity—and its façade also renders Moser's poster legible. The poster makes repeated and direct references to the location of the Secession exhibition, connecting with the urban experience of its Viennese public. Familiarity with the building provides a level of recognition to the poster, making it user friendly. And while appreciation of the poster may exist on many levels—the local, the historical—it relates it to its own time and audience, demonstrating an effective approach to visual communication. Moser's XIII Secession poster demonstrates that even well-trodden territory can yield new discoveries in the history of design.

David Raizman is professor in the Art and Art History Department in the Westphal College of Art and Design at Drexel University in Philadelphia and author of *History of Modern Design* (Laurence King and Prentice-Hall Publishers, 2004; 2nd expanded and revised edition, 2010). He coedited with Professor Carma Gorman (Southern Illinois University, Carbondale) the book *Objects, Audiences, and Literatures: Alternative Narratives in the History of Design* (Newcastle, Cambridge Scholars Press, 2007). In October 2009, Raizman was a research fellow at the Wolfsonian-Florida International University museum and library conducting research on nineteenth-century world's fairs in relation to the design, production, and reception of furniture.

(Vienna Secession Building): Christine Bastin et Jacques Evrard

no. 63

SELECTED BY WARD SUTTON | McCARTHY: PEACE POSTER | DESIGNED BY BEN SHAHN

Ben Shahn's 1968 poster for presidential candidate Eugene McCarthy completely broke the mold of staid, graphically bland campaign posters.

The font and illustration styles remain striking and hip (notice Shahn's influence on contemporary illustrators such as Edwin Fotheringham), and its design is still defiantly radical more than forty years later.

The poster has a brilliant design that I never seem to get tired of. But it's also inspiring to see how Shahn combined his political feelings with his art in a way that avoided being heavy handed and yet had such graphic strength.

Shepard Fairey's 2008 poster for then U.S. presidential candidate Barack Obama may have helped usher in a new political era, but in terms of graphic approach, Shahn's poster was more risky. Notice that there is no graphic representation of the candidate himself, but instead, a dove decorated in stripes ingeniously conveying a patriotic pacifism. Indeed, the message of this poster is what appears in its boldest lettering: Peace. Fairey was selling Obama, branded as "Hope." Shahn was selling Peace, branded as "McCarthy." It may not have gotten McCarthy elected, but in my opinion, it's the most interesting campaign poster ever created.

When I moved to New York in 1995, I had twin passions for politics and posters. I began scavenging the city for books of old posters and going to poster exhibitions—I was a junkie. One of the books I discovered was *Prop Art* (1972), which presented an amazing collection of political graphics. Within it was Shahn's poster (unfortunately in black and white). I found some books of Shahn's work, but the image of the poster wasn't in them. I found a brochure from a poster dealer that had a color reproduction of Shahn's poster on it! I hung on to that and put it in a scrapbook of things that inspired me.

My career has been focused on honing my abilities to express my ideas, especially political ideas, and how to make my artwork as strong and effective as it can be. I'm constantly experimenting between subtle and sledgehammer, turning the dial up and down with what I do. This piece somehow manages to do it all with amazing grace—I refer to it often whether I'm working on a concert poster, a political cartoon, or an editorial illustration.

Ward Sutton's cartoons appear in the *New Yorker*, the *New York Times*, the *Village Voice*, the *Onion*, and many other publications. He has created concert posters for musicians such as Beck, Pearl Jam, and Phish, as well as posters for John Leguizamo's Broadway show *Freak* and the 2000 Sundance Film Festival. His book *Sutton Impact: The Political Cartoons of Ward Sutton* was published in 2005. He currently creates "Drawn to Read," illustrated book reviews for the *Barnes & Noble Review*.

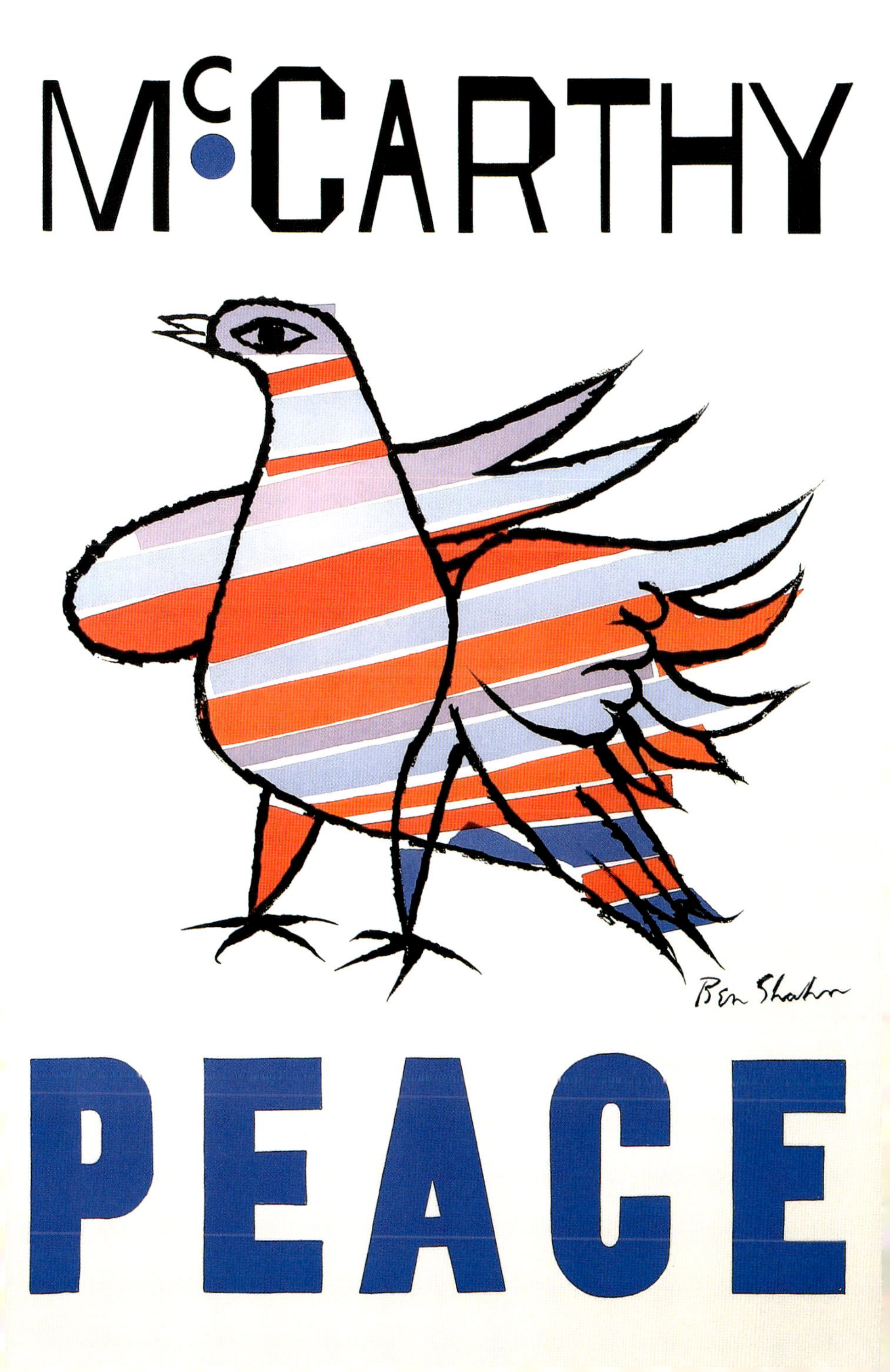
McCARTHY
Ben Shahn
PEACE

no. 64

SELECTED BY MARIAN BANTJES | YENI MOSQUE, ISTANBUL (1597–1640) | DESIGNER UNKNOWN

It is my opinion that Islamic art, particularly from the fourteenth to the seventeenth century, contains everything we have ever desired or required in perfection of design. It combines mathematical precision and intricacy with beauty. It balances intense and mind-boggling detail with perfectly balanced form. There is message and meaning within that message. There is incredibly sophisticated planning and form, but at the same time, pure emotionalism. Every nuance and detail is worked to within an inch of its life without giving up liveliness. The Islamic artists did it better than the Christians, and better than the Modernists. They embraced and embodied the best of type, illustration, and craft. What more could you possibly ask for?

Marian Bantjes has been variously described as a typographer, designer, artist, and writer. Working from her base on a small island off the west coast of Canada, her personal, obsessive, and sometimes strange graphic work has brought her international recognition. Following her interests in complexity and structure, Bantjes is known for her custom typography, detailed and lovingly precise vector art, her obsessive handwork, and her patterning and ornament. Her book, *I Wonder*, is due out in the fall of 2010, published by Thames & Hudson.

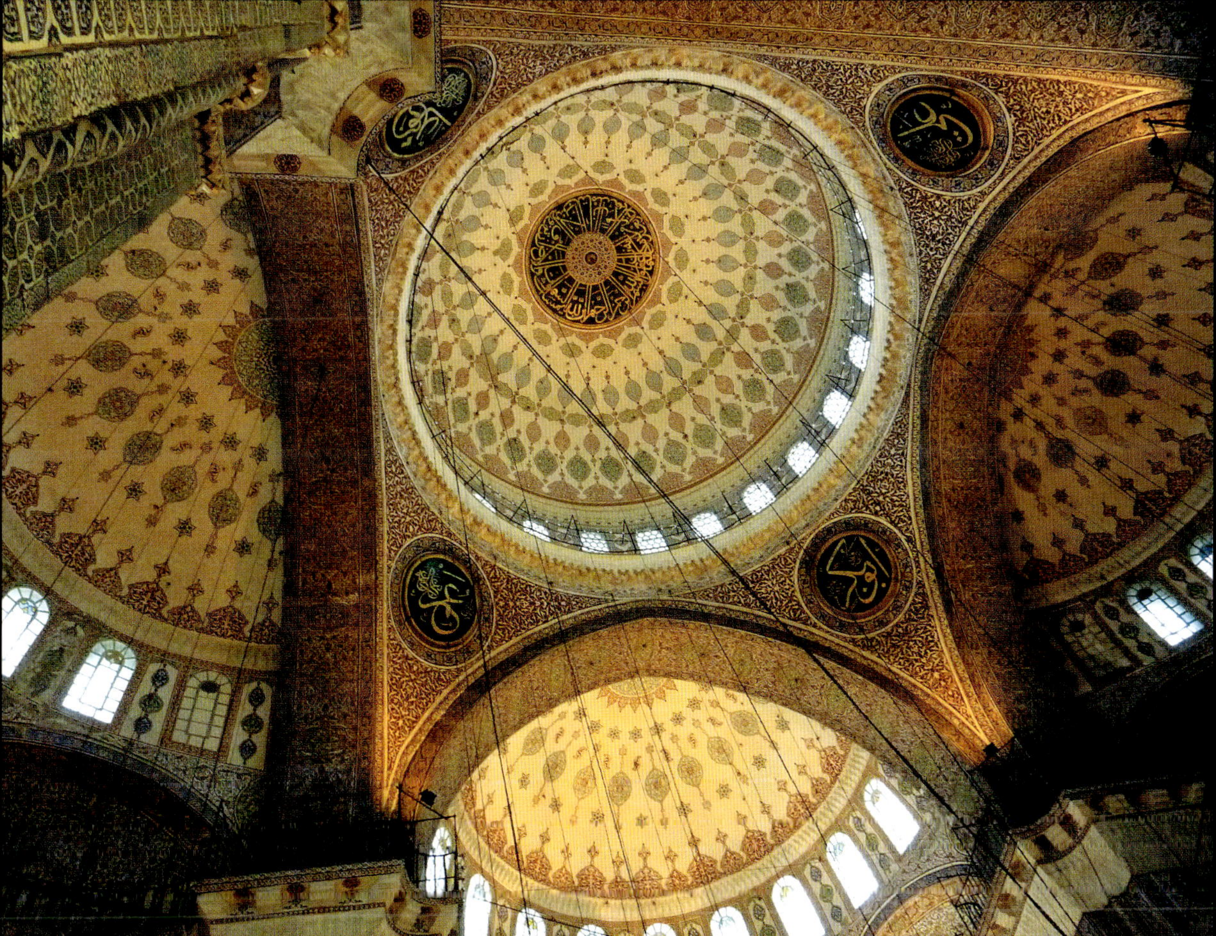

no. 65

SELECTED BY MAJID ABBASI | KORANIC EXEMPLA | ILLUSTRATED BY MORTEZA MOMAYEZ

Morteza Momayez (1936–2005) is undoubtedly Iran's founder of modern graphic design and illustration. In addition to creating immortal works of graphic design, such as great posters, gorgeous logos and logotypes, and book covers, he also bequeathed brilliant illustrations that are rare and matchless on their own account, and whose effects on his generation and other generations to come are beyond doubt.

By reviewing the illustrations at the early *Qajar* dynasty, which were made for different lithographic print books, it appears that for the first time, the cornerstones of illustration formed at that period in a primitive way from common painting of the time. Iranian illustration was rooted in Qajar period, when it tried to take advantage of techniques of the time.

Momayez, for the first time, published his illustrations in *Ketab-e Hafte* (*The Book of the Week*), whose editor in chief used to be Ahmad Shamloo (1925–2000). There, he could present his techniques in different styles. He was a nonpareil in designing and using tools like metal pen, ink, and different pencils; his illustrations vividly exhibited the stories and were well adapted and loyal to the texts. "The importance of a work is not only about reflecting an illustration which includes a story; a good work produces a deeper belief and a higher comprehension of the story and gives the reader more energy, motivation, and enthusiasm to carry on studying," said Momayez.

The *Koranic exempla* collection was produced by putting black ink on very thick glossy cardboard. Then the dried ink was scraped off to create the finished form. Momayez noted, "These illustrations, like a sculptor's sculptures, were carved slowly in order to take shape." Creating this collection of twenty-two illustrations took about six months.

Momayez was the founder of graphic design department in the Faculty of Fine Arts, University of Tehran, and taught there for more than thirty-five years until his death. "He was the one who adapted

Joseph's brothers drop him into the well

our illustration to the present time. Actually, the world of modern painting somehow entered Iranian graphics by him," says Farshid Mesghali, illustrator and graphic designer, university professor, and chairman of Iranian Graphic Designers Society (IGDS).

Majid Abbasi was born in 1965 in Tehran, where he still lives today. He graduated from the Faculty of Fine Arts at the University of Tehran in 1996 in visual communication. It was in this same year, having already enjoyed numerous freelance design commissions, that Abbasi set up his prestigious studio, Did Graphics Inc., with partner Firouz Shafei. Also a lecturer at the University of Tehran, following Morteza Momayez's invitation to join the university's Faculty of Fine Arts from 2003 to 2007, Abbasi is the editor of *Neshan*, the Iranian graphic design magazine, and is also a founder of the 5th Color, a collective formed by what he describes as "the new generation of Iranian graphic designers."

Plotting to abduct Lughman the Sage

Devastation of Shad-da d's Eden

Advent of Islam

The War of Ababil and Elephant Army

Untitled

no. 66

SELECTED BY DEBORAH SUSSMAN | COLLAGE | DESIGNED BY ALAN FLETCHER

Among the great delights created by Alan Fletcher, cofounder of Pentagram in London, was a series of collages that he sent to friends, using "found" letters, combined to create a monogram using the friends' initials. Like everything he did, concept and aesthetic were inseparable. And he always made it look so easy.

In this case, he used a couple of torn and folded pieces of printed characters. My initials, DS, are made of lowercase *d* and a cap *S* so that, when turned upside down, it says SP. Which happens to be the initials of my firm, Sussman/Prejza. If he had used a cap *d* the double entendre wouldn't exist. What a clever guy.

Design, like all art, transforms one thing into another—enabling us to see things differently. In experiencing the juxtaposition of unlike elements, we broaden our understanding and appreciation of the world. So, sometimes, small surprises yield insights that are treasures.

Alan was a star from the beginning. When we were both invited to speak at the first of a series of graphic design conferences in Mexico, I was treated as a celebrity. Alan was treated like a rock star.

Some years ago at an AGI Congress in Toronto, we were asked to partner in a dual presentation. Alan showed drawings of flowers that he'd just made in the middle of a sleepless night. I showed a model of a deconstructed rose icon/sculpture/fountain being designed for one of our projects.

We had an asymmetrical relationship.

Deborah Sussman, a pioneer in environmental graphic design, was trained at the office of Charles and Ray Eames. She founded Sussman/Prejza, whose celebrated "urban branding" projects include city identities; cultural and performing arts centers; retail, corporate and university campuses; and U.S. embassies. S/P developed the "look" of the 1984 Olympic Games in Los Angeles. Other clients include Disney, Hasbro, the Museum of the African Diaspora, Amgen, and S.C. Johnson.

Deborah Sussman

№ 67

SELECTED BY KEN GARLAND | **LILLIPUT** | **ART DIRECTED BY STEFAN LORANT**

In July 1937, the first issue of the monthly *Lilliput* appeared. Though ostensibly a British periodical, it was conceived, edited, and part owned by a Hungarian exile, Stefan Lorant. Born Istvn Lrnt in 1901, he had been a photographer, film cameraman, and film director in Austria and Germany, and in 1933 was editor of the highly successful pictorial publication Munchner *Illustrierte Presse*. When the Nazis marched into Munich in March of that year, he was immediately arrested without charge and spent six and a half months in prison, after which he fled to Hungary and went to Britain.

Lorant brought with him an unrivaled ability and experience as a photojournalist. Immediately on his arrival in Britain in 1934, he was recruited by Odhams Press to start a photo magazine, *Weekly Illustrated*. Successful though it was, he had in mind a periodical of his own; and so, three years later, he borrowed enough cash to start *Lilliput*.

What made this production unique? First of all, its size: As its title suggested, it was very small, only 7¾ × 5½ inches (19.7 × 14 cm). To the best of my knowledge, no other magazine of the time was anywhere near as small; it slipped easily into a jacket pocket or handbag. Secondly, it combined writing of the very best quality with photographs (unconnected with the text) of equal quality. Thirdly, it introduced the British public to the endlessly satisfying delights of what Lorant called doubles—pairs of photographs on opposite pages, hitherto unrelated but brought together in an ironic, suggestive, or merely ridiculous montage. Fourthly, it was the first regular platform for the brilliant documentary photography of Will Brandt, who would go on to even

Lilliput

THE POCKET MAGAZINE FOR EVERYONE

AUGUST VOL. 5 No. 2

LOVE NUMBER 6ᴰ

more success in *Picture Post*, another hugely popular periodical launched by Lorant in 1938. Fifthly, the first 147 issues (until 1949) were gloriously embellished with covers illustrated by another refugee from Hitler's Germany, Walter Trier. With remarkable consistency and even more remarkable variety, each cover featured a young man, a young woman, and a small terrier.

As a child of eight, I was a devoted patron of *Lilliput* from its launching. The monthly ritual of unveiling the array of *doubles* is a keenly remembered delight to this very day; and I was surely not the only future graphic designer or photographer to be so entranced by them. Though it is almost forgotten as an original and unique contribution to our craft, it thoroughly deserves a place in your list of paragons.

Lorant left the United Kingdom in 1940, dismayed at being treated as a hostile alien, and settled in the United States for the rest of his long life (he died in 1997). Though he wrote many fine books—twenty in all—and enjoyed a vigorous working life to the end, it is as the founder and editor of *Lilliput* and *Picture Post* that he deserves to be best remembered.

OLD GERMANY

NEW GERMANY

Ken Garland was art editor of *Design* magazine from 1956 to 1962, when he left to establish his own graphic design studio as Ken Garland and Associates. Among his many clients were Galt Toys, Race Furniture, Barbour Index, the Butterley Group, William Heinemann, Paramount Pictures, Harper & Row, Otto Maier Verlag, the Science Museum, Cambridge University Press, the Ministry of Technology, Jonathan Cape, the Arts Council, the Royal Parks Agency, and the Barbican Gallery. He has contributed many articles to design periodicals in the United Kingdom, United States, Europe, and Japan. His own publications include *First Things First: A Manifesto* (self-published, London, 1964), *Graphics Handbook* (Studio Vista, London/Reinhold Publishing, New York, 1966), and more. He was a visiting lecturer at the University of Reading (1971–1999), the Royal College of Art (1977–1987), Central School of Art and Design (1986–1991), and the National College of Art and Design, Dublin (1982–1992). He has lectured widely in the United Kingdom, United States, Canada, Portugal, Norway, Denmark, Germany, and Bangladesh.

no. 68

SELECTED BY | **PONTRESINA** | **DESIGNED BY**
RETO CADUFF | | **HERBERT MATTER**

When Swiss designer Herbert Matter, at the age of twenty-seven, started his now iconic poster series for Swiss tourism clients in the early 1930s, he had just come back from a stint in Paris, where he collaborated with A. M. Cassandre, Fernand Léger, and Le Corbusier.

In Switzerland, his French-inspired flair met the rigid and Bauhaus-influenced ideas of his fellow "foto grafiker" friends such as Max Bill. The result culminates in a series of posters that had nothing to do with the illustrative process that dominated poster design at that time. It was fresh, modern, and provocative, and it took the vocabulary from surrealism and constructivism and applied it to the commercial realm.

With this work, Matter secured himself a place in the graphic design pantheon early on. A few years later, he interviewed with Alexey Brodovitch for a job at *Harper's Bazaar* in New York. His *Pontresina* poster hung on the wall behind Brodovitch's desk.

To me, the Matter posters represent an important step in the early stages of modernism, a design era that still exudes a huge influence on me. Matter, as one of the great unknown arbiters of this movement, was so interesting that I made a film about him called *The Visual Language of Herbert Matter*. If you can design an object that still looks as fresh as the Pontresina poster does after decades have passed, you truly understand what makes graphic design work.

Reto Caduff, born in Zurich, began his career as a typographer and graphic designer. During those studies, he discovered the work of Herbert Matter. Wanting to express himself in other forms than just on paper, Caduff worked as a host for Swiss National Radio and owned a record label. While directing music videos for his signed acts, he discovered a great passion for the moving image. He joined Swiss National Television, where he worked as a producer and director. In 1994, he moved to New York, working as a designer, photographer, and filmmaker.

engelberg
trübsee

schweiz   suisse   switzerland

no. 69

SELECTED BY LOUISE FILI | SIGNS OF ITALY | DESIGNERS UNKNOWN

For years and years, I have been documenting the vernacular signage of Italy. Whenever I travel there, I make a point of going to a city I haven't yet been to, just to photograph the signs. The mix of Stile Liberty (or Art Nouveau), Art Deco, and post-Fascist lettering; scripts, neon, and hand-painted specimens are a great source of inspiration. The signs are so beautifully rendered as to make all contemporary methods seem inferior.

The signs were made by skilled craftsmen—with emphasis on "men." No women were employed in this specialist's profession. They doubtless learned their craft from previous generations. Some garnered their styles from books in which templates for letters provided the aesthetic basis for the respective periods. They worked on glass, wood, and metal. The ones on glass, however, are the most luminescent. I have hundreds of photos arranged in small albums, by city and town.

I refer to them often, whether for a specific commission, including reference for a logo or sign (or cookbook), or just to transport me back to Europe. I never tire of looking at them. And nothing makes me happier than to see a modern shoe store that will show the respect to retain a wonderful old sign from its former life as a pasticceria.

Louise Fili is principal of Louise Fili Ltd., a New York–based graphic design firm that focuses on restaurant identities and specialty food packaging. She has also written and designed books on graphic design and Italy, including *Italianissimo* (Little Bookroom).

Bar

BAR S. CALISTO

La Torinese

Gelateria

Trattoria

l'artistica

CARAMATI

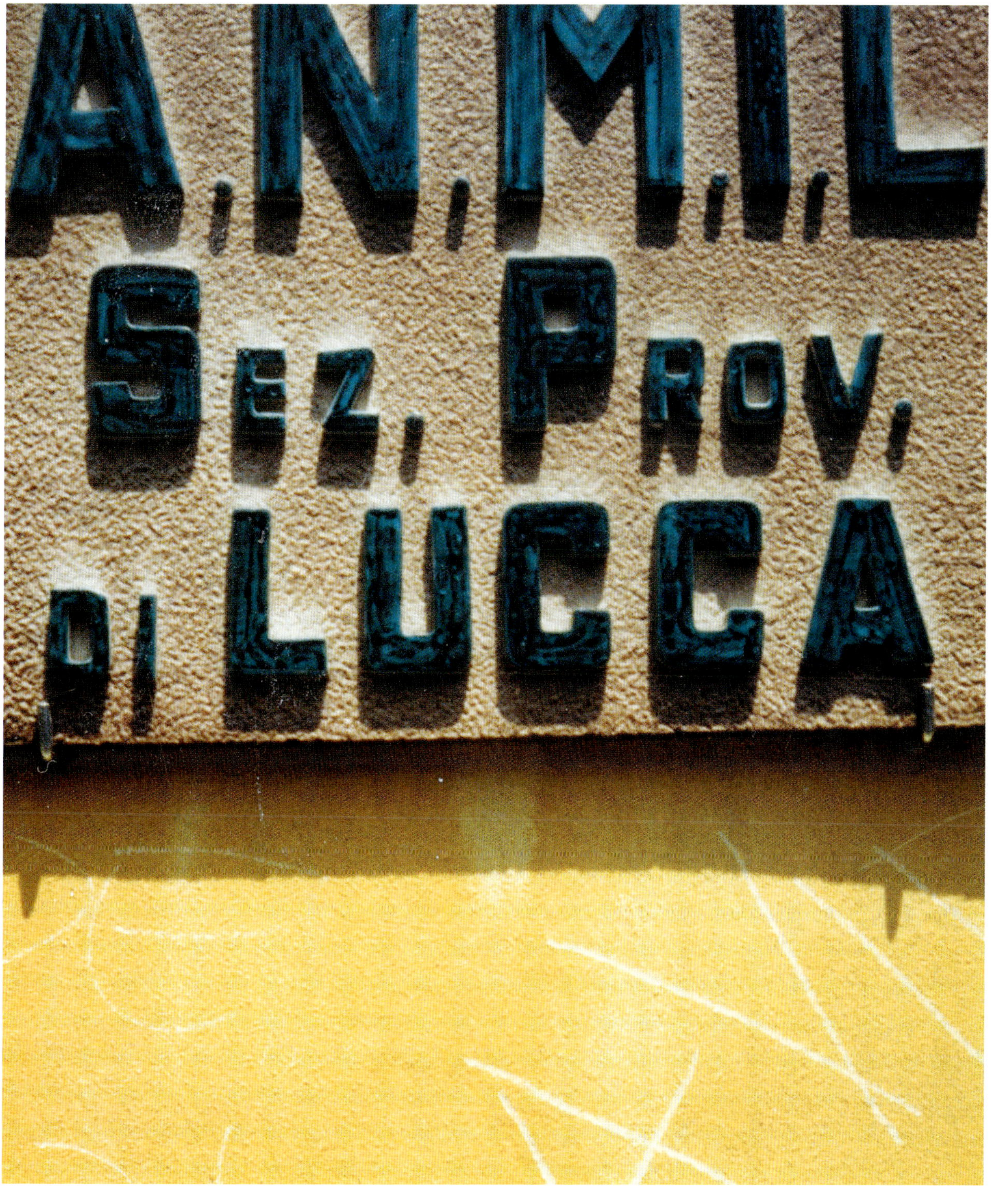
A.N.M.I.L
SEZ. PROV.
DI LUCCA

no. 70

SELECTED BY KRZYSZTOF LENK | REQUIEM FOR 500 THOUSAND | **DESIGNED BY** LESZEK HOLDANOWICZ

This Polish poster was designed by Leszek Holdanowicz in 1963 for the documentary movie *Requiem for 500 Thousand*, on the history and tragic end of the Warsaw Ghetto under German occupation during World War II.

It looks like a simple layout built from easily recognizable elements: a menorah and candle flames. Only with a closer look at the flames, one can discern the hands emerging from darkness, signing to us with simple gestures of people swallowed by the ghetto fire—or perhaps only their souls trying to tell us something. In the history of posters, in Poland and beyond, we could count only a handful of works that are equally moving and timeless. Struck by its power, I was unable to take my eyes off it, and even today, I am moved by it still. Each year, I show it to my young students and can see that they, too, share the same experience, and are forever impressed by the image.

Krzysztof Lenk is a designer and educator, specializing in information design and typography. He's been professor of graphic design at Rhode Island School of Design since 1982. Before coming to RISD, he had been faculty at School of Art and Design in Lodz (Poland) since 1973. Before coming to the United States, he worked as a designer, design director, and consultant for clients in Poland, France, and Germany on a variety of editorial and publication design projects. Between 1990 and 2000, Lenk had been a partner and a creative director at Dynamic Diagrams, a consulting company specializing in information and interface design. His most recent book, *Projects and Doodles*, is an overview of a fifty-year design career.

REQUIEM DLA 500 TYSIĘCY

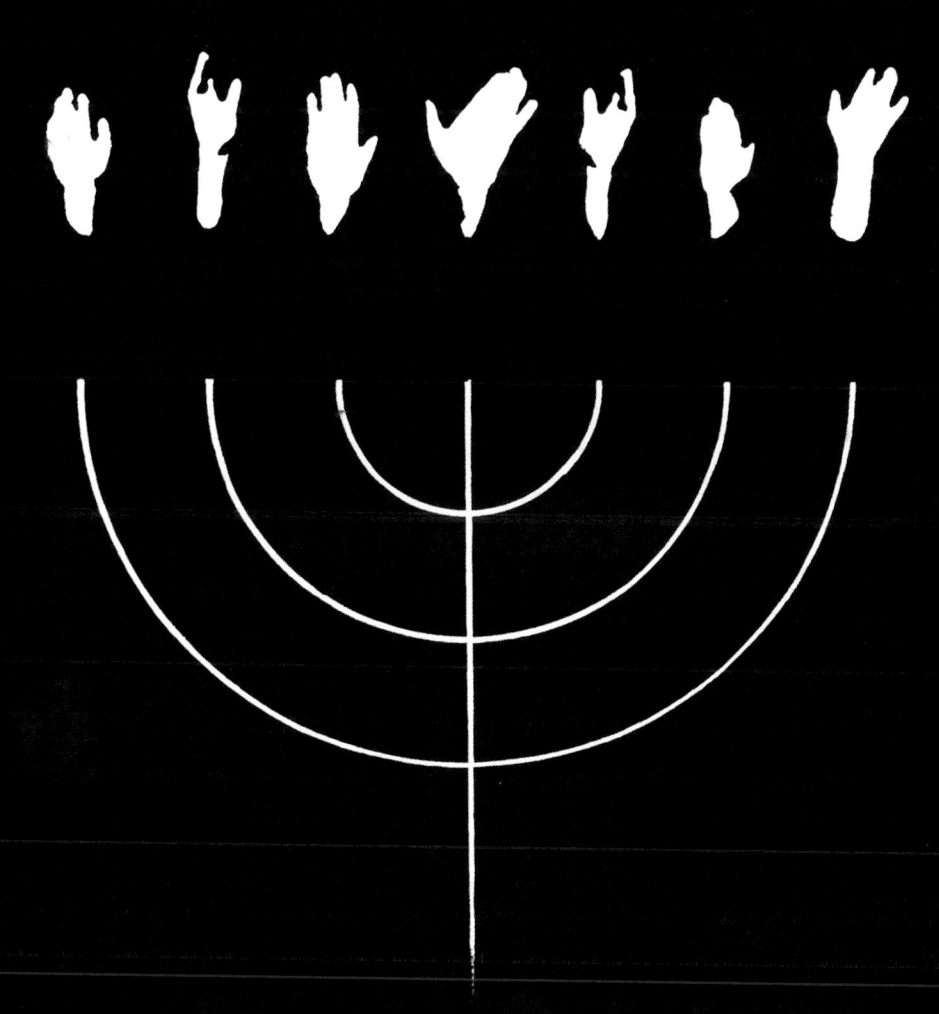

Realizacja: Jerzy BOSSAK i Wacław KAŹMIERCZAK
Wytwórnia Filmów Dokumentalnych w Warszawie

no. 71

SELECTED BY MONIKA PARRINDER | MOTORWAY SIGNS

DESIGNED BY MARGARET CALVERT & JOCK KINNEIR

There's an oft-quoted motorway sign that when heading out of London on the M1, simply points north. The experience on the road—where a sign can suddenly embody the enigma of travel—is also poignant for Margaret Calvert, a designer of the British system together with Jock Kinneir.

As she recalled in a radio interview with historian Joe Kerr, testing of the signage had been largely hypothetical, and she saw them first when speeding up the M1 in a car hired especially for the opening occasion. Mesmerized by the sheer scale of the signs and the expanse of empty road, they missed their junction—and the ceremony itself.

More frequently, drivers comprehend signage in a subconscious way. In Will Self's "Scale", this is the inspiration for the main character's innovation Motorway Verse; poetry that aims to "breathe reality into the land." Powering westward out of London:

Jnctn 1. Uxbridge. Jnctn 1A. (M25) M4.
Jnctn 2. Slough A365. No Services.On M40...[1]

When it's poorly received, he explains, "Naturally, it is necessary that readers imaginatively place themselves in a figurative car that is actually driving up the aforementioned motorway."

Self's character uses the rhythm of signs to judge time-scale as he ramps down speed to his exit. But at Jnctn 2, they have got the distances wrong. He crashes.

That's the way it is in reality. If good road signage draws attention only to itself when it doesn't work, then, conversely, indifference is seen as a tribute to the supreme functionalism (readable/modular) of its design. But design's significance lies in the way it helps us make sense of our world.

Today, we speed along the Internet at breakneck velocities, but on the motor highway, this signage is still poignant. Motorway signs lay marker to a twentieth century transformed by speed.

Monika Parrinder is a writer and lecturer based in London. She is cofounder, with Colin Davies, of LimitedLanguage.org, which is a platform for generating writing on visual and sonic culture, and coauthor of the book *Limited Language: Rewriting Design—Responding to a Feedback Culture* (Birkhäuser, 2010).

[1] "Scale" in Will Self, *Grey Area* (London: Penguin Books, 1996), p. 105

A 217 Reigate, Sutton, Kingston (A 240)
8
Leatherhead (A 243)
Heathrow (M 4), Watford & (M 1)
M 25
Reigate 5
Leatherhead 10
Heathrow 31
Watford 47

no. 72

SELECTED BY DEBBIE MILLMAN | MORTON SALT UMBRELLA GIRL | DESIGNER UNKNOWN

Joy Morton started the Morton Salt Company in 1910 with a novel idea: By adding magnesium carbonate to salt crystals, moisture would not affect the granules and lumps and clumps could be avoided in damp, humid weather. This allowed for a uniquely consistent, smooth pour. In 1911, after a number of clunky iterations, a clever advertising slogan touting the brand's benefit was created, and "When It Rains, It Pours" has been in use ever since.

In 1914, design history was made in the form of an illustration that graced Morton's cylindrical package. It featured an image of a mop-headed little girl rendered in yellow and blue; she carried an oversize umbrella warding off rain in one hand and a canister of pouring salt in the other. But what made this illustration so remarkable was neither the style nor the craft; rather, this was the first time a logo was developed as a telegraphic metaphor to describe a product's innovative benefit. The image of the Morton umbrella girl was a puzzle to be figured out, and her enigmatic stance has since influenced marks such as I (Heart) NY, FedEx, and amazon.com.

Rumors have long abounded about the umbrella girl's origin, but executives at the Morton Salt Company insist that she is simply a figment of a long-forgotten artist's imagination. She's been redrawn numerous times over her long career, but her iconic attributes remain: the skip in her step, her joyful expression, and the fact that after nearly a century of selling salt, Morton has never given the umbrella girl a name.

Debbie Millman is president of the design division at Sterling Brands, where she has worked on the redesign of over 100 global brands. She is also president of AIGA, the largest professional association for design, a contributing editor at *Print* magazine, a writer at FastCompany.com, chair of the Master's in Branding Program at the School of Visual Arts, and the author of *Look Both Ways: Illustrated Essays on the Intersection of Life and Design* (HOW Books, 2009), and *How to Think like a Great Graphic Designer* (Allworth Press, 2007).

When it rains it pours

Morton Salt • Plain or iodized

no. 73

SELECTED BY MIRKO ILIĆ | **PROCES, KAFKA, 1964** | **DESIGNED BY ROMAN CIESLEWICZ**

Most theater posters produced up to 1964 were very literal and painterly. They were either illustrations with type on them, like the influential Polish posters of the time, or were the opposite—mostly type with some illustration.

The Swiss posters mostly used minimal colors and typography (Helvetica). For this poster, Roman Cieslewicz managed to take the best of both worlds and create something totally new.

For the image, Cieslewicz posterized a black-and-white photograph, a technique developed by Martin Weber in the 1940s. He created the head of the main character, Joseph K., to be bigger than his body, giving the character a childlike, fragile appearance. He cleverly repeated the same face, each time reduced in size. The upper lip and chin of the bigger head becomes the hair/forehead of the smaller head, creating an organic, shrinking person, as the main character continues to diminish in the play. Meanwhile, from a distance, it almost looks like a tie. In the play, Joseph K. must face and go through various parts of an institution, continually blocked by their closed doors. The simple red frame without the bottom horizontal line actually becomes the very symbol of a door frame. And because the poster was created in a Communist, oppressed Poland, the red door frame has an additional meaning.

The treatment of typography is also quite interesting. The typeface, a version of the art-nouveau typefaces such as those designed by J. H. Kaemmerer around 1915, is small and minimal. It was unusual to see the author's name *Kafka* in black against the white chopped corner—which is effective, making a counterbalance against the white word *proces*. The word *proces* also becomes the person's handkerchief, making his appearance more formal.

I was always fascinated with this poster at first glance. It is a simple poster but is actually loaded with symbolism. When I was in my twenties, I had a chance to meet Roman Cieslewicz in Croatia, where he was redesigning the magazine *Start*. I was working as an illustrator and, by that time, I was already familiar with his work, but meeting him in person gave me a chance to see how gentle and thoughtful he was. That reconfirmed my opinion about his work and influenced my own way of thinking even more.

Mirko Ilić is a writer (author of various publications, some in collaboration with Steven Heller), professor (with Milton Glaser at the Cooper Union and the School of Visual Arts), designer (his company, founded in 1995, is mainly known because of the creation of strong concepts), and, definitively, one of the most influential figures in the world of design.

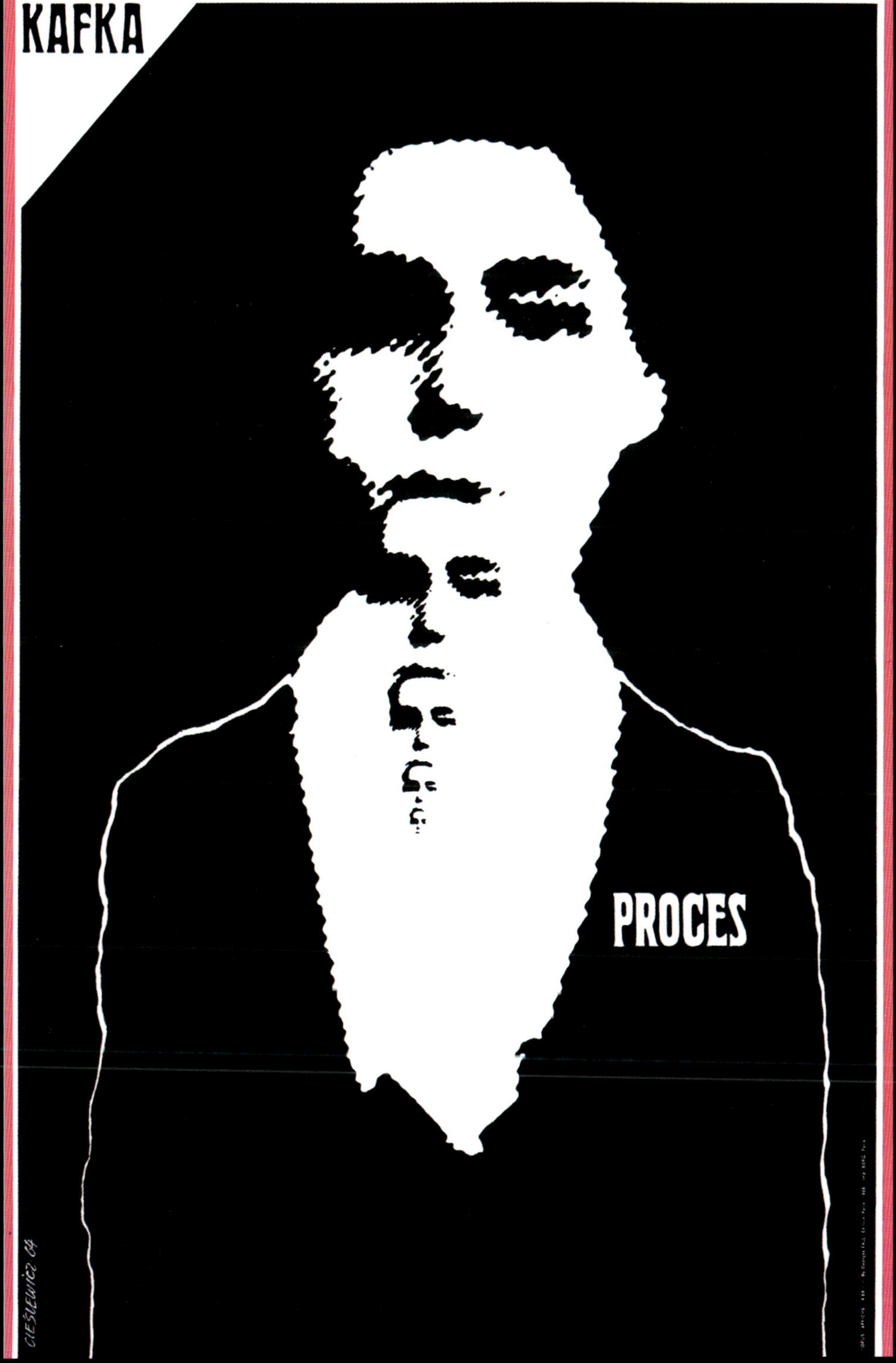

KAFKA
PROCES
CIEŚLEWICZ 64

no. 74

SELECTED BY MARSHALL ARISMAN | SEEING IS NOT BELIEVING | DESIGNED BY ROBERT WEAVER

Robert Weaver's (1924–1994) small poster under the title *Seeing Is Not Believing*, printed in the 1970s, was commissioned by Silas H. Rhodes, founder of the School of Visual Arts. More than a poster, it is a visual essay that shows a photograph transforming into a drawing. The art is quintessential Weaver. He was the undisputed pioneer of contemporary illustration. He introduced the element of time by splitting the page and working sequentially. Functioning more like a writer than an illustrator, he often told more than one story in his visual essays.

With the advent and popularity of the graphic novel, Weaver foreshadowed how a story could be told over thirty years ago. It is only in recent times that his pictorial genius is being recognized as a turning point for developing storylines.

At first glance, *Seeing Is Not Believing* is a casual acknowledgment of how photo reference is used by an illustrator or fine artist. This is not a tracing but an active interpretation of what makes figuration so intriguing. Instead of the camera lens, we bear witness to the act of drawing. Instead of being dispassionate viewers or witnesses, we watch the creative process developing in front of our eyes. It is no accident that Weaver chose a photograph of a man from the early 1900s. There is nothing distinctive or special about the man or what he is doing. Our focus becomes the drawing, Weaver's intent. Seeing art emerge as the reality is believing. *Seeing Is Not Believing* is Weaver's endless pictorial game playing.

When he was inducted into the Society of Illus-

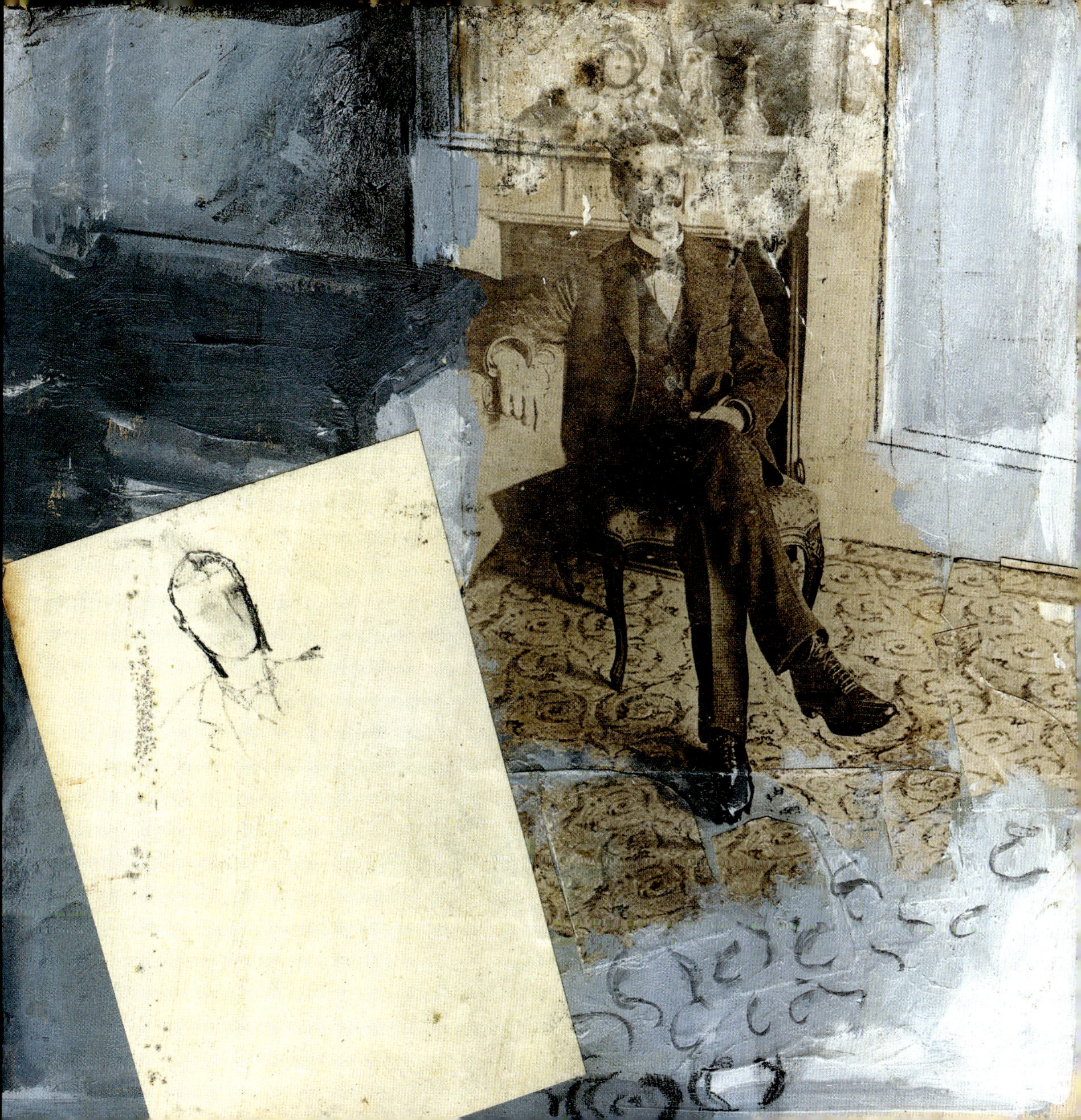

trators Hall of Fame in 1985, he asked me to introduce him. Knowing how he hated organizations, clubs, and awards, I eagerly awaited his acceptance speech.

Comparing himself to J. Edgar Hoover, he said, "I suppose the Society of Illustrators would rather have me inside the tent pissing out than outside the tent pissing in!" Amen.

Marshall Arisman's paintings have been widely exhibited both internationally and nationally, and his work may be seen in the permanent collections of the Brooklyn Museum, the National Museum of American Art, the Smithsonian Institution, the Metropolitan Museum of Art, as well as in many private and corporate collections. His original graphic essay *Heaven Departed*, in which paintings and drawings describe the emotional and spiritual impact of nuclear war on society, was published in book form by Vision Publishers (Tokyo, 1988). He is chairman of the MFA degree program at the School of Visual Arts in New York City. Arisman was the first American invited to exhibit in mainland China. His series, *Sacred Monkeys*, appeared at the Guang Dong Museum of Art in April 1999.

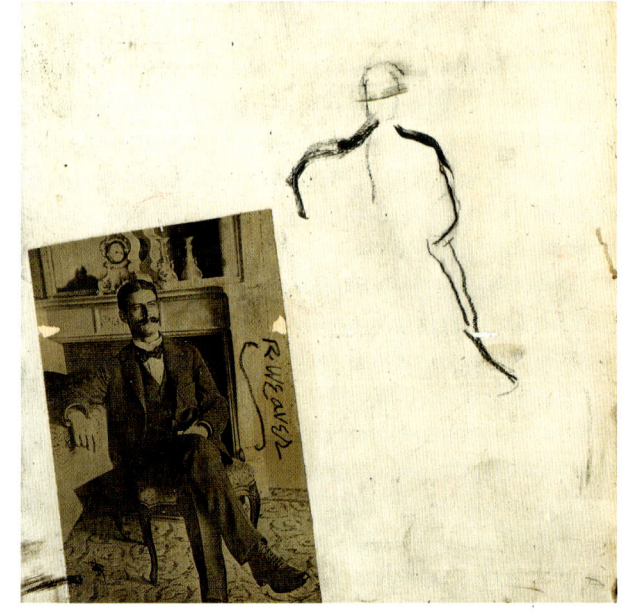

/ 203 /

no. **75**

SELECTED BY DAVID TARTAKOVER | COMMERCIAL ART OF PALESTINE, 1938 | DESIGNED BY FRANK KRAUSZ

The original design which is gouache on paper, (23.5 × 25.8 cm) was printed on the cover of the *Association of Jewish Commercial Artists* in Palestine catalog issued in 1938. This publication was a landmark in the history of Israeli graphic design.

Until the 1930s, there was hardly any commercial art in Palestine. The wave of immigration of Jews who fled the Nazi regime also brought to the country experienced graphic artists and advertising experts. In this publication, twenty-one pioneers of graphic design showed their work to a society that was not yet aware of the importance of their profession.

In the '70s, I started my research of the history of graphic design in Israel. This led me to meet Franz Krausz, (1905–1998), the creator of this piece. Krausz, whom I consider the best graphic artist of his generation, immigrated to Palestine from Berlin in 1934. His work as a poster artist is connected to the work of well-known German artists like Lucian Bernhard and Ludwig Hohlwine. As a poster designer, I've chosen this piece because it relates to posters and to the way posters were distributed in their golden age. It describes a situation that hardly exists. The round Litfas Pillar that was invented in Germany by Alfred Litfas in 1854 was prominent in the public urban space, until it was replaced by the gigantic advertising billboard.

Another reason for choosing this image is anecdotal: The photograph of the kids—one dressed like a "billboard," and the other one as a poster hanger—was taken over fifty years ago. The kid inside the billboard is me. The headline on the upper poster says "Learn a Trade!," which I did.

David Tartakover has operated his own studio in Tel Aviv since 1975, specializing in culture and politics. He is known for his self-produced posters dealing with the Israeli–Palestinian conflict. His work has won numerous prizes in Israel and abroad. Among them are Gold Medal, 8th Lathi Poster Biennial, Finland (1989) and Grand Prix, Moscow International Poster Biennial (2004). He collects and researches history of Israeli design and is also the curator of design exhibitions in Israel and abroad. Among the books he has published is a lexicon of the 1950s in Israel, *Where We Were, And What We Did*. For his contribution to Israeli design and culture, he was awarded the Israel Prize (2002).

no. 76

SELECTED BY MAURO ZENNARO | LETTERS IN POMPEII | DESIGNER UNKNOWN

I saw for the first time this picture in Edward M. Catich's *The Origin of the Serif,* and I immediately fell in love with it. The letters of the word LVCRETI-SATRI are beautiful—elegant and regular narrow roman capitals, surely painted by an anonymous *scriptor* (professional writer). I went to look for them at Pompeii archaeological site, but I was bitterly disappointed: That wall didn't exist anymore. I photographed what remains today: the two last red letters *RI* under a protective glass.

During World War II, the Anglo-American carpet bombings destroyed part of Pompeii. A kind archaeologist of the Pompeii Archaelogical Supervision Board advised me to search in Rome's American Academy library. I found not one, but two different pictures of the inscription, shot by an American photographer in the 1930s. The words *Lvcreti-Satri* in the two different walls are identical. The writer was a great master.

These letters are unique. Their narrow shape is due to the limited space on the walls of ancient Roman towns: They were full of writings. It was an advertisement for a circus show featuring beast huntings and gladiator fights offered by the wealthy Lucretius Satricus. The anonymous writer painted them at the beginning of April A.D. 79 In August he died under Vesuvius's eruption.

They aren't as famous as the Trajan inscription and are made of an accomplished alphabet, but these letters are perfect. I've copied them many times and even designed my own typeface, but I still love the original the best. I pretended to be an ancient Pompeii scribe to design the lacking letters, and it's been an exciting experience.

Mauro Zennaro was born in Rome in 1953, graduated in architecture, and studied palaeography and calligraphy. He has been working as a graphic designer for several public institutions (Italian libraries, museums, municipalities) and designing typefaces. He teaches in a professional graphic design high school and in the master's in type design of the Department of Architecture Valle Giulia of Rome's La Sapienza University. He is the author of *Calligrafia: Fondamenti e Procedure* (Viterbo, Nuovi Equilibri, 1997) and *Alphabeto Romano* (Roma, Edizioni dell'Elefante, 1988), and he writes articles for graphic design magazines.

This picture is in the American Academy in Rome's Library, no. 10376F (published in Edward M. Catich, *The Origin of the Serif: Brush Writing and Roman Letters*, The Catfish Press, 1968).

American Academy in Rome's Library, no. 2525.

The Pompeii inscription as it is now.

/ 208 / i heart design

no. **77**

THE CENTURY DICTIONARY
FIRST ISSUED 1889–1891, FINAL EDITION 1914

SELECTED BY | **PRINTED AND PUBLISHED BY** | **EDITED BY**
SCOTT-MARTIN KOSOFSKY | THEODORE LOW DE VINNE | WILLIAM DWIGHT WHITNEY

It was an undertaking so enormous—eventually a half million entries, nearly 8,500 pages, and some 10,000 wood engravings—that its printer and publisher, Theodore Low De Vinne, had to quickly construct an extension at 21 to 23 East 4th Street to his already massive plant on Lafayette. Nothing was impossible in New York in 1889.

The project at hand was *The Century Dictionary*, a work that would forevermore set a standard for clear typography and seamless organization and establish America's standing as a center of scholarship.

De Vinne (1828–1914), the preeminent American printer of his day, was a largely self-educated man who became a respected and prolific scholar of the history of his craft. He, above all others, brought impeccable craftsmanship to printing in the age of machines. His greatest achievement in the *Dictionary*, though, was its typography. Everything that had to be differentiated was differentiated—never too much or too little.

- Entries: 8 pt. Ionic bold, a slab serif face in upper- and lowercase (in earlier dictionaries, entries were always in caps)
- Etymologies and definitions: 8 pt. Modern roman and italic
- Demarcations of secondary entries: 8 pt. bold Modern figures with words in 6 pt. Ionic bold
- Quotations: 6 pt. Modern roman; author's name in italic

That's seven fonts, plus accents and symbols, and Greek for etymologies. Each compositor—scores of them—stood before specially made stands and type cases that gave them access to all the fonts at once.

Scott-Martin Kosofsky designs, produces, edits, composes, writes, and makes types for books in Lexington, Massachusetts, where he is a partner in the Philidor Company. He specializes in complex typographic books, especially in Jewish religion and history, and in interesting photography books, with occasional forays into music, art, and graphic design.

borized or moss-agate," Wright. Also spelled *arborise.*

arborolatry (är-bọ-rol′ạ-tri), *n.* [< L. *arbor*, a tree, + Gr. λατρεία, worship.] Tree-worship.
Few species of worship have been more common than arborolatry. *S. Hardy*, Eastern Monachism, p. 216.

arborous (är′bọ-rus), *a.* [< *arbor*[1] + *-ous*.] Consisting of or pertaining to trees.
From under shady arborous roof.
Milton, P. L., v. 137.

arbor-vine (är′bọr-vīn), *n.* [< *arbor*[1] + *vine*.] A species of bindweed. The *Spanish arbor-vine* of Jamaica is an ornamental species of *Ipomœa, I. tuberosa.*

arbor-vitæ (är′bọr-vī′tē), *n.* [L., tree of life: see *arbor*[1] and *vital*.] **1.** In *bot.*, a common name of certain species of *Thuja*, a genus belonging to the natural order *Coniferæ. Thuja occidentalis* is the American or common arbor-vitæ, extensively planted for ornament and for hedges.
2. In *anat.*, the arborescent or foliaceous appearance of a section of the cerebellum of the higher vertebrates, due to the arrangement of the white and gray nerve-tissue and their contrast in color. See cut under *corpus*. — **Arbor-vitæ uterinus**, an arborescent appearance presented by the walls of the canal of the neck of the human uterus, becoming indistinct or disappearing after the first gestation.

arbour, *n.* See *arbor*[2].

arbrier (är′bri-ėr), *n.* [OF., also *arbreau, arbret, arbriet*, < *arbre*, a tree, beam: see *arbor*[1].] The staff or stock of the crossbow.

arbuscle (är′bus-l), *n.* [< L. *arbuscula*, a little tree, dim. of *arbor*, a tree.] A dwarf tree, in size between a shrub and a tree. *Bradley.*

arbuscular (är-bus′kū-lär), *a.* [< L. *arbuscula*: see *arbuscule*.] Resembling an arbuscule; tufted.

arbuscule (är-bus′kūl), *n.* [< L. *arbuscula*, a little tree: see *arbuscle*.] In *zoöl.*, a tuft of something like an arbuscle, as the tufted branchiæ of an annelid; a tuft of cilia.

arbusta, *n.* Plural of *arbustum.*

arbustive (är-bus′tiv), *a.* [< L. *arbustivus*, < *arbustum*, a plantation of trees: see *arbustum*.] Containing copses of trees or shrubs; covered with shrubs; shrubby.

arbustum (är-bus′tum), *n.*; pl. *arbustums*, *arbusta* (-tumz, -tä). [L., < *arbos, arbor*, a tree: see *arbor*[1].] A copse of shrubs or trees; an orchard or arboretum.

arbute (är′būt), *n.* [Formerly also *arbut*, < L. *arbutus*: see *arbutus*.] The strawberry-tree. See *arbutus*, 3.

arbutean (är-bū′tē-an), *a.* [< L. *arbuteus*, pertaining to the arbutus, < *arbutus*: see *arbutus*.] Pertaining to the arbute or strawberry-tree.

arbutin (är′bū-tin), *n.* [< *arbutus* + *-in*[2].] A glucoside ($C_{25}H_{32}O_{14} + H_2O$) obtained from the bearberry (*Arctostaphylos Uva-ursi*) and other plants of the heath family. It forms tufts of colorless acicular crystals soluble in water and having a bitter taste.

arbutus (com- Strawberry-tree (*Arbutus Unedo*).
monly är-bū′tus), *n.* as a Latin word, är′bū-tus), *n.* [Formerly also *arbute, arbut* = F. *arbute*. — It. *arbuto*, < L. *arbūtus*, the wild strawberry-tree; prob. akin to *arbor, arbos*, a tree.] **1.** A plant of the genus *Arbutus.* **2.** The trailing arbutus (see below). —
3. [*cap.*] A genus of evergreen shrubs or small trees of southern Europe and western North America, natural order *Ericaceæ*, characterized by a free calyx and a many-seeded berry. The European *A. Unedo* is called the strawberry-tree from its bright-scarlet berries, and is cultivated for ornament. *A. Menziesii* is the picturesque and striking madroño-tree of Oregon and California, sometimes reaching a height of 80 feet or more. — **Trailing arbutus**, the *Epigæa repens*, a fragrant ericaceous creeper of the United States, blooming in the spring, and also known as *May-flower* (which see).

arc[1] (ärk), *n.* [Early mod. E. also *ark*; < ME. *ark, arke*, < OF. (and F.) *arc* = Pr. *arc* = Sp. Pg. It. *arco*, < L. *arcus, arquus*, a bow, arc, arch, akin to AS. *earh*, ᛒ E. *arrow*, q. v. Doublet *arch*[1].] **1.** In *geom.*, any part of a curved line, as of a circle, especially one which does not include
Arc.
a point of inflection or cusp. It is by means of arcs of a circle that all angles are measured, the arc being described from the angular point as a center. In the higher

mathematics the word *arc* is used to denote any angular quantity, even when greater than a whole circle: as, an arc of 750°. See *angle*[3].
2. In *astron.*, a part of a circle traversed by the sun or other heavenly body; especially, the part passed over by a star between its rising and setting.
The brighte sonne
The *ark* of his artificial day hath ronne
The fourthe part.
Chaucer, Prol. to Man of Law's Tale, l. 2.
3. In *arch.*, an arch. [Rare.]
Turn *arcs* of triumph to a garden-gate.
Pope, Moral Essays, iv. 30.
Arc boutant (F.), a flying buttress. — **Arc doubleau** (F.), in *arch.*, the main rib or arch-band which crosses a vault at right angles and separates adjoining bays from each other. — **Arc formeret** (F.), the arch which receives the vaulting at the side of a vaulted bay. — **Arc ogive** (F.), one of the transverse or diagonal ribs of a vaulted bay. — **Complement of an arc.** See *complement.* — **Concentric arcs**, arcs which belong to circles having the same center. — **Diurnal arc**, the apparent arc described by the sun from its rising to its setting: sometimes used of stars. — **Elevating arc**, in *gun.*, a brass scale divided into degrees and fractions of a degree, and fastened to the breech of a heavy gun for the purpose of regulating the elevation of the piece; or it is sometimes fixed to the carriage under the trunnions. When secured to the gun itself, a pointer is attached to a ratchet-post in the rear of the piece, and indicates zero when the gun is horizontal. — **Nocturnal arc**, the arc described by the sun, or other heavenly body, during the night. — **Similar arcs**, of unequal circles, arcs which contain the same number of degrees, or are the like part or parts of their respective circles. — **Supplemental arcs**. See *supplemental*. — **Voltaic arc**, in *elect.*, a brilliant band of light, having the shape of an arc, produced by the passage of a powerful electrical current between two carbon-points. Its length varies from a fraction of an inch to two inches, or even more, according to the strength of the current. Its heat is intense, and on this account it is used for fusing very refractory substances. It is also used for illuminating purposes. See *electric light*, under *electric.*

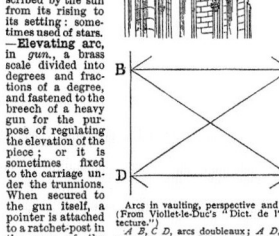

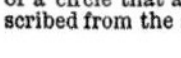

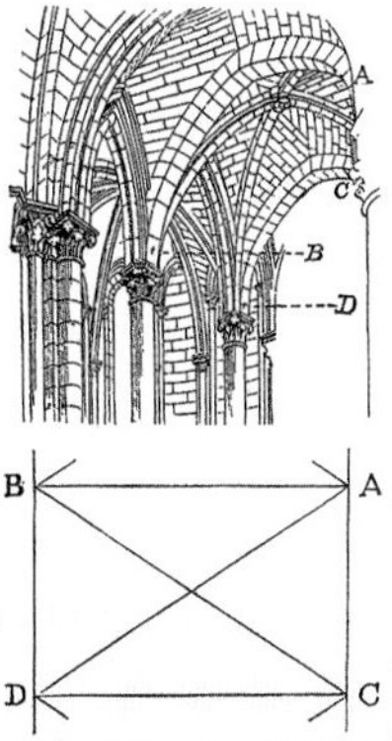

arc[2], *n.* Obsolete form of *ark*[2].

arca (är′kä), *n.* [L., a chest, box, safe; in eccles. writers, the ark: see *ark*[2].] **1.** In the early church: (*a*) A chest for receiving offerings of money. (*b*) A box or casket in which the eucharist was carried. (*c*) A name given by St. Gregory of Tours to an altar composed of three marble tablets, one resting horizontally on the other two, which stand upright on the floor. *Walcott*, Sacred Archæol. — **2.** [*cap.*] [NL.] A genus of asiphonate lamellibranch mollusks, typical of the family *Arcidæ* (which see); the ark-shells proper. [Sp., = *harquebusier*.] A musketeer; a harquebusier.
Here in front you can see the very dint of the bullet Fired point-blank at my heart by a Spanish *arcabucero*.
Longfellow, Miles Standish, i.

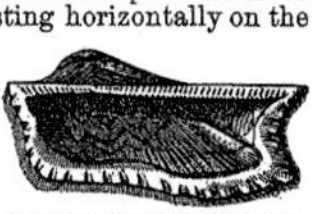

Arcadæ (är′ka-dē), *n. pl.* See *Arcidæ.*

arcade (är-kād′), *n.* [< F. *arcade*, < It. *arcata* = Sp. Pg. *arcada*, < ML. *arcata*, an arcade, < L. *arcus*, arc, bow: see *arc*[1], *arch*[1].] **1.** Properly, a series of arches supported on piers or pillars. The arcade is used especially as a screen and as a support for a wall or roof, but in all architecture since the Roman it is also commonly used as an ornamental dressing to a wall. In this form it is known as a *blind arcade* or an *arcature*, and is also called *wall-arcade.*
2. A simple arched opening in a wall. [Rare.]
— **3.** A vault or vaulted place. [Rare.] — **4.** Specifically, in some cities, a long arched passageway; a covered avenue, especially one that is lined with shops.

arcaded (är-kā′ded), *a.* Furnished with an arcade.

Arcadian (är-kā′di-an), *a.* and *n.* [< L. *Arcadius, Arcadia*, < Gr. Ἀρκαδία.] **I.** *a.* **1.** Of or pertaining to Arcadia, a mountainous district of Greece in the heart of the Peloponnesus, or to its inhabitants, who were a simple pastoral people, fond of music and dancing. Hence — **2.** Pastoral; rustic; simple; innocent. — **3.** Pertaining to or characteristic of the Academy of the Arcadians, an Italian poetical (now also scientific) society founded at Rome in 1690, the aim of the members of which was originally to imitate classic simplicity. Sometimes written *Arcadic.*
II. *n.* **1.** A native or an inhabitant of Arcadia. — **2.** A member of the Academy of the Arcadians. See I.

Arcadianism (är-kā′di-an-izm), *n.* [< *Arcadian* + *-ism*.] Rustic or pastoral simplicity, especially as affected in literature; specifically, in Italian literature about the end of the seventeenth century, the affectation of classic simplicity.

Arcadic (är-kā′dik), *a.* [< L. *Arcadicus*, < Gr. Ἀρκαδικός.] Same as *Arcadian.* — **Arcadic poetry**, pastoral poetry.

arcana, *n.* Plural of *arcanum.*

arcane (är-kān′), *a.* [< L. *arcanus*, hidden, < *arcere*, shut up, *arca*, a chest. Cf. *arcanum.*] Hidden; secret. [Rare.]
The luminous genius who had illustrated the demonstrations of Euclid was penetrating into the *arcane* caverns of the cabalists. *I. D'Israeli*, Amen. of Lit., II. 294.

arcanum (är-kā′num), *n.*; pl. *arcana* (-nä). [L., neut. of *arcanus*, hidden, closed, secret: see *arcane*.] **1.** A secret; a mystery: generally used in the plural: as, the *arcana* of nature.
The very *Arcanum* of pretending Religion in all Wars is, That something may be found out in which all Men may have interest. *Selden*, Table-Talk, p. 105.
Inquiries into the *arcana* of the Godhead. *Warburton.*
The Arabs, with their usual activity, penetrated into the *arcana* of wealth. *Prescott*, Ferd. and Isa., i. 8.
2. In *alchemy*, a supposed great secret of nature, which was to be discovered by alchemical means; the secret virtue of anything. Hence — **3.** A secret remedy reputed to be very efficacious; a marvelous elixir. — **The great arcanum**, the supposed art of transmuting metals.
He told us stories of a Genoese jeweller, who had *the great arcanum*, and had made projection before him several times. *Evelyn*, Diary, Jan. 2, 1652.

arcature (är′kā-tūr), *n.* [< ML. *arcatura*, < *arcata*: see *arcade*.] In *arch.*: (*a*) An arcade of small dimensions, such as a balustrade, formed by a series of little arches. In some medieval churches open arcatures were introduced beneath the cornices of the external walls, not only as an ornament, but to admit light above the vaulting to the roof-timbers.

(*b*) A blind arcade, used rather to decorate a wall-space, as beneath a row of windows or a cornice, than to meet a necessity of construction.

arc-cosecant (ärk-kō-sē′kant), *n.* In *math.*, an angle regarded as a function of its cosecant.

no. 78

SELECTED BY CHRIS PULLMAN | MUSICA VIVA | DESIGNED BY JOSEF MÜLLER-BROCKMAN

In the mid-'60s, when I was just learning about design and typography at Yale, Modernism was the style du jour. I was intellectually turned on by the minimalism (one font, usually Akzidenz in just a few sizes), the rules (flush left, ragged right, the logic of the grid), and the idea of a "universal" aesthetic where content of any variety could be accommodated in this rational system.

Switzerland was then the mecca of European Modernism, and Joseph Müller-Brockmann, one if its key practitioners, had just published what might have been the first pedagogical book on the subject: *The Graphic Artist and His Design Problems*.

I opened it up and there on page 124 was this amazing poster from 1960.

I was jolted, because it seemed to me to represent the irreducible, can't-get-more-basic-than-this exemplar of Swiss Modernism.

It was as if every Swiss poster of the previous decade was reverse engineered, gradually eliminating all pictorial elements and all hierarchical and clarifying typographic signals until the only thing left was one uninflected, flush left, ragged right, one-size, one-weight, run-on block of text. And then, into this dense message, the bare minimum of clarity was added: commas between phrases; a faint hint that it contained three paragraphs; and then those four red elements denoting the content: the name of the concert series and the three performers.

Gone are Müller-Brockmann's geometric illustrations and iconic photographic images of the '50s. From this baseline, type-as-image start-over sprang a series of beguiling and increasingly complex typographic compositions for *Musica Viva*.

For me, this deliberate process of moving from simple/uninflected/opaque to complex/articulated/clear informed my own early typography as a teacher and encouraged me in my own work to see typography itself as an image.

Chris Pullman served as vice president for design for WGBH, public broadcasting, in Boston, from 1973 to 2008, which supplies about 30 percent of the PBS prime-time schedule and the bulk of pbs.org websites. He and his staff were responsible for the visual personality of WGBH as expressed through its on-air titles, credits, animation, promotional and sales support, classroom materials, and interactive media. In 2002, he was honored with the AIGA Medal for excellence over a lifetime of work.

dienstag, den 7. januar 1958 schweizerische erstaufführungen musica viva
20.15 uhr großer tonhallesaal andré jolivet
12. volkskonzert cinque danses rituelles
der tonhalle-gesellschaft ernst krenek
zürich zweites klavierkonzert
als drittes konzert luigi nono
im zyklus «musica viva» «y su sangre va vienne cantando» karten fr. 1.-, 2.- und 3.-
leitung hans rosbaud musik für flöte und kleines orchester vorverkauf tonhallekasse hug
solisten alfred baum klavier bernd aloys zimmermann jecklin kuoni
andré jaunet flöte sinfonie in einem satz genossenschaftsbuchhandlung

no. **79**

SELECTED BY | IRON MAIDEN: PIECE OF MIND | DESIGNED BY
CHARLES WILKIN | | DEREK RIGGS

I honestly had no idea who Iron Maiden was when I bought *Piece of Mind* in 1983 at age fourteen, but I just knew by looking at the cover it would piss off my parents. In that split second, this album cover transformed my teenage rebellion into inspiration and ultimately became the reason I'm a designer/illustrator today. Even after all these years, Eddie's image motivates me to kick ass and take names later.

Perhaps these days I'm just being nostalgic or looking to rekindle the fearlessness of youth now long gone, but clearly Derek Riggs's illustrations still inspire me to make art.

Even if you're not a fan of heavy metal you have to admit Derek Riggs has created some truly iconic covers for Iron Maiden over the years. Riggs's style is unforgiving, raw, and perhaps even juvenile in comparison to today's conceptual design and polished illustration techniques, yet his images are undeniably captivating. Riggs's creation of Iron Maiden's mascot, Eddie, in 1980 has since become a global trademark and what many still consider the gold standard in heavy metal branding, defining not only a band but also an entire genre of music. Eddie's zombielike eyes and the clumsy, angular logotype effortlessly resonate with fans. This simple yet elusive connection with people is something all great design seems to have in common—a universal trait I believe we all aspire to as designers, regardless of style or method. Riggs's consistent achievement of design's Holy Grail is why I personally consider him an equal among album cover legends like Roger Dean, Peter Saville, Stefan Stagmeister, and Mark Farrow.

Charles Wilkin is proprietor of the studio Automatic Art and Design. Started in 1994, Automatic strives to bridge the gap between personal expression and commercial expectations. Automatic has worked with clients such as Target, Mattel, Pentagram, Burton Snowboards, Chronicle Books, and Australian *Vogue*. Wilkin has lectured across the United States and published his monograph *Index*-A in 2003 through German publisher Die-Gestalten. His work has also been archived in the permanent collections of the U.S. Library of Congress and the Museum of Decorative Arts, Hamburg, Germany.

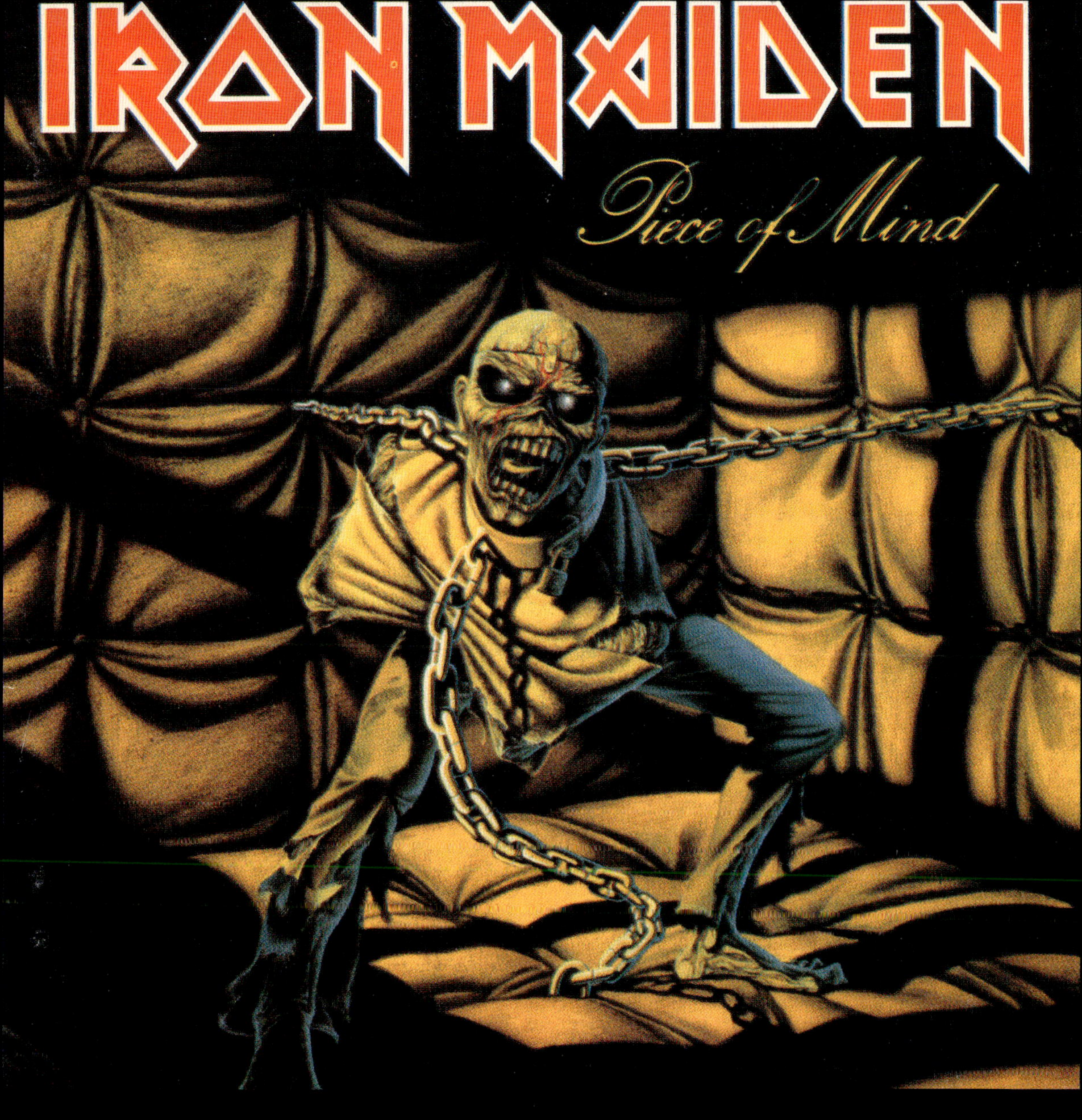
IRON MAIDEN
Piece of Mind

no. 80

SELECTED BY ALISSA WALKER | HIGHLY PRIZED, 1967 | DESIGNED BY SISTER MARY CORITA KENT

When I first moved to Los Angeles, I would take long runs high into the hills around my Hollywood house to learn the lay and splay of the land—to clear my head from the unsettling visual cacophony of this strange city, where beauty coexisted uncomfortably close with ugliness.

Almost every day I ran by the Immaculate Heart College, oblivious to its significance, until one day I noticed a tiny sign on the gate written in what looked like hastily dashed script: Corita.

For twenty years during the '60s and '70s, a Catholic nun named Sister Mary Corita Kent ran a tiny printmaking studio here that became an internationally recognized art institution, one visited by Buckminster Fuller, Saul Bass, and Charles Eames. Her messages of peace and love were tempered with a raw, visual urgency, ushering in a new language of democratized design that would influence an era of protest banners and Pop Art. In the spring, her students organized a massive public art show on the school's lawn for Mary's Day, unfurling banners out the windows and stacking silkscreened cardboard boxes into towers, as they whirled between them in a pastel blur of sundresses and hats sewn from daisies.

Kent took her cues from what she called "marvelously unfinished Los Angeles," gathering imagery from field trips to car washes and supermarkets. The serigraph *highly prized* was ripped quite literally from the streets of L.A., slathered in traffic-cone orange paint, and transformed into an appropriately messy, hand-scrawled celebration of urbanity, freedom, and hope. All this, I marveled, happened right up the street from my new home.

Years later, I attended a Mary's Day celebration. Wearing a floral dress and carrying a screenprinted sign, I walked onto that same grassy hill poised at the edge of the endless gray grid and gazed out over the city that I now so proudly called my home. It was Corita Kent's radical work that taught me how to truly embrace Los Angeles, for all its freeways and freakishness, all its ugliness and unfinishedness. This serigraph now hangs in my living room.

Alissa Walker is a writer, curator, and event producer whose work can be seen in publications like *Fast Company* and *Dwell*, at events like the GOOD Design series, which asks designers around the country to tackle urban problems, and as cocurator of the 2010 California Design Biennial at the Pasadena Museum of California Art. She lives in Los Angeles, where she eats gelato almost every day and hardly ever drives a car.

I CARE. I CARE ABOUT IT ALL.

FREEWAY ENTRANCE 1960

IT TAKES TOO MUCH ENERGY NOT TO CARE. THE WHY OF WHY WE ARE HERE IS AN INTRIGUE FOR AWHILE SCENE IT. THE HOW IS WHAT MUST COMMAND THE LIVING. WHICH IS WHY I HAVE LATELY BECOME AN INSURGENT AGAIN.
LORRAINE HANSBURY